Off the Beaten Path®
THE DAKOTAS

OFF THE BEATEN PATH® SERIES

NINTH EDITION

Off the Beaten Path®
THE DAKOTAS

A Guide to Unique Places

LISA MEYERS McCLINTICK

Globe
Pequot

Guilford, Connecticut

Globe Pequot

An imprint of Rowman & Littlefield
Off the Beaten Path is a registered trademark of Rowman & Littlefield

Distributed by NATIONAL BOOK NETWORK

Copyright © 2015 by Rowman & Littlefield
Text design: Linda R. Loiewski
Maps: Equator Graphics © Rowman & Littlefield

British Library Cataloguing in Publication Information Available

Library of Congress Cataloging-in-Publication Data is available on file.

ISBN 978-0-7627-9674-8
ISBN 978-1-4930-1745-4 (e-book)

∞™ The paper used in this publication meets the minimum requirements of American National Standard for Information Sciences—Permanence of Paper for Printed Library Materials, ANSI/NISO Z39.48-1992.

Contents

About the Author

Lisa Meyers McClintick has been a journalist for more than 25 years, with the last 15 focused on travel writing and photography. She specializes in covering the Dakotas, Minnesota, and Wisconsin, along with any destinations that include family attractions, adventure travel, living history, hands-on learning, funky cafes and farm stands, and quirky places off the beaten path. She frequently writes for *Midwest Living*, *USA Today*'s *Go Escape* magazine, the *Minneapolis Star Tribune*, and *Family Vacation Critic*. She also wrote *Day Trips® from the Twin Cities* for Globe Pequot. You can find many of her travel features at LisaMcClintick.com or on her blog 10000Likes.com, or follow her @LisaMcClintick on Twitter.

She lives in St. Cloud, MN, with her husband, Bob, who grew up near Sioux Falls, South Dakota, and their children: Jon, 15, Katie and Kylie, 11, and their sidekick, Gracie, a rescue dog who relishes road trips.

Acknowledgments

Special thanks goes to my husband and kids, who adore the Dakotas and have accompanied me on many ambitious road trips or held down the fort at home when I've been traveling solo. We've hiked North Dakota's Badlands while it was snowing (in June—surprise!), playfully mugged our way down the Enchanted Highway, enjoyed magical performances under the moon and stars, followed Lewis and Clark, dug for fossils and hunted for rocks, ridden horses through the Black Hills National Forest, and climbed on boulders that give mothers minor heart attacks.

Huge thanks also go to my parents, Rik and Lyn Meyers, who inspired my travel bug at an early age, coached me through writing and photography, and instilled a love of nature and road trips.

Cheers, too, to South Dakota Tourism, North Dakota Tourism, regional chambers of commerce, and the folks I've met across the Dakotas who have chimed in with amazing expertise and helped me find the most intriguing, memorable, and scenically stunning places to go. And, finally, thank you to my agent, Julie Hill, for making this project possible.

Missouri R.

CENTRAL
NORTH DAKOTA

EASTERN
NORTH
DAKOTA

WESTERN
NORTH DAKOTA

Bismarck ★

Fargo ■

ALONG
THE
MISSOURI
RIVER

NORTHEASTERN
SOUTH DAKOTA

Watertown ■

WESTERN
SOUTH DAKOTA

Pierre ★

Rapid City ■

SOUTHEASTERN
SOUTH DAKOTA

Sioux Falls ■

Missouri R.

Introduction

If you've had the privilege of admiring Mount Rushmore in person, you know it's more than an Eighth-Wonder-of-the-World kind of monument. It's a place that hums with national pride with an entrance that waves the colors of all 50 states and offers an unforgettable look at presidents representing American ideals such as independence and strength, freedom and equality.

You'll hear languages from across the globe and see kids who've gleefully hit the jackpot for the license plate game in Mount Rushmore's parking lot.

Truly this is a place powerful enough to draw people from around the world, but travelers who are wise know to stay, to linger, and to explore. No matter what road they take—east, west, north, or south—it's easier to ditch crowds and get off the beaten path. Travelers can discover places that feel as authentic and pristine as they were more than 200 years ago when Lewis and Clark and their Corps of Discovery made their historic journey into the Dakotas and across the continent.

These are, after all, two of the country's six least-populated states (which also include Montana, Idaho, Wyoming, and New Mexico). North Dakota and South Dakota claim fewer than 10 people per square mile. That makes most of North and South Dakota off America's beaten path. Case in point: North Dakota's Badlands may be a top destination for Dakotans, but Theodore Roosevelt National Park—which protects the scenic Badlands—is one of America's least-visited national parks despite its stunning beauty. It's also why I've included North and South Dakota's biggest attractions, as well as the under-the-radar gems and lesser-known adventures, in this guide for exploring both states.

You'll find Native Americans who proudly share their heritage with vibrant powwows, music, and artwork that continue their traditions and legacy of storytelling. You can stand on a bluff above the Missouri River to picture vast villages from the 1700s, tour an earth lodge, or sleep in a tipi that lets you watch the stars at night.

At South Dakota's Custer State Park or North Dakota's Theodore Roosevelt National Park, feel the power of a buffalo herd thundering across grasslands, watch a mother nuzzle her cinnamon-colored calf, and marvel at the resonant grumble of a one-ton buffalo as he ambles in front of your car—then takes a dirt bath in the ditch.

Both North and South Dakota proudly marked 125 years of statehood in 2014. And while that's perfect timing to celebrate their remarkable past and a rich cast of characters from Crazy Horse and General Custer to L. Frank Baum and Laura Ingalls Wilder, neither of these states has hit the pause button.

While much of the country has quietly ridden out a national recession and tough times, the Dakotas have boomed and thrived. Every city is growing—and quickly. North Dakota's population grew by 7 percent in just three years. Construction of much-needed housing is catching up. North Dakota added 24 new hotels with 2,236 rooms in just 2013, with about 100 new or expanded hotels since 2010.

Much of the growth is driven by North Dakota's oil boom. New technology makes it possible to tap the Bakken and Three Forks formations that spread across the northwest part of the state and into Montana and Saskatchewan. North Dakota has risen to the No. 2 oil-producing state in the country, behind Texas and in front of Alaska, by pumping out an average of 911,000 barrels a day.

The two Dakotas already had an energy legacy with lignite coal, hydroelectric power from dams harnessing the mighty Mississippi River, and wind turbines that pinwheel across the horizons, especially on the prairie coteau that rises along the eastern edge of the states.

Agriculture, including both farming and ranching, also anchors the economy, continuing the dream of pioneers who first settled the state and worked tirelessly to put down roots and claim a homestead. Their rural warmth and welcome, an echo of Old World heritage, a get-it-done work ethic, and a sense of pride still ripple through small towns (and cities, too).

The Dakotas are two of America's best states for hitting the road and slowing down, for hearing yourself think and soaking in sights such as a V of geese gliding into a prairie pothole gilded by a sunset, or wild horses roaming among buttes or plains. You can see a storm build from miles away before it thunders dramatically across wheat fields before quietly casting a rainbow across a pasture of black cattle. Word of advice: Keep your camera handy. These moments of beauty make it easy to understand why the

Dakotas are so popular with birders, wildlife photographers, artists, campers and backpackers, hunters, and fishermen.

Geographically, both North Dakota and South Dakota are generously endowed with pristine lakes, clay-streaked buttes, thick forests, blue-tinged prairies, and, of course, the mighty Missouri River. The Mighty Mo splits both states into East River and West River, with the flatlands of East River coveted for their agriculture, and the hills and forests of West River praised for their beauty and frontier inspiration. The states were almost split into East and West Dakota, but a north and south division prevailed as statehood was approved for both Dakotas in 1889. That decision 126 years ago ultimately offered them both diversity in landscape and economy.

sizeandgrowth

South Dakota ranks 14th in the nation for its size of 75,956 square miles. North Dakota ranks 19th with 69,299 square miles. While both states are thriving and growing, they rank almost at the bottom nationally for population. South Dakota sits at 46th, North Dakota at 48th.

In those early years, Germans, Scandinavians, and Czechs flocked to South Dakota. Germans from Russia, Icelanders, and Scandinavians headed to North Dakota. Both states also are home to many tribes of Dakota (Sioux) and Chippewa.

Some American travelers still snub the Dakotas (and the Midwest in general) as fly-over land. But those of us in the Heartland, as well as growing numbers of European and global travelers, know better. Yes, the drives to get from here to there can be long—even mind-numbing—but the reward is an authentic American experience.

It's here, off the beaten path from most of the country, where you can also walk in the footsteps of Laura Ingalls Wilder and Sitting Bull. You can excavate mammoth bones, spelunk in some of the world's longest caves, mountain bike a world-class trek through the North Dakota Badlands, find your inner cowboy, and enjoy some of the nation's best bird watching, hunting, and fishing. You can dance to Norwegian fiddles, polka with Germans, tell stories over a crackling campfire, or lose yourself in the brilliant splendor of a powwow where rhythmic drumming echoes like a dozen heartbeats.

This is a land rich with the history of explorers, treasures to be discovered, and adventures yet to be lived. Enjoy finding yours.

North Dakota Fast Facts

Population: 723,393
Capital: Bismarck
State tree: American elm
State flower: Wild prairie rose
State bird: Western meadowlark
Nickname: Peace Garden State
State drink: Milk
State fruit: Chokecherry

BIGGEST CITIES

Fargo: 109,779
Bismarck: 64,751
Grand Forks: 53,456
Minot: 43,746

TOP INDUSTRIES

Energy: Oil, gas, lignite coal and coal gasification, wind power, and ethanol fuel production
Crops: North Dakota ranks first in the nation for producing flaxseed, canola, durum wheat, dry edible beans, dry edible peas, spring wheat, honey, lentils, sunflowers, barley, and oats.
Livestock: Beef, dairy cattle, and hogs
Tourism

SPEED LIMITS

You can cruise up to 75 mph on interstates, 70 mph on four-lane divided highways, and 65 mph on two-lane highways.

ROAD CONDITIONS

Get updates on weather-related road conditions, closings, or work zones at dot.nd.gov/travel-info-v2.

TIME ZONES

Most of North Dakota uses the Central time zone, but the southwest corner goes by Mountain time. North Dakota also observes daylight saving time.

HELPFUL INFO

North Dakota Tourism
(701) 328-2525
ndtourism.com

Pride of North Dakota
Locally made gifts and products
prideofdakota.nd.gov

North Dakota Grape and Wine Association
ndgwa.org

North Dakota Bed and Breakfast Association
ndbba.com

South Dakota Fast Facts

Population: 844,877
Capital: Pierre
State tree: Black Hills spruce
State flower: Pasque flower
State bird: Chinese ring-necked pheasant
Nickname: The Mount Rushmore State
State animal: Coyote
State fish: Walleye
State insect: Honey bee
State fossil: Triceratops
State mineral: Rose quartz
State gemstone: Fairburn agate
State sport: Rodeo
State dessert: Kuchen

BIGGEST CITIES

Sioux Falls: 164,676
Rapid City: 70,812

TOP INDUSTRIES

Agriculture: In the country's top 10 states for hay, sunflower, rye, honey, corn, soybeans, wheat, and cattle production
Tourism

TIME ZONES

South Dakota has two time zones: Central for its eastern half, Mountain for the west. Daylight savings goes into effect on the first Sunday in April to the last Sunday in October.

SPEED LIMITS

Travelers can drive up to 75 mph on the interstate. Most other highways are 65 mph.

ROAD CONSTRUCTION

For updates, call (605) 773-3571.

HELPFUL INFO

South Dakota Tourism
(800) 732-5682
travelsd.com

South Dakota Specialty Producers Association
Farm market products, meats, honey, and wines
sdspecialtyproducers.org

Bed and Breakfast Innkeepers of South Dakota
southdakotabb.com

Winter Driving Tips in the Dakotas

- Listen to the forecast before departing and postpone travel if inclement weather is expected.

- Check winter driving sites such as safetravelusa.com for construction and road condition updates or call 511 for current winter driving reports.

- Carry a fully charged cell phone.

- Avoid traveling alone. Inform others of your timetable and primary and alternate routes.

- Keep your gas tank near full to avoid ice in the tank and the fuel lines.

- Adjust your speed to the conditions and increase following distances.

- Remember that bridges and overpasses are usually more slippery than other parts of the road.

- Always carry a survival kit in your vehicle. Your kit should be equipped with a can of sand or kitty litter; tire chains; flashlight with extra batteries; candles and matches; an empty coffee can (to be used to burn the candles for heat and to melt snow for water); caps, mittens, boots, and sleeping bag or blanket for everyone; nonperishable foods, such as granola bars or dried fruit; booster cables; battery-operated radio with extra batteries; and first-aid kit.

Weather

Summer: Warm (sometimes hot) days and cool nights are the norm from mid-June to mid-September.

Fall: Comfortable warm weather through September and crisp cool weather into November is typical.

Winter: Below freezing from December to early March, alternating with milder weather. Snowfall is prevalent, providing excellent conditions for winter sports.

Spring: Mostly sunny days late March to mid-June with scattered rain showers or the more rare snow showers through early May.

Restaurant and Accommodation Pricing

The restaurant cost categories refer to the price of entrees without beverages, desserts, taxes, or tips. Those listed as inexpensive are $10 or less;

moderate, between $10 and $20; and expensive, $20 or more. Places to stay listed as inexpensive are $100 or less per double per night; moderate, $101 to $200 per night; and expensive, $201 or more per night.

Northeastern South Dakota

By a fortunate accident of nature, the northeastern area of South Dakota, also known as the Glacial Lakes Region, features prime boating and recreational areas, with 16 state parks and two national wildlife refuges. Serendipity appeared in the form of glaciers some 20,000 years ago, and more than 120 lakes and miles of prairies were left when the glaciers retreated. This area is referred to as the Young Drift Plains by geologists, but residents simply call it the Lakes Region. For the most part the area is swampy plain, dotted with lakes and marshes. The notable exception is the wide, flat valley of the James River. I-29, which runs north-south, and US 12, which runs east-west, help keep travel and commerce flowing from Sioux Falls, in the southeastern corner of the state, to Rapid City, in the west.

Aberdeen Area

We'll begin on US 12 in the northwest corner of the James River valley, anchored by **Aberdeen,** which was first settled by the Arikara Indians, who introduced farming to the region. Established Americans from the East Coast

NORTHEASTERN SOUTH DAKOTA

NORTH DAKOTA
SOUTH DAKOTA

SISSETON LAKES AREA

Aberdeen
Ipswich
ABERDEEN
AREA
Webster
Milbank

Faulkton
Redfield
James R.
Watertown

BROOKINGS
Huron   De Smet
Brookings

Flandreau

SOUTH DAKOTA
MINNESOTA

0   30 mi
0   30 km

and newly arrived pioneers from Scandinavian countries, Germany, Russia, and the British Isles were to follow by train and wagon and on foot. Established in 1881 near the Milwaukee Railroad, the town was named for Aberdeen, Scotland, the hometown of Alexander Mitchell, president of the railroad. Aberdeen soon became known as the Hub City in recognition of the rail lines that converged here—at least nine of them in 1890—like spokes on a wagon wheel. These days the community has more than 1,400 businesses and more than 26,000 residents, making it the third largest city in South Dakota. Agriculture and manufacturing still anchor the economy, while the city provides a regional hub for services and education. Northern State University, a public university established in 1901, and Presentation College, a small four-year Catholic college, bring history, higher learning, and the arts to the Aberdeen area.

> ## wheretoretire
>
> *CNN Money Magazine* named South Dakota the No. 1 state for retiring and featured Aberdeen in 2014.

You can wander through the whimsical world of *Wizard of Oz* author L. Frank Baum's imagination at Aberdeen's **Storybook Land** on US 281. It includes **Land of Oz** with Dorothy's farmstead (complete with special effects to simulate a tornado), a petting zoo with farm animals, a Yellow Brick Road that leads to Munchkin Land (a small cornfield that is planted

NORTHEASTERN SOUTH DAKOTA'S
TOP HITS

Bramble Park Zoo	Ingalls Homestead
Children's Museum of South Dakota	Redlin Art Center
Dacotah Prairie Museum	South Dakota Art Museum
Fort Sisseton State Park	South Dakota State Fair
Gladys Pyle Historic Home	Storybook Land & Wylie Park

The Man Behind *The Wizard of Oz*

The area's best-known resident was L. Frank Baum, author of numerous children's books including a 12-book "Oz" series that inspired *The Wizard of Oz*, one of America's all-time favorite Hollywood musicals. *The Wizard of Oz* movie debuted in 1939, 20 years after Baum's death, and his stories are still influencing popular culture with *Oz the Great and Powerful* hitting movie theaters in 2013.

L. Frank Baum moved to Aberdeen from New York in 1888 and opened a variety store called Baum's Bazaar that fall. Unfortunately, he was lacking the necessary business skills and had a track record of barely supporting his wife, Maud, and their sons. The daydreamer who loved to act and entertain didn't always please his formidable mother-in-law, Matilda Josyln Gage, a famed suffragist.

While Baum often bounced between jobs in his younger years—and he stayed in Aberdeen only until 1891—South Dakota was where he found a way to let his writing skills flourish. After closing the store, he bought the town newspaper. He renamed it the *Aberdeen Saturday Pioneer* and proved to be a top-notch journalist. Baum's stories were witty, satirical, and sometimes controversial, but the town's happenings were always reported with great passion. Writing let Baum tap the storytelling skills he would use with his boys at bedtime and lean on his love of playwriting and acting.

By 1896 and at the age of 40, he was writing *Mother Goose in Prose* and *Father Goose, His Book* and on his way to becoming America's first successful children's author. By 1890, when his first "Oz" book was published, it became an instant hit. Scholars suggest that the populist prairie might have inspired the Land of Oz, a fairyland where the common man and woman become hero and heroine and self-reliance saves the day.

He died in 1919, leaving the world a legacy of Yellow Brick Roads, ruby slippers, winged monkeys, and a dreamy land somewhere over the rainbow.

and harvested annually), the Scarecrow's and Tin Man's homes, the Haunted Forest and Lion's Den, and the Wicked Witch's Castle. The Wizard Balloon Ride offers a view of the park from about 32 feet in the air.

Other larger-than-life exhibits at Storybook Land were inspired by fairy tales and nursery rhymes, such as "Jack and Jill Went Up the Hill," "Cinderella," "Jack and the Beanstalk," and "Humpty Dumpty." Kids can climb aboard Captain Hook's ship, ride a carousel, slide down the Tin Man's giant metal legs, crawl through a tunnel to watch prairie dogs at the zoo, and explore a medieval castle. The zoo also includes buffalo, elk, sheep, deer, and geese.

Admission to Storybook Land is free, although rides are extra, including a trip aboard the scale-model replica of the 1863 C.P. Huntington that chugs and whistles its way around the park.

The *Visitor Center* stays open 10 a.m. to 9 p.m. between Memorial Day and Labor Day weekends, with shorter hours in the spring and fall (roughly April 15–October 15). Call the park at (605) 626-7015 for more information or go to aberdeen.sd.us.

Surrounding Storybook Land, you'll find *Wylie Park,* with 200 acres of recreation that includes a lake, picnicking, paved trails, and golf. With *Thunder Road,* you can race go-karts or minigolf past a volcano spew-

rollthrough thepark

If you're seeking a whimsical way to get around the sprawling Wylie Park, *Rollout Bike Rentals* provides choppers, surreys, tandem bikes, pedal go-karts and John Deere Tractor bikes. Call (605) 255-1139 or go to rolloutbikerentals.com for details.

ing flames (605-225-8541; thunderroad.info). Events are held throughout the year, including *Haunted Forest* the third weekend in October. Visitors are guided through 13 spooky scenes led by ghoulish guides. A matinee walk-through is available for younger children, who are invited to wear costumes and collect candy at every scene (aberdeenhauntedforest.org).

Lake Minne-Eho, Wylie Park's man-made lake with more than 1,000 feet of shoreline, features an unsupervised swimming area and is stocked each year for those under age 16 to try their fishing skills. You can rent paddleboats or canoes to get onto the water. On a few Saturdays in the summer, you can catch the *Aqua Addicts Ski Shows.* Check the Parks and Recreation guide at aberdeen.sd.us for specific times.

Kids craving a cooler destination on sizzling summer days can shoot down a 280-foot raft slide, a 215-foot body slide, or an enclosed 125-foot slide at the outdoor *Aberdeen Aquatic Center.* The large complex includes an 8-lane lap pool, diving boards, and a lazy river. Day passes are $5.25–$7.25. Call (605) 626-7015 or go to aberdeen.sd.us/aquatics for more information.

Wylie Park Campground offers paved roads and camp pads, 115 RV campsites, a dozen camping cabins, 2 larger cabins, and a 3-bedroom deluxe cabin that sleeps 8 and has kitchen and bathroom facilities. For reservations, call (605) 626-3512 or toll-free (888) 326-9693.

You can learn more about author L. Frank Baum and about life in Brown County at downtown Aberdeen's free **Dacotah Prairie Museum,** tucked into an 1880s bank building rising grandly from Main Street. Walk through the luxurious brass-ceilinged, velvet-curtained Pullman passenger car, watch model trains chug through old Aberdeen, peek into an Arikara earth lodge and a Lakota tipi, and marvel at a 7-ton African elephant in the wildlife gallery. If you have kids in tow, print out a scavenger map before your visit. Museum galleries are open from 9 a.m. to 5 p.m. Tues through Fri and 1 to 4 p.m. Sat and Sun.

aninsidelook atfarms

If you can plan ahead and travel in a group of 10 or more, Aberdeen's Convention and Visitors Bureau puts together special tours of wheat farms, cattle ranches, a pheasant farm, sculptor Ben Victor's studio, or a chance to visit the area's *Hutterite Colonies*, a self-sustaining rural community that has changed little in more than 400 years.

From April 15 to October 15, the museum also opens the **Granary Rural Cultural Center,** where you can look at artwork in the 1928 granary and walk the grounds where sculptures and interpretive signs tell about life in the fertile valley where the James River squiggles across the landscape. To reach this historic farm, which also includes a 1912 town hall, head west on Highway 12 and north on Highway 10 until you reach 128th Street. It's about 20 miles northeast of Aberdeen. For more information on the granary and Dacotah Prairie Museum, call (605) 626-7117 or go to dacotah prairiemuseum.com.

If you love history, leave time to stroll the **Highlands Historical District,** on North Main Street between 12th and 15th Avenues, encompassing 17 homes built between 1907 and 1969. The district earned the lofty title of Highlands because it rose 3 feet higher than the commercial sector, which was located in a slough. When the first houses were built, only prairie grass covered the area, so young trees were brought up from along the James River and transplanted here to line the sedate streets. Many architectural styles have melded in the district over the years, and the result is a

Aberdeen Railway Station Canteen

Aberdeen cemented its reputation as *Pheasant Capital of the World* and Home of the Pheasant Sandwich with a simple intention to support soldiers during World War II. The town set up a canteen in 1943 at the 1911 Milwaukee Depot as thousands of troops flowed through it and arrived hungry. Red Cross and USO volunteers served what was available, and soon soldiers were raving about the pheasant sandwiches. Word spread quickly, demand skyrocketed, and the railroad fueled the fame by advertising these sought-after sandwiches in national magazines.

Aberdeen-area volunteers put in 24-hour shifts making and serving sandwiches, and locals gave up their own wartime rations for items such as butter to feed the troops. Others in the region and across the state helped with supplemental pheasant hunts, and a local meat locker kept up to 1,000 birds stashed and ready for soldiers. The canteen fed an average of 500 soldiers a day with a record number hitting 1,500 on their busiest day. The canteen operated through March 1946, serving an estimated 586,000 troops and forever linking pheasant to local hospitality.

You can view a documentary on the canteen at the Depot from 8 a.m. to 5 p.m. Mon through Fri.

Aberdeen's famous pheasant sandwiches:

Finely chop 3 cups cooked pheasant, 2 hard-boiled eggs, half a medium onion, and ½ cup celery. Add 2 grated carrots and 2 teaspoons pickle relish, plus salt and pepper to taste. Stir in enough mayonnaise or salad dressing to blend nicely and spread the mix onto bread.

—Courtesy of the WWII Pheasant Canteen

fascinating study in both modern and classical structures. Call (800) 645-3851 or go to visitaberdeensd.com for more information.

When you reach the dead end of 2nd Avenue Northwest, you have arrived at an isolated, strangely ominous home called ***Easton's Castle.*** Drive by and inspect the Jacobean revival architecture that was popular in England in the 1830s. Multiple windows, peaked roofs, and gables distinguish this style. Samples of the home's French-made wallpaper, which remains intact, have been documented in the Cooper Hewitt Museum of Design of the Smithsonian Institution.

If you visit Aberdeen in the fall, you'll be in good company as pheasant hunters flood into eastern South Dakota and roam across its rich grasslands with bird dogs at their side. The Aberdeen area alone has more than 350,000 acres of public and private hunting lands with several counties that estimate more than 200 pheasants per square mile. Hunters who bag one of 100 specially banded birds can win prizes from $100 to $1 million—like a feathered lottery. If you're new to the sport, you can find many outfitters to ease you into it and find the best hunting locations. Call (605) 225-2414 or go to huntfishsd.com for more information.

While you're downtown, be sure to leave time to browse Aberdeen's Main Street, peppered with shops, restaurants, and the 1926 French art deco **Capitol Theatre,** which hosts new movies, Aberdeen Community Theatre productions, and the annual South Dakota Film Festival. The **Red Rooster Coffee House** at 202 South Main St. also provides night life by hosting local musicians playing everything from old-time jams and bluegrass to cover bands and rock. The coffee house also has an art gallery, hot sauce shop, and fair trade gift store, and serves croissant sandwiches, soup, bagels, hummus sandwiches, nachos, and baked goods. Visit redrooster.ning.com for information or call (605) 225-6603.

As you head east or west of Aberdeen on US 12, take a little time to ponder this route's rich history as one of the country's first transcontinental highways, dubbed the **Yellowstone Trail.** J. W. Parmley, known as the "Father of the Yellowstone Trail," bought his first automobile in 1905 and spearheaded the idea of connecting rural communities from Minneapolis to Yellowstone National Park with "one main good road." That idea then expanded to one good road "from Plymouth Rock to Puget Sound."

Parmley lived just west of Aberdeen in the cozy burg of **Ipswich.**

airboatrides

You don't have to be in the Everglades to experience a unique way to zip across marshes and shallow ponds. Ken's Airboat Service at (605) 530-2430 can take up to six passengers into this area's remote and beautiful wetlands.

You can learn more about him and local history at the **J. W. Parmley Museum** at 319 Fourth St. Like other notable South Dakotans, he had a thing for geology and showcased his family's eccentric array of rocks, shells,

South Dakota Hunting Seasons

Pheasant (traditional)
mid-Oct to early Jan
(preserve)
Sept to Mar

Prairie Chicken
mid-Sept to mid-Oct

Dove
Sept to mid-Oct

Waterfowl
Early Oct to early Dec

East River deer (firearms)
mid-Nov to early Dec
(archery)
late Sept to Dec

Turkey
Spring and fall

and minerals collected during his family's travels when he built the two fireplaces in their home. An iron fence post, allegedly from a fence around Sitting Bull's grave when his remains were buried at Fort Yates, forms part of one fireplace. Another quirk of the 1919 home: Mr. Parmley considered himself a practical man (and lost his previous home to a prairie fire), so this one was built mostly from concrete, including floors and bathtubs. For more information call (605) 426-6580 or visit ipswich-sd.com. The home, along with *Parmley Western Land Office,* is open Memorial Day through Labor Day, Wed, Fri, and Sun from 2 to 5 p.m.

Ipswich, platted in 1883, boasts some of South Dakota's finest fieldstone architecture. Check out its First Baptist Church, the community library (a charming Hansel-and-Gretel-like stone structure), and on its lawn the mysterious Prayer Rock, a giant boulder with handprints supposedly carved by a Native American medicine man. At the city park, you'll also find Memorial Arch that once arced over the Yellowstone Trail. It was reconstructed after a storm and like Parmley's fireplaces boasts an eclectic collection of stones from all 50 states, calcite crystals from the Badlands, fossils, and even stones brought back from World War II by soldiers stationed on Pacific Islands.

If traveling the Yellowstone Trail gets you in the mood to road-trip, take advantage of the Dakotas' excellent birding in the prairie pothole region.

About 40 miles northeast of Aberdeen, *Sand Lake National Wildlife Refuge* boasts 21,451 acres of wildlife and waterfowl in grasslands, forest, lake, and marsh. The area surrounding the refuge was once vast, rolling grassland interrupted only by the slow-moving curves of the James River. Settlers arrived in 1887 and brought sweeping changes to the landscape. Farming and grazing depleted essential wildlife habitat, causing waterfowl to dwindle to alarmingly low numbers by the 1930s.

Congress established Sand Lake in 1935 to preserve critical habitat for nesting and migrating waterfowl, and it was also designated a Wetland of International Importance in 1971—one of only 16 such sites in the US. Today millions of ducks, geese, and other wildlife make Sand Lake their home. In fact, 266 species of birds have been recorded at the refuge since 1935, including white pelicans, snow geese, and western grebes, which are known for their almost comical mating dance that has them skittering upright across the water.

Most people choose to drive through the refuge. A nicely illustrated, self-guided auto-tour guide is available. Along the 15-mile route there are 12 numbered stations, which correspond to symbols and text in the brochure. Station Two, for instance, affords an overlook where two important duck-nesting habitats can be seen. Station Eight is perfect for birders. Great horned owls occasionally roost here, and mallards, pintails, and the smaller blue-winged and green-winged teal also can be seen. If you're craving more of a bird's-eye view, climb the 108-foot observation tower built by the

TOP ANNUAL EVENTS

Arts in the Park
Aberdeen, June
Contact the Aberdeen Arts Council,
(605) 226-1557

Laura Ingalls Wilder Pageant
De Smet, last weekend in June and
first two weekends in July
(800) 776-3594

**Northeast South Dakota Celtic Faire
and Games**
Third full weekend in September
nesdcelticfaire.com

Storybook Land Festival
Aberdeen, July
Contact the Aberdeen Arts Council,
(605) 226-1557

South Dakota Film Festival
Aberdeen, September
(605) 725-2697
southdakotafilmfest.org

South Dakota State Fair
One week starting Labor Day weekend
(800) 529-0900
sdstatefair.com

Civilian Conservation Corps in 1936. Another good observation point is the Sand Lake Overlook in the Columbia Day Use Area.

To reach the refuge from Aberdeen, take US 12 east to CR 16 (Bath Corner, 7 miles east of Aberdeen). Drive 20 miles north, through Columbia, to the refuge entrance. You can tour the Wildlife Drive 7 days a week, from daylight to dark, between early Apr and mid-Oct. The visitor center and main office are open Mon through Fri, 8 a.m. to 4:30 p.m. and some additional weekends depending on the availability of volunteers. Visitor center restrooms have access 24 hours a day. For more information, call (605) 885-6320 or visit fws.gov/sandlake.

If you drive about 50 minutes west of the Sand Prairie National Wildlife Refuge, you'll find another excellent spot for birding at *Samuel H. Ordway Jr. Memorial Preserve.* At 7,800 acres, it's the Nature Conservancy's largest tract of preserved prairie in South Dakota. You can find it about 8 miles west of Leola, a small town that sits at the intersection of Highways 10 and 45. Look for a parking area just off Highway 10. Trails include a new self-guided lichen trail with more than 30 species identified, along with the chance to see spring and summer wildflowers, granite boulders and potholes left by glaciers, tipi rings, and a ruined homestead. You may also be able to see some of the Conservancy's herd of 250 bison from the fence in the nature trail area. There are no facilities, so bring sunscreen, plenty of

let'splayball

If you continue east on US 12, you'll find the *birthplace of American Legion baseball* in Milbank, home to 3,640 people on the South Dakota–Minnesota border (about 47 miles northeast of Watertown). American Legion baseball began at a 1925 convention of that organization in Milbank. A historical marker commemorating the birth of American Legion baseball is located near the community baseball field. Former American Legion players include Yogi Berra, Johnny Bench, Jim Palmer, Frank Robinson, Greg Gagne, and Jack Morris.

Baseball fans should also consider a trip to tiny Lake Norden (pop. 467) about 27 miles south of Watertown, following Highway 81 and heading east on Highway 28. It's home to the **South Dakota Amateur Baseball Hall of Fame.** It chronicles 100 years of amateur baseball with photos and mementos of its best players. It's open 9 a.m. to 7 p.m. May through Oct.

water, and bug repellent. Call (605) 439-3475 for more information or go to nature.org.

Only an hour's drive from Aberdeen (take SD 45 south from Ipswich, then go west on US 212) is the **Pickler Mansion** in **Faulkton,** a friendly town of 785 people. John A. Pickler served four terms as South Dakota's first US representative-at-large, and his wife, Alice W. Alt Pickler, campaigned for the suffrage cause. Fellow suffragette Susan B. Anthony was one of the more famous guests in the home, and some of her original letters found here are on display.

The home, a 20-room Victorian house on the prairie, is complete with a secret room and a 2,550-book library that features Civil War and congressional sections. Called the Pink Castle (its distinct pink color was chosen by pioneer artist Charles T. Greener in 1894), the mansion is open daily from Memorial Day through Labor Day from 1 to 4 p.m. and at other times by appointment. Call (605) 598-4285 for a guide. Admission is $5 per person.

Faulkton is called the Carousel City because it is home to the state's only electrically operated permanent 1925 Parker carousel. The carousel features 19 original aluminum-cast horses. Located on 9th Avenue South, the **Happy Times Carousel** can be enjoyed for free Wed 7 to 8 p.m. and from 3 to 5 p.m. and 6:30 to 8 p.m. Sat and Sun during the summer season. Call (605) 598-4285 for hours of operation.

Sisseton Lakes Area

If you travel 53 miles east of Aberdeen on US 12, you reach **Webster,** which sits on the cusp of an area dense with glacial lakes. Start with a visit to the **Day County Museum** (214 Eighth Ave. West; 605-345-3765), in the basement of the Day County Courthouse. Artifacts include Native American bow and arrows, spears, arrowheads, beautiful beaded items, stone tools, a drummer's stick, and three beaded war clubs. Among the farm equipment used by early-day settlers are cow and sheep bells, single and double oxen yokes, an iron hoe, and a hand corn planter. One of the more unusual items is a hair wreath made in 1865 from human hair, which was either crocheted, knitted, or wound around cardboard to make flower petals. The free museum is open 2 to 5 p.m. Mon, Wed, and Fri.

For an utterly eclectic museum experience, Webster also includes the ***Museum of Wildlife, Science, and Industry of Northeastern South Dakota.*** The assortment of 23 buildings includes a shoe-shaped one housing a shoe collection, farmhouses, a jail, church, post office, and oddities such as the world's largest hairball. Open daily mid-May through mid-Oct. Call (605) 345-4751 or check sdmuseum.org for more details.

If you head 10 miles east on US 12 and turn north on 444th Avenue, you can find the ***Blue Dog State Fish Hatchery*** at 44437 139A St. in Waubay. Considered the largest hatchery in the state, the 53-acre facility produces 70 million fish a year. Stop at the visitor center and aquarium to learn how they harvest eggs, incubate them, and rear northern pike, walleye, yellow perch, large and smallmouth bass, bluegill, and crappie to stock the state's lakes. They also raise cold-water species, such as trout and Chinook salmon in the winter. Stop by between 8:30 a.m. and 4 p.m. Mon through Fri.

If you head back to Webster and follow Highways 25 and 17 for about 23 miles, you'll reach ***Fort Sisseton State Park*** at 20641 SD Highway 1806, Fort Pierre. Here, you can step back into the western frontier at this 1864 site originally called Fort Wadsworth. To see it truly come to life with the bang of muzzleloaders, a whiff of black powder, and the clip-clop of cavalry horses, catch the annual Fort Sisseton Festival the first weekend in June. There also is a visitor center and museum, plus a self-guided tour of the buildings, open the weekend before Memorial Day through Sep-

> ## tip
>
> If you're going birding, bring binoculars, a good camera, and a helpful guide such as the *Northeastern South Dakota Glacial Lakes Birding Guide*. If you cannot find a copy at tourism offices, download one at gfp.sd.gov/wildlife/docs/glacial -lakes-birding.pdf.

tember. The park offers camping, cabins, boating, canoeing, hiking, and fishing. See sdgfp.info/parks or call (605) 448-5474 for details on hours and other information.

Two other notable state parks within 30 miles also are worth exploring. ***Roy Lake State Park*** at 11547 Northside Dr. in Lake City is only 20 minutes from Fort Sisseton State Park and offers a large, nicely shaded lakeside campground and camping cabins. With canoe and kayak rentals, hiking, a boat launch, beach, disc golf, and fishing, it's an ideal pick for a weekend of family camping. (Worth noting: Families have been sharing meals along this shore since AD 1300 or earlier, according to burial mounds and artifacts found nearby.) Call (800) 710-2267 or visit campSD.com for site reservations at either Fort Sisseton or Roy Lake.

If you follow winding CR 10 east of Highway 10 (a good map will help), you'll reach **Sica Hollow State Park.** Sica, a native word pronounced "she-cha," means evil or bad with Dakota lore telling of reddish bogs thought to be the blood of their ancestors and of other mysterious happenings. These days the Trail of Spirits is a nationally designated trail and considered a scenic hike into the woods, along waterfalls and through patches of wildflowers.

You can find campsites here as well, along with snowmobile trails and cross-country skiing in the winter. Roy Lake is another good option for skiing.

One of the most pleasant ways to enjoy the gorgeous scenery of this region and its coteau topography is to take a trail ride with **Prairie Sky Ranch,** 44370 109th St. near tiny Veblen. It's a gorgeous view and fantastic experience to spend a night in one of their cabins on the coteau—even with a storm rolling in and offering Mother Nature's sound-and-light show. Like most private South Dakota ranches or bed-and-breakfasts, hunters are their main customers. Your best bet is to make reservations before those seasons open. Call (605) 738-2411 or go to prairieskyranch.com for more information.

The Coteau des Prairies is the highest point between Winnipeg, Manitoba, Canada, and the Gulf of Mexico and the Appalachians and the Black Hills. Lewis and Clark referred to it as the "mountain of the prairie" on their 1814 expedition maps. Today it's best known as an area where wind turbines pinwheel across the horizon and take advantage of coteau-influenced winds, especially on the southeast portion in Minnesota.

Coteau des Prairies

The often overlooked but beautiful **National Natural Landmark** known as Coteau des Prairies ("hills of the prairie") is a wedge-shaped plateau that rises more than 2,000 feet above the flat prairie of South Dakota, stretches 100 miles in width, and runs 200 miles, crossing into both southwestern Minnesota and Iowa.

From Sica Hollow State Park, head back to Highway 10 and head east toward Sisseton. About 3.5 miles west of town you'll see the ***Joseph N. Nicollet Tower and Interpretive Center,*** which is dedicated to the French mapmaker who could very well be a sort of real-life Lieutenant Dunbar from the Academy Award–winning movie *Dances with Wolves.* (The Kevin Costner movie, by the way, was filmed in South Dakota.) Nicollet spent 1838 and 1839 creating the first accurate map of the vast area between the Mississippi and Missouri Rivers. He was trained as an astronomer in Paris, and he took highly accurate notes in his journals that recorded more than his precise mathematical calculations. Like those of the fictional Dunbar, Nicollet's journals also illuminated a love for the prairies and respect and understanding of native people. He wrote in 1839 of the Coteau des Prairies (Hill of the Prairies):

May I not be permitted to introduce a few reflections of the prairies? . . . Their sight never wearies . . . to ascend one of its undulations, moving from wave to wave over alternate swells and depressions; and finally to reach the vast interminable low prairie, that extends itself in front, be it for hours, days or weeks, one never tires; pleasurable and exhilarating sensations are all the time felt. . . . I pity the man whose soul could remain unmoved under such a scene of excitement.

Today, the 75-foot observation tower with three floors affords a breathtaking view of the great valley carved by glaciers some 40,000 years ago. On clear days you should be able to see North Dakota, Minnesota, and South Dakota.

The "mother map" of the Midwest is displayed at the foot of the tower. Nicollet was the first person to create maps that showed elevations and topography changes. He also included many of the Native American names for rivers, lakes, and other natural features, many of which are still used today. He presented the map to the US Senate in 1841. Original artwork by nationally recognized wildlife artist John S. Wilson also is displayed in the Interpretive Center, as are paintings depicting the Dakota Indian people Nicollet described in his journals. The tower is open May through Oct, 10 a.m. to 5 p.m. Mon through Fri and 1 to 4 p.m. Sun. Call (605) 698-7621 for more information.

The Legend of Sam Brown

The Dakotas are rich with legends great and small. One such hero is Sam Brown, who in 1866 was chief scout for Fort Wadsworth, now known as Fort Sisseton. He was told of an approaching Sioux Indian war party, and Sam sent a warning message to a fort farther north. Sam mounted his horse and set off to scout a camp 60 miles west. When he arrived, he discovered that the war party was simply several Indians delivering word of a new peace treaty. Sam knew that to prevent bloodshed, he must intercept his warning. Struggling through the freezing rain and snow of a ruthless spring blizzard, he managed to reach the fort by morning. But as he slipped from his horse, exhausted and half frozen, he was unable to stand. Sam Brown's heroic 150-mile ride cost him the use of his legs. He never walked again.

While you're in the area, stop by the *Stavig House Museum* at 112 First Ave. NW in Sisseton. The museum follows the lives of Norwegians in the area through many walks of life, from entrepreneur to humble fisherman. During the summer, the three-story 1916 Victorian home is open from 10 a.m. to 4 p.m. Thurs through Sat, 1 to 4 p.m. Sun. Open by appointment and for special events in the winter. A guided tour costs $5. Call (605) 698-4561 for more information or visit sissetonmuseums.org for information on both Nicollet Tower and the museum.

Watertown

From Sisseton take US 12 east to I-29 and go south until you reach the crossroads of I-29 and US 212. It is here that you will find *Watertown.* Known as the Lake City, Watertown quite naturally lives up to its name; the town is situated along the Big Sioux River and is bordered by Lake Kampeska and Lake Pelican. Originally called Kampeska, the settlement owed its initial boom to the railroads. These days it's a mostly agriculture-based community (population 21,995), diversified in small grains, row crops, and livestock.

No Watertown traveler can miss seeing its best-known attraction—the Redlin Art Center—with its grandiose hilltop location and 24 massive granite columns that make it visible for miles. It may be tempting to skip if you think you've seen enough of artist Terry Redlin's work on Boy Scout tins, calendars, and puzzles, but the several floors inside tell a touching tale of a humble artist from Watertown who poignantly captured scenes of everyday midwestern life that he called "romantic realism."

You can view Redlin's entire collection of more than 150 original paintings—from early sketches and wildlife scenes to the stirringly patriotic *America the Beautiful.* His "An American Portrait" series depicts a single home through several decades starting when the family's son was young and climbing trees to when a military officer arrives with news of the young man's death. There's a reason they keep a box of tissues near the video about those paintings. The center is also home to a collection of artifacts from ***Langenfeld's Ice Cream and Dairy,*** owned and operated by the family of Terry's wife, Helene. The center closes on major holidays, but its sprawling grounds make it a popular spot for watching Watertown's Fourth of July fireworks. The art center is open 9 a.m. to 5 p.m. Mon through Fri, 10 a.m. to 4 p.m. Sat, and noon to 4 p.m. Sun, with longer hours in the summer months. Admission is free. Call (877) 873-3546 or visit redlinart .com for more information.

seekredlin's inspirations

While at the Redlin Art Center, grab information on a ***Watertown driving tour.*** It highlights landmarks and locations from the area that were included in Redlin's paintings.

Don't miss a trip into Watertown's sizable historic downtown. Besides numerous secondhand shops, there are several places worth checking out. ***Past Times Coffee House and Restaurant*** at 16 W. Kemp Ave. (605-882-5813; pasttimesrestaurant .com) offers walls filled with local memorabilia to browse while waiting for a Cranny Granny (grilled turkey sandwich with cranberries), a Cow Tipper (roast beef sandwich with garlic pepper cream cheese), or bread pudding made with their homemade caramel rolls.

The ***Watertown Confectionery*** (116 E. Kemp Ave.; 605-753-5249; watertownconfectionery.net) features addictive chocolate-covered crushed jalapeño potato chips and other sweet treats, but it has become an even bigger draw for home brewers, winemakers, and even soda pop fans who come for classes, kits, and ingredients to make their own beverages, from a foamy stout and frothy root beer to special-occasion wines.

b&binthe country

The Dakota Inn Bed and Breakfast, 45587 177th St., offers a pastoral country setting with grazing sheep and big-sky views that would fit right in with a Terry Redlin painting. The house built in 2008 includes four guest rooms and three bathrooms, six miles from Watertown. Call (605) 520-2521 or go to dakotabandb.com.

Across the street, *Birchtree Gallery and Framing* offers stained glass, mosaic, and lapidary art classes, along with a nice variety of local artwork (605-881-0626; birchtreeframing.com). You can also admire paintings and catch local musicians at the elegant Goss Opera House just down the block at 100 E. Kemp. Lovingly restored, this historic building's main floor offers an elegant, eclectic spot for drinks, coffee, ice cream, and date-night dinners. Be sure to ask if you can take a peek at the 1889 opera house upstairs. It features lakeside murals and a Pied Piper leading a line of children (605-878-4677; gossoperahouse.com).

Pop into the *Codington County Heritage Museum* in a former Carnegie Library at 27 First Ave. SE, if you're interested in local history. Exhibits are heavy on war memorabilia, plus Indian, pioneer, and railroad artifacts. It's open 10 a.m. to 5 p.m. Mon through Fri in the summer and 1 to 5 p.m. in the off-season, along with 1 to 5 p.m. Sat. Admission is free; donations are accepted. Call (605) 886-7335 or visit cchsmuseum.org for more information.

pheasantsgo wild

The Bramble Park Zoo was started in 1912 as a display of pheasants and waterfowl donated by Frank Bramble. Bramble also was instrumental in getting South Dakota to put 250 pairs of Chinese ringneck pheasants into the wild in 1911. They—obviously—thrived and have become a key part of South Dakota's culture.

If you meander into the residential area on the north side of town, you'll find more history at the *Mellette House* (421 Fifth Ave. NW). South Dakota's first governor, Arthur C. Mellette, was appointed governor of the Dakota Territory by President Benjamin Harrison and later was elected governor of the new state of South Dakota. Free guided tours offer insight into South Dakota life in the

Buffalo Ridge

Buffalo Ridge Resort, 45 miles southeast of Watertown and near the Minnesota border, ranks among South Dakota's more intriguing places to stay. The centerpiece is the 19-room Herrick Hotel, a classy and art-filled transformation of the former South Dakota's first School for the Blind and Visually Impaired that opened in 1900. The resort opened in 2009 on the edge of Gary, population 225. The shaded, peaceful setting makes it a destination wedding spot and business retreat—especially for people in the wind industry that thrives in this region. The property includes more than 30 campsites and a tipi, walking trails, trout fishing at Lake Elsie, and the Rock Room Bar and Grill. Call (605) 272-7777 or go to buffaloridge.com for more information.

1880s as seen through one of its leading families. Artifacts in the Victorian-era rooms include Maggie Mellette's china painting, crazy quilts made by the maid, and Indian beadwork and sashes. The home is open May 1 through Oct 1, Tues through Sun from 1 to 5 p.m. Call (605) 886-4730 or visit mellettehouse.org.

If you're traveling with children, don't miss **Bramble Park Zoo,** which brings you face-to-face with playful lemurs, a white Bengal tiger, and black bears among more than 500 mammals, reptiles, and birds from around the world as well as those native to the Great Plains. The zoo's small size keeps it relaxed and easy to get close to animals, especially free-roaming birds such as a scarlet ibis and peafowl that trail you like hungry shadows. Indoors, the Terry Redlin Environmental Center includes dioramas with mounted animals and a variety of aquariums. On weekends in the summer, zoo keepers offer special talks. The zoo is open year-round, weather permitting, from 10 a.m. to 7 p.m. in the summer, and from 10 a.m. to 4 p.m. in the winter. Admission ranges from free for ages 2 and under to $8 for adults. Call (605) 882-6269 or visit brambleparkzoo.com for general information and special events.

Brookings

If you take I-29 south from Watertown for 44 miles, you'll reach the state's largest university, South Dakota State University, in **Brookings,** home to

22,943 people. The university enriches the community in many ways, from ice cream to an art museum, from gardens to college games that thrum with Jackrabbit pride.

It also boasts one of the state's best family attractions: *The Children's Museum of South Dakota* at 521 Fourth St. Even if you don't have kids or grandkids along or a few hours to explore its locally inspired exhibits, it's worth stopping by to see this inspirational and clever reuse of a historic school built in the 1920s. You can grab a hot or frozen coffee or a full meal (including a playful grilled cheese that looks like an owl) at the museum's *Coteau Cafe* in an open and airy atrium added onto the school in 2010. The many windows offer an entertaining view of the prairie-themed outdoor play area. Summer's definitely the best time to visit because you can watch kids fishing in a pond, splashing in a river, going through the prairie grass maze, and digging up dinosaur fossils. The big hit for most: a baby T. rex and his mama, who both pack a roar and move realistically enough to send some kids scurrying. The museum's open 10 a.m. to 5 p.m. Mon through Sat and noon to 5 p.m. Sun. Admission is $6/person, but you can dine here without going into the museum. Call (605) 692-6700 or visit prairieplay.org for more information.

Across the street at 424 Fifth St. is another example of the town's creative architectural transformations. What was once a 1958 bank with drive-through lanes is now home to a boutique and the *Old Market Eatery and Bar* (605-692-5757; oldmarketeatery.com). The drive-through area was enclosed in glass to become a heated porch that's perfect for dining on balmy summer days when the breeze wafts through and the sun shines in. Try one of their citrusy salads, hand-cut market fries, fragrant hummus made with basil, and desserts such as tangy rhubarb upside-down cake.

While downtown, take a stroll to admire the colorful summer landscaping. The community's support of gardening shouldn't be a surprise when it's home to *McCrory Gardens and State Arboretum,* at 6th Street and 20th Avenue. With 20 acres of formal display gardens and 45 acres of arboretum, it's called the prettiest quarter section in the state, and a visitor center built in 2012 makes an impressive entrance. Visitors can wander 14 formal theme gardens and a rose garden with more than 30 varieties, an herb garden, a sensory garden, a children's maze, a historic gas station renovated as a garden cottage, and a memorial to Governor George S.

Old-fashioned Hamburgers and Malts

For a blast from the past, don't miss **Nick's Hamburgers** at 427 Main, a local institution since 1929. Their burgers were priced at a nickel and haven't gone above $1.48. That means even money-strapped college students should be able to hop onto one of the red vinyl bar stools and splurge on fries, homemade pie, or a thick shake to go with it. They're open 11 a.m. to 7 p.m. Mon through Fri, 11 a.m. to 4 p.m. Sat. Call (605) 692-4324 or go to nickshamburgers.com.

Mickelson. You can check out what's up and coming in the trial garden for All-America seed selections and explore a "green" building constructed with straw bales for insulation and crowned with sedum on the living roof. Admission is technically free, but a $6 donation per adult and $3 per child is suggested. Call (605) 688-5921 or visit sdstate.edu/ps/mccrory for more information.

You'll find several good stops at South Dakota State University's campus along Medary Avenue.

The *South Dakota Art Museum,* at the intersection of Harvey Dunn Street, features permanent galleries, changing exhibitions featuring national and international artists, lectures, workshops, guided tours, and a gift shop packed with artsy and regionally made gifts. The absolute must-see: Harvey Dunn's *The Prairie Is My Garden,* one of Dunn's most iconic paintings that took inspiration from his childhood as the son of South Dakota homesteaders. Dunn's painting *Something for Supper* was among 20 stamps that honored America's greatest illustrators in 2001. Dunn was one of eight artists chosen to document World War I as it was happening and was so prolific in later decades that he once produced more than 55 paintings in 11 weeks. The museum has more than 112 of Dunn's works, but also honors other notable South Dakota artists. Oscar Howe is among its featured Native American artists, and children's book illustrator Paul Goble is featured in a child-friendly exhibit and puppet theater. The museum is open from 10 a.m. to 5 p.m. Mon through Fri, from 10 a.m. to 4 p.m. Sat. It's also open noon to 4 p.m. Sun Apr through Dec. Admission is free, although $2–$3 donations are encouraged. For more information, call (605) 688-5423 or visit south dakotaartmuseum.com.

About a block away at the intersection of Medary Avenue and 11th Street you'll find the *South Dakota Agricultural Heritage Museum.* Giant harvesters, tractors, and displays of engines show the evolution of farming technology and South Dakota's influence on building and improving the machinery that gathers the state's crops. Among the engines is the Briggs and Stratton brand, founded and built by South Dakota State University graduates. The museum also includes a "Life on the Land" gallery with an original Dakota Territory claim shanty and replica of a 1915 farmhouse. Exhibits rotate, but all offer a slice of life on the farm. It's open 10 a.m. to 5 p.m. Mon through Sat, as well as 1 to 5 p.m. Sun Apr through Dec. Admission is free, and you can call (605) 688-6226 or visit sdstate.edu/agmuseum for more information.

If you're looking for a tasty souvenir of Brookings's agricultural heritage, head back across Medary Avenue to the *Dairy Bar* in the Alfred Dairy Science Hall. Pride in SDSU ice cream can be felt throughout the region, and the campus claims to have invented cookies-and-cream ice cream in the 1970s. You can choose from several riffs on the standard cookies-and-cream, which may be minty or sweetened with extra caramel. The Dairy Bar, remodeled in 2011 to feel polished and welcoming, offers 60 rotating flavors of ice cream throughout the year, such as sweetly nutty butter almond, peanut butter revel, and tangerine sherbet. You can also find cheese varieties, butter, and milk. All products are made at the SDSU Davis Dairy Plant (also rebuilt in 2011), which involves students in processing 18,000 pounds of milk a week. The Dairy Bar is open 7:30 a.m. to 6 p.m. Mon through Fri (605-697-2585; sdstate.edu/ds/plant).

Ice-cream aficionados should also beeline to the *Pheasant Restaurant and Lounge* in the southwest section of Brookings at 726 Main Ave. South. It has been serving the area since 1949, but third-generation general manager Michael Johnson has transformed it into a chic eatery with an outdoor patio, frequent jazz and live music nights, local wines and microbrews, appetizers like pheasant lettuce wraps, fresh twists on juicy burgers (think crostini burger or bison burger with Thai seasoning), and wildly creative ice cream. The restaurant also has a classy Coteau des Prairies olive oil and vinegar bar in the lobby with exotic flavors that infuse the restaurant's menu with light, zingy salad dressings, zippy marinades, and even unusual desserts. Artisan ice cream maker Trevor Clements crafts out-of-the-box flavors such as 18-year-old balsamic, Swedish lingonberry, sweet corn, coffee ice cream with candied bacon, and a zippy cayenne ginger Fireworks ice cream with Pop Rocks for pop. He also makes sorbets such as peach Riesling or watermelon basil. If you want a sweet way to enjoy a beer, try the dulce de leche ice cream in a Brau Brothers oatmeal stout. Plan on leaving absolutely stuffed and wanting to try more. For details on daily specials, scheduled musicians, or hours, call (605) 692-4723 or go to pheasantrestaurant.com.

South of Brookings and 30 miles north of Sioux Falls is the **Royal River Casino** (877-912-5825; royalrivercasino.com), located in **Flandreau** off I-29. The casino, owned by the Santee Sioux tribe, has rejuvenated the community of 2,301 residents. The town, situated along the Big Sioux River, was first settled in 1869 by 25 Christian Santee Sioux families who bravely gave up their tribal rights—and their surnames—so that they could homestead.

Religious themes recur in Flandreau through several historic churches built in the 1800s. Most notable is the **First Presbyterian Church** on North SD 13, the oldest continuously operating church in South Dakota.

Local events include the **Good Old Summertime Festival** during the Fourth of July and the Santee Sioux Powwow during the third week of July when residents don their full regalia to perform traditional ceremonies.

De Smet

Generations of Laura Ingalls Wilder fans from across the globe have found their way to tiny **De Smet** (population 1,082), the real setting for *Little House on the Prairie*, 42 miles west of Brookings at the intersection of SD 25 and US 14 (also part of the Laura Ingalls Wilder Historic Highway that runs from Wisconsin to South Dakota). Fresh-faced little girls and even grown-ups in crisp gingham bonnets evoke the stories of the town's most famous writer each summer during the **Laura Ingalls Wilder Pageant,** and the saplings that Pa Ingalls planted so long ago are now mature cottonwoods. Laura moved here as a child in 1879, and the prairie town figured prominently in six of her pioneer adventure books.

You can see many sites mentioned in the books. Start with the Laura Ingalls Wilder Historic Homes Tour where you can see the railroad surveyor's shanty where the family first lived in De Smet, the schoolhouse where Laura went to school, a replica of the Brewster school where she first taught, and the final house Pa built for his family in 1887 after giving up the homestead. It's filled with artifacts, exhibits on Laura's career and that of her journalist daughter, Rose, exhibits of the "Little House" books (including editions printed in other languages) and their illustrator Garth Williams, plus fascinating information on the real people who inspired these beloved stories. Admission is $12 for adults; $6 for children 5 and older. Call (605) 854-3383 or go to discoverlaura.org for more information. De Smet also offers maps for visiting some sites on your own, including Silver Lake and the cemetery where Charles, Caroline, and Carrie Ingalls are buried.

Most visitors time a trip to De Smet to catch the July pageant, performed during three weekends on the open prairie a mile southeast of De Smet. Gates open at 6 p.m. when kids can take a ride in a horse-drawn wagon as they wait for the 8 p.m. show time. Guests find a seat on benches or in their own chairs as the sun is setting, and kids scramble up front with blankets and popcorn. Each year's script takes inspiration from different books with *By the Shores of Silver Lake* inspiring the 2015 pageant and *The Long Winter* planned for 2016. Visit desmetpageant.org or call (800) 880-3383 for advance tickets.

For kids, the best attraction is roaming the Ingalls Homestead, a quarter section that Pa Ingalls claimed in 1880. Kids will love finding farm cats, seeing newborn foals or calves, ducking into a sod house, exploring barns, trying out pioneer chores like laundry, and taking a buggy to the one-room schoolhouse where the bell rings to announce classes. The homestead also offers a few campsites and the chance to sleep in a handful of covered wagons (a fresh twist on a camping cabin). The open prairie can get hot by day, but it's also on a small rise, which helps cool it down by night and offers spectacular views of the sky. The homestead's open 9 a.m. to 7 p.m. daily Memorial Day weekend through Labor Day weekend with shorter hours throughout September. Admission is $10 per person over the age of 5. For details, call (800) 776-3594 or visit ingallshomestead.com.

Huron

To truly experience a place, you need to attend its state fair. **South Dakota's State Fair** claims one of the biggest ag-focused fairs in the nation and celebrates 130 years in 2015. It's a true dose of Americana, a place where home-canned goods, roller coasters, livestock, machinery, race cars, rodeos, 4-H, and deep-fried foods all converge for five days in early September.

Gates open 7 a.m. to 8 p.m. Daily admission is $5 for adults and $3 for kids age 6 to 15. Visit sdstatefair.com or call (800) 529-0900 for more information.

The *Dakotaland Museum* is also located on the fairgrounds with more than 5,000 artifacts celebrating the heritage and history of Huron and Beadle County. It includes the entire Kouf family mammal and bird collection. Admission is $1 for kids 6–12; $3 for adults. The museum is open from 9:30 to 11:30 a.m., 1 to 4 p.m., and 6:30 to 8:30 p.m. Mon through Fri; and 1 to 4 p.m. and 6:30 to 8:30 p.m. weekends and holidays. For more information, call (605) 352-4626.

Huron, population 12,592 and the Beadle County seat, also is home to the first elected female US senator, Gladys Pyle, who served in the Senate during the 1930s. This pioneering feminist's home, the *Pyle House Museum* (376 Idaho Ave. SE), is open to the public. The 1894 Queen Anne–style building features stained glass, ornately carved golden oak woodwork, and Gladys's original furnishings. The home is open from 1 to 3:30 p.m. daily or by appointment. Admission is $1.50. Call (605) 352-2528 or visit huronsd.com for more information.

fishingformore

Walleye dominate the fishing scene in northeastern South Dakota, and most are caught trolling over hard gravel or sand bottoms. Other fish found in the area are smallmouth and largemouth bass, white bass, bullheads, yellow perch, and northern pike. More than 120 glacial lakes dot the northeastern landscape of the state. Anglers who travel to this rolling farm and ranch country will find that the lakes range in size from several acres to more than 16,000 acres. There are 14 state parks and recreation areas and several municipal and private campgrounds in the region. Resorts can be found at most of the larger lakes, but a few of the glacial lakes remain undeveloped and may be surrounded by private land.

Also in the annals of political and state history is Hubert H. Humphrey, the former senator and vice president of the US. He worked at his father's Huron drugstore during the Great Depression, and the still-operating *Humphrey Drugstore* retains some of that mid-1930s atmosphere and Humphrey family memorabilia at 233

An Angel in South Dakota

South Dakota considers Cheryl Ladd its Hollywood Girl, even though more than 30 years have passed since the Huron-born blond beauty portrayed Kris Munroe in *Charlie's Angels*. The popularity of the series never seems to wane, especially with big-screen remakes of the series starring Lucy Liu, Drew Barrymore, and Cameron Diaz.

Ladd was born Cheryl Stoppelmoor in Huron in 1951. She was a cheerleader and waited on cars at The Barn, a local carhop. Her singing—Ladd joined a local band in high school—proved to be her ticket to stardom. After years of acting classes, appearances in commercials, and guest-starring roles on TV, Ladd joined *Charlie's Angels*. She also has recorded two albums, *Cheryl Ladd* and *Dance Fever,* which were big successes in Japan.

Ladd has continued to act in movies and TV. She also writes children's books with her husband, Brian. Their daughter, Jordan Ladd, also caught the acting bug. She was in the hit film *Never Been Kissed.*

Dakota Ave. South. Humphrey's nephew now runs the store, which is open from 8:30 a.m. to 6 p.m. daily. Call (605) 352-4064 for more information.

Another way to learn the community's history is to check out its "Murals on the Town," a project that uses buildings as canvases with scenes from farming to the arrival of the railroad.

Located 15 miles northeast of Huron, ***Lake Byron*** has consistently been one of the top producers of trophy walleye. Expect to catch perch, crappie, pike, and bullheads as well on this 1,750-acre lake. If you're not into dropping a line, try water-skiing, ski-boarding, camping, or picnicking.

Where to Stay in Northeastern South Dakota

ABERDEEN

AmericInn Lodge and Suites
310 Centennial St.
(605) 225-4565
(800) 634-3444
Moderate

Best Western Ramkota Hotel
1400 8th Ave. NW
(605) 229-4040
aberdeen.bwramkota.com
Moderate

Foote Creek B&B
12841 383rd Ave.
(877) 922-1617
footecreek.com
Moderate

TownePlace Suites by Marriott
402 Norwood St. S
(605) 725-3500
marriott.com
Moderate

BROOKINGS

Fairfield Inn and Suites
3000 Lefevre Dr.
(605) 692-3500
(866) 508-0257
fairfieldinn.com
Moderate

Hampton Inn and Suites
3017 LeFevre Dr.
(605) 697-5232
brookingssuites
.hamptoninn.com
Moderate

Holiday Inn Express Hotel and Suites
3020 Lefevre Dr.
(605) 692 9060
hiexpress.com
Moderate

DE SMET

The Prairie House Manor Bed and Breakfast
209 Hwy. 25 S
(605) 854-9131
(800) 297-2416
prairiehousemanor.com
Moderate

FLANDREAU

Royal River Casino and Hotel
607 Veterans St.
(877) 912-5825
Moderate

HURON

Super 8 Motel
2189 Dakota Ave.
(605) 352-0740
Inexpensive

WATERTOWN

Best Western Ramkota
1901 9th Ave. SW
(605) 886-8011
watertown.ramkota.com
Moderate

Dakota Sioux Casino
16415 Sioux Conifer Rd.
(605) 882-2051
(800) 658-4717
Moderate

Days Inn
2900 9th Ave. SE
(605) 886-3500
daysinn.com
Moderate

Where to Eat in Northeastern South Dakota

ABERDEEN

Maverick Steaks and Cocktails
720 Lamont St.
(605) 225-1314
maverickssteak.com

Minervas Restaurant and Bar
1400 8th Ave. NW
(605) 226-2988
minervas.net
Moderate to expensive

Palm Garden Cafe
602 S. 3rd St.
(605) 725-4240
Inexpensive

Sammy's Restaurant & Omelette Shop
212 S. Main St.
(605) 229-4753
Inexpensive

SELECTED CHAMBERS OF COMMERCE

Aberdeen Convention & Visitors Bureau
10 Railroad Ave. SW
PO Box 78
Aberdeen, 57402
(605) 225-2424 or (800) 645-3851
visitaberdeensd.com

Brookings Area Chamber of Commerce and Convention Bureau
414 Main Ave.
PO Box 431
Brookings, 57006
(605) 692-6125
brookingssd.com
brookingschamber.org

Huron Chamber & Visitors Bureau
1725 Dakota Ave.
Huron, 57350
(605) 352-0000 or (800) 487-6673
huronsd.com

Sisseton Chamber of Commerce
1608 Highway 10, Suite 10
Sisseton, 57262-0221
(605) 698-7261
sisseton.com

Watertown Area Chamber of Commerce and Convention & Visitors Bureau
1200 Mickelson Dr., Suite 308
PO Box 225
Watertown, 57201-6113
(605) 753-0282 or (800) 658-4505
watertownsd.com

BROOKINGS

Cottonwood Bistro
1710 6th St.
(605) 692-8938
cottonwoodcoffee.com
Inexpensive

Sake Japanese Restaurant
724 22nd Ave. South
(605) 692-2888
Moderate

DE SMET

Ward's Store and Bakery
127 Calumet Ave.
(605) 854-3688
Inexpensive

HURON

Prime Time Tavern
2110 Dakota Ave. S
(605) 352-7631
Moderate

SISSETON

Crossroads Restaurant
Dakota Connection Casino
46102 Hwy. 10
(605) 698-4273
dakotanationgaming.com
Moderate

WATERTOWN

Charley's
100 E. Kemp St.
(605) 878-3100
Moderate to Expensive

Good to Go Market and Grill
18 N. Broadway
(605) 753-5555
Inexpensive

Off the Clock Chop House
206 E. Kemp Ave.
(605) 878-2467
Moderate to Expensive

Southeastern South Dakota

With more than 40 museums and galleries, countless parks, and the state's biggest metropolis, southeastern South Dakota easily claims the most cosmopolitan corner of the state. It deftly proves that life on the prairie can be chic. It can be pretty in pink, too. Look closely at the landscape—especially at Palisade State Park and at Sioux Falls' Falls Park—and you can see the rosy shades of pink quartzite. You might see that same rosy color glittering off the region's highways as you leave the city behind and head into the countryside to enjoy the parks, small towns, and great outdoors of southeastern South Dakota. The region is easily accessible via east-west I-90 or north-south I-29.

North of Sioux Falls

Tucked between Lake Madison and Lake Herman, the town of Madison is a popular recreation spot. Formed by melting glacial ice thousands of years ago, the 1,350-acre Lake Herman was named for Herman Luce, who settled here in the 1870s with his son. The cabin they built, lived in, and used as a survey office is available for tour in *Lake Herman State Park.*

SOUTHEASTERN SOUTH DAKOTA

Wessington Springs

NORTH OF SIOUX FALLS

Garretson

MINNESOTA

Mitchell

Madison

MITCHELL

Sioux Falls

Canton

James R.

SIOUX FALLS, VERMILLION, AND YANKTON

MISSOURI NATIONAL RECREATION RIVER

S.D.

IOWA

Missouri R.

SOUTH DAKOTA

Yankton

NEBRASKA

Vermillion

N

0   30 mi

0   30 km

On Lake Madison the Chautauqua summer program was a pioneer's favorite pastime from 1891 to 1933. People gathered to hear lectures and concerts, watch plays, and engage in lively debates. The **Smith–Zimmermann Heritage Museum** on Madison's Dakota State University campus is home to the Chautauqua Collection, which is considered one of the most important in the Midwest. While you're here be sure to look at the Civil War memorabilia, the covered wagon, period clothing, and 1880s parlor. The museum is open from noon to 4 p.m. Tues through Fri or by appointment. Admission is free. Call (605) 256-5308 or visit smith-zimmermann .dsu.edu.

Two miles west of Madison, **Prairie Village** is a living museum of an authentic pioneer town. Attractions include antique tractors, an 1893 steam carousel, a sod house, and a log cabin. For more than 50 years, the annual Threshing Jamboree in August has embraced an array of pioneer-worthy events that include horse-powered grain threshing, antique tractor pulling, weaving, and quilting. The village is open 10 a.m. to 5 p.m. Mon through Sat and 11 a.m. to 5 p.m. Sun from Mother's Day until Labor Day. Admission is $5 for adults, $2 for children age 6 to 12, and free for children under 6. For an additional fee, the carousel is open daily, and train rides are offered on Saturday. Call (605) 256-3644 or go to prairievillage.org for more information.

The annual **Quarry Days** celebration is held the last weekend in June in **Dell Rapids,** and the event shows the civic pride this small town has for its quartzite quarries 3 miles east of I-29 and only 15 miles north of the I-29 and I-90 intersection. The bounty of quartzite quarries is handsomely displayed as building stone in walls and foundations throughout the downtown district. Many of the buildings, which showcase Victorian, Romanesque revival, and neoclassical revival architectural styles, are listed on the National Register of Historic Places. The dells were formed more than 12,000 years ago by strong currents of water passing over exposed Sioux quartzite fissures. Native Americans called it *imnizeusteca,* or "canyon."

Winston Churchill once said, "We shape our buildings, and afterwards they shape us," and Dell Rapids' architecture has magnificently primed the community's cultural scene. You can pick up a Dell Rapids Walking Tour guide at the **Dell Rapids History Museum,** 407 E. 4th St., then hit the streets. First stop: Seeing the art deco glamour on the facade of the 1938

SOUTHEASTERN SOUTH DAKOTA'S
TOP HITS

Corn Palace	National Music Museum
Dakota Discovery Museum	Old Courthouse Museum
Falls Park	Palisades State Park
Great Plains Zoo and Delbridge Museum	Prairie Village
Lewis and Clark Recreation Area	Sioux Falls downtown
	Washington Pavilion

Dells Theatre at 511 E. 4th St. It still has its original paint, seats, stage curtain, and light fixtures.

Another glamorous building is the *Grand Opera House,* built in 1888. Located at 425–427 E. 4th St., it is where special occasions are celebrated in Dell Rapids. Check out the calendar of events online at dellrapidsgrandoperahouse.com or call (605) 428-3580.

Stay the night in the 1908 *Rose Stone Inn,* 504 E. 4th St., for another experience of small-town intimacy and the iridescence of quartzite, which is the inn's main building material. Originally built as an inn for traveling salesmen and now on the National Register of Historic Places, the inn offers 5 guest rooms furnished with fashionable pieces from the late-19th and early-20th centuries. Room rates range from $95 to $150 per night for two people, including breakfast. Open year-round. Call (605) 428-3698 or visit rosestoneinn.com.

Drive southeast of Dell Rapids and walk in the footsteps of the legendary outlaw Jesse James near *Garretson.* At *Devil's Gulch,* a rocky chasm at least 20 feet across and 50 feet deep, the notorious outlaw stymied a posse trying to catch him after the infamous failed bank robbery in Northfield, Minnesota. The story goes like this: The James brothers were chased into eastern South Dakota. When Jesse reached Devil's Gulch, he reined in his horse and stared into the forbidding chasm. Jesse turned, retraced his steps to get a running start, let out a whooping battle cry, and dug his spurs into his horse. The horse bounded forward. Time stood still; then the bandit lurched forward as his mount landed. He had made it. The posse, too dumbfounded by Jesse's daring jump to follow, simply milled about as the outlaw rode off. Today you can stand on a footbridge that spans Devil's Gulch and picture yourself visiting the site in 1876, just like Jesse James.

Stop in the gift shop for a copy of the seven-point walking trail map that provides additional history and insight to the geography in the area. Call (605) 594-6721 for more information.

Each June, the escapades of the James brothers are celebrated during the *Jesse James Roundup Days* at Split Rock Park, just north of Garretson off SD 11. A Dutch oven cook-off, craft fair, chuck wagon feed, and theater production commemorate the nefarious, although exciting, James brothers' connection to South Dakota. The park is a perfect place for camping, hiking, and other outdoor sports.

To get onto the water, contact Jesse James Pontoon Rides at (605) 594-2225. Owner Bruce Rekstad narrates a pretty wild tale while the boat moves slowly up and down the creek. He grew up in the area and played in a cave that was apparently a hideout of Frank and Jesse James. Call (605) 594-2225.

Spectacular quartzite chasms are a drawing card, too, in *Palisades State Park,* southwest of Garretson. The view is breathtaking, and the waters here are an inviting and dreamy blue. Colorful red quartzite pinnacles and formations with 50-foot vertical cliffs line Split Rock River, which winds through the park. Please take note of the many posted signs that say "Don't jump off the cliffs," and then follow that advice, even if you see others doing it. Each summer, someone jumps into the water below onto a big rock under the water line, and the best you can hope for is a broken leg and a $100 fine. Notice, too, the unique architecture of the WPA (Works Progress Administration) of the 1930s, which features a dam with a waterfall, a bathhouse, bridges, and a rock wall with a flower garden. You can camp at the park or stay in the camping cabins that overlook the river. At a minimum, plan on bringing a picnic lunch, taking a hike, and bringing a camera to capture the scenery. If you're more ambitious, the park's pinnacles—especially the King and Queen rocks—may be tempting to climb. For campsite or cabin reservations, call (605) 594-3824.

Near *Baltic* (10 miles north of exit 402 on I-90 and 15 miles north of Sioux Falls) is the *Earth Resources Observation Systems (EROS) Data*

Center, which houses the government's central archives for nonmilitary satellite images and aerial photography. That requires the largest mainframe computer in the state and the largest computer complex in the Department of the Interior. The center operates an archive with more than 8 million photographs of the US taken from aircraft and more than 3 million world-wide images acquired by sensors aboard several satellites. The complex reproduces and disseminates data to scientists throughout the world and assists users in the application of such photographs. It definitely offers a fresh way to admire the earth. They even have a series that shows all the topographical obstacles faced by Lewis and Clark and their Corps of Discovery in 1804–1806. Audiovisuals in the lobby will take you on an engrossing 30- to 45-minute self-guided tour from 8 a.m. to 4 p.m. Mon through Fri. Guided tours are offered at 10 a.m. and 2 p.m. Free admission. Visitors are required to show government-issued identification. Some older state driver's licenses are not acceptable; they do not fit enhanced security standards. Bring a passport as backup ID, or call (605) 594-6511 or visit eros.usgs.gov for more details.

Sioux Falls

With a population of 164,676 and continually growing, *Sioux Falls* ranks as the largest city in the state. If you count its entire metropolitan area, it's close to 243,513 residents and has increased by 22 percent since 2000. For visitors, that means there are even more chic boutiques, funky restaurants, and artsy destinations to discover.

A good starting point is *Falls Park,* where the Big Sioux River rumbles across a series of postcard-worthy waterfalls and beautiful rosy quartzite formations that first drew hardworking pioneers and big dreamers. They were able to harness the river's power to start businesses and a fledgling community in 1865. You can wander past the ruins of *Queen Bee Mill,* one of the first businesses to harvest the river's power and grind locally grown wheat.

The former Sioux Falls Light and Power Company (built in 1908) provides a pretty setting for the *Overlook Cafe,* a popular place to grab a light meal or ice cream. The *Falls Park Visitor Information Center* offers additional information on Falls Park and other Sioux Falls attractions, and includes a five-story *observation tower* and elevator. Don't miss that chance—it's the best way to see the remarkable path and iconic rocks of the Big Sioux River. The Horse Barn Arts Center adds an artsy touch with gallery shows and other activities. The Wells Fargo Park Sound and Light Show spectacularly outlines the history of Sioux Falls. You can watch the show nightly during the summer months after sunset. Call (605) 367-7430 for more information.

Richard F. Pettigrew, who convinced an eastern investor to finance the construction of the huge, seven-story 1,200-barrel-per-day Queen Bee flour mill, also had an idea to use the river's power to slice petrified wood, which was briefly trendy at the turn of the 20th century as America's up-and-coming millionaires were building grand homes. The practice stopped when conservationists found a way to protect Arizona's petrified wood supply.

You can see the unique, colorful beauty of those petrified wood cross-sections on the exterior of the 1889 **Pettigrew Home and Museum** at 131 N. Duluth Ave., which is open for tours. Besides developing the mill, Pettigrew became South Dakota's first full-term US senator. R. F. Pettigrew also was a seasoned traveler who collected artifacts from all over the world and left them for the community to see. They're shown in conjunction with natural history and cultural artifacts from the Siouxland area, such as Native American objects and the home's 5,000-volume research library that contains Pettigrew's personal papers. The site is open from 9 a.m. to 5 p.m. Mon through Sat, and from noon to 5 p.m. Sun May 1 through September 30. After that, it's noon to 5 p.m. every day. Admission is free. Call (605) 367-7097; siouxlandmuseums.com.

Just next door you'll also find the **Victorian House B&B**. After a day of exploring, leave time to also stroll the neighborhood and admire the grand homes built in the late 1800s and early 1900s within **St. Joseph's Cathedral Historic District,** stretching between 4th and 10th Streets and bordered by Prairie and Spring Streets. At the B&B, you can relax on the wrap-around porch or cozy up to the outdoor fireplace on the patio. The home has 3 second-floor rooms for guests. Call (605) 310-7482 or go to thevictorianbed andbreakfast.com for more information.

Head east and downhill to reach downtown. Whet your appetite for history and discover the heritage of the area in the **Old Courthouse Museum,** 200 W. 6th St., a restored structure listed on the National Register of Historic

Exploring Downtown

You could easily spend a weekend strolling, dining, and shopping your way through **downtown Sioux Falls.** The main downtown, anchored by Phillips Avenue, stretches for several blocks that are kept lively with artwork and the fair-weather energy of outdoor cafes. If you cross the Big Sioux River at E. 8th Street, you'll reach the up-and-coming, refreshingly hip **East Bank,** where boutiques, cafes, and restaurants infuse historic railroad buildings with great shopping and dining, and Hill City–based winery Prairie Berry opened an impressive restaurant/winery/marketplace in 2014.

You can find public parking in ramps behind Shriver Square and across from the Washington Pavilion for downtown (free on evenings and weekends) and at the Eighth and Railroad Center for the East Bank, which has free parking.

Here's a look at our favorite stops, but you'll want to get a map and guide to decide for yourself given the wealth of choices. For more information, go to dtsf.com.

West Bank

CH Patisserie
309 Phillips Ave.
Exquisite pastries, macaroons, and sweets, as well as pastry classes.

Child's Play Toys
233 S. Phillips Ave.
Creative toys, games, and upscale children's clothing and accessories.

Great Outdoor Store
10th Street and 1st Avenue
Moisture-wicking clothing and gear needed to enjoy outdoor recreation.

Holsen Hus
225 S. Phillips Ave.
Scandinavian books, jewelry, linens, and home decor.

Home Porch
217 Phillips Ave.
A variety of keepsakes and gifts made in South Dakota.

Mama Lada's
116 W. 11th St.
Homey enchiladas in this small but appealing cafe that also serves cool sangrias.

The Market on Phillips
204 S. Phillips Ave.
Fine wines, artisan cheeses, and other foodie finds for an upscale picnic.

Mrs. Murphy's Irish Gifts
219 S. Phillips Ave.
All things Celtic, from sweaters to Claddagh rings.

Phillips Avenue Diner
121 S. Phillips Ave.
Hearty breakfasts, juicy burgers, or a Crazy Shake.

Prairie Star Gallery
207 S. Phillips Ave.
Nationally known artwork and traditional crafts created by South Dakota Native Americans.

Minerva's, at 301 S. Phillips Ave., has long been considered one of the best restaurants in the city. A classy establishment, the restaurant is perfect for special occasions, dates, or any time you just want excellent food and impeccable service. Appetizers such as pheasant ravioli, almond duck strips, coconut shrimp, and crabmeat artichoke pique the taste buds. Main course options include Cajun chicken linguine, and Italian sausage and pepper pasta—musts for carb lovers. Meat-and-potato enthusiasts will find a mouthwatering selection of top sirloin, roast prime rib of beef, rib eye, filet mignon, and New York strip-sirloin steaks.

Its adjacent *Paramount Wine Bar* offers a more casual option for drinks and lighter plates. Don't miss trying a strawberry-basil martini dusted with black pepper. It's as fragrant as it is tasty. They also serve chislic, an eastern South Dakota specialty. Stop by between 8 and 11 p.m. Thurs and Fri for live music.

Minerva's is open from 11 a.m. to 2:30 p.m. and 5 to 10 p.m. Mon through Sat. Limited bar menu served 2:30 to 5 p.m. Mon through Sat. (Dinner reservations are suggested.) Call (605) 334-0386 or go to minervas.net. Minerva's also has a sister restaurant called *Spezia,* which is known for its Sunday brunch but also has great pizzas in a more casual setting. Spezia is located at 4801 S. Louise Ave.; (605) 334-7491.

East Bank

Josiah's Coffee House and Cafe
101 S. Reid St.
Breakfast and lunch with paninis, quinoa and black rice salad, pizzas, and coconut cupcakes.

Prairie Berry
322 E. 8th St.
Both wine and beer flights (with its new Miner Brewing Company line), plus pizzas, appetizers, sandwiches, and salads to enjoy indoors or on its patio, plus gourmet foods to go.

Queen City Bakery
324 E. 8th St.
Savory quiche, homemade granola, decadent cakes like Brooklyn Blackout (devil's food with sea-salt caramel), pies, and supersize cookies such as milk chocolate hazelnut praline.

8th and Railroad Center
401 E. 8th St.
Packed with cool cafes and shops such as *Aviena Vintage/Modern* with creatively upcycled clothing, accessories, and refurbished furniture; *Rug and Relic*'s huge selection of exotic textiles and cool boots crafted with rugs; *K Restaurant* with modern American cuisine; and *Sanaa's* with its bright colors and a fragrant whiff of Middle Eastern spice from its fresh salads, savory meats, *fatayers* (flaky pita pockets), and sweet desserts.

Places. The massive quartzite stone building served as the county courthouse from 1890 to 1962. The first-floor exhibits bring to life the history of early settlers and the Plains Indians, along with the art and cultural significance of Siouxland. A handsomely laid-out building, the Old Courthouse is decorated with 16 murals of different sizes, created by the Norwegian artist Ole Running in 1915. You also can find the Queen City Mercantile at the museum, where local and regional books, crafts, old-fashioned toys, holiday collectibles, souvenirs, and exhibit-related items are for sale. The Old Courthouse Museum is open from 8 a.m. to 5 p.m. Mon through Fri, from 9 a.m. to 5 p.m. Sat, and from noon to 5 p.m. on Sun. The museum also stays open until 9 p.m. on Thurs. Free admission. Call (605) 367-4210 or visit siouxlandmuseums.com.

trivia

Chislic, deep-fried cubes of beef or sheep, is a specialty usually found in southeast South Dakota, occasionally on menus, at food stands or fairs.

Three blocks from the museum, at the intersection of N. Phillips and 8th Street, you can get a brochure for downtown's beloved *SculptureWalk,* which has been bringing big, impressive, and conversation-sparking artworks to the city every year for more than a decade. On one corner, kids may climb over a pair of bears while a Native American releases an eagle across the street and a dinosaur emerges from recycled materials down the street. You can also download the information at sculpturewalksiouxfalls.com.

Native Art

If a visit to the Visual Arts Center or downtown's Prairie Star Gallery stirs your interest in Native American art, time a return visit for the annual *Northern Plains Indian Art Market,* organized by Sioux Falls' Sinte Gleska University and Rosebud Sioux Reservation in late September. The country's largest art market devoted to Northern Plains tribes includes painting, sculpture, beadwork, jewelry, quillwork, and other unique styles such as ledger art, in which Native Americans would draw stories in old ledger books because they didn't have the luxury of blank art paper. For more information, go to npiam.org.

Sioux Falls Parks

Sioux Falls has more than 80 parks in its 3,154-acre park system. There's also a 26-mile paved bike trail that wraps around the city and follows the Big Sioux River Greenway. You can get details by calling (605) 367-8222 or going to siouxfalls .org/parks.

Among the favorite parks is **Terrace Park,** 1100 W. 4th St. The Shoto–Teien Japanese Gardens are located here next to Covell Lake. Built from 1928 to 1936, the gardens feature a lush array of flowering trees and shrubs, pagodas, and lanterns. The Terrace Park Aquatic Center is a perfect jumping-off point, too, with swimming pools and water slides.

A full-scale cast of Michelangelo's *David* stands in the heart of Sioux Falls at **Fawick Park** (located on 2nd Avenue between 10th and 11th Streets). Thomas Fawick, a Sioux Falls philanthropist and industrialist who made a fortune as an inventor, gave the city the statue in 1972. The statue of *David,* fully in the buff, created enormous controversy when it first arrived. To mollify public opinion, the statue was placed facing away from traffic, and trees were planted to screen it from the street. (Fawick later gave the city the sculptor's statue of Moses, which was placed on the Augustana College campus.)

At 12th and Kiwanis Streets, the **USS South Dakota *Battleship Memorial*** in Sherman Park is a patriotic sample of World War II naval history. The battleship, which participated in every major battle in the Pacific from 1942 to 1945, was the most decorated of World War II. Parts of the actual battleship punctuate a concrete outline of the ship's width and length. Visitors can walk through the concrete configuration and learn about the military personnel who gave their lives while serving on this vessel. A gift shop is open daily 10 a.m. to 5 p.m. Memorial Day through Labor Day. Call (605) 397-7060.

Nostalgic yet hip, funky yet classy, *Zandbroz Variety* (605-331-5137; zandbroz.com) at 209 S. Phillips Ave. offers a fresh blend of fine pens in antique cupboards, fine papers, books, cards, baskets, jewelry, gourmet foods, and other nifty things for giving (or keeping for yourself). Part of the charm is the way everything is displayed, often with vintage cabinetry from the drug-store days and a lot of color. The back room, once a popular soda fountain and coffee bar, now has a wealth of used books and carefully chosen vintage items—all keeping an emphasis on variety.

Sioux Falls' Family-Friendly Fun

Great Plains Zoo and Delbridge Museum combines the rugged expanse of a North American plain, the wild recesses of an African veldt, and the quiet beauty of the Australian Outback. Located at 805 S. Kiwanis Ave. (0.5 mile east off I-29, exit 79 to 12th Street), the Delbridge Museum of Natural History houses one of the largest collections of mounted animals in the world. The zoo is known for its big cat collection, which includes cheetahs and tigers. But there are also wallabies and delicate flamingos, and bears that look more cuddly than they really are. This zoo is recognized nationally for its innovative partnership with the local children's hospital. Cameras in many of the animal habitats stream live video to the patient rooms, entertaining and educating children who otherwise might not visit the zoo for a long, long time. Open daily year-round. Zoo hours are from 9 a.m. to 6 p.m. Tickets are $6.80 for adults, $6 for senior citizens, $3.80 for children ages 3 to 12, and admission is free for children 2 years of age and younger. Call (605) 367-7059 or visit gpzoo.org.

Sioux Falls Outdoor Campus, an initiative of the state game, fish, and parks department, gets people in touch with the outdoors through workshops and hands-on exhibits. Classes include everything for the outdoors from canoeing and kayaking to fishing, hiking, gardening, bird watching, rock climbing, and more. All classes are free and most are just one or two sessions. This is also a place to come and enjoy without taking a class. There's a small museum with wildlife exhibits, camping information, and the like. A butterfly garden, 4 picnic shelters, and a hiking trail are included on the property at 4500 S. Oxbow Ave. Call (605) 362-2777; outdoorcampus.org.

The city is rightfully proud of its ***Washington Pavilion of Arts and Science,*** a creative transformation of the city's Washington High School at the corner of 11th and Main Streets. Its oldest section opened in 1908 and was expanded over the years, becoming a visually distinctive, 255,000-square-foot building constructed of native Sioux quartzite. The roof balustrade and dentiled cornices are visible from many downtown Sioux Falls locations. The high school closed in 1992 until it was reopened with new purpose in 1999. It has since been a place where visitors can be touched by extraordinary artwork or dig in with interactive science displays.

The Pavilion's ***Visual Arts Center*** features 7 galleries of changing exhibits, including Native American artists, regional and national contemporary visual arts exhibitions, and a hands-on children's gallery. The Visual Arts

Sertoma Butterfly House and Marine Cove, 4320 Oxbow Ave., isn't a day-long excursion like a sprawling zoo, but you'll want to linger and enjoy the beauty here. Give yourself time to study vibrant corals, anemones, and tropical fish in the many aquariums, reach into the Midwest's only shark and stingray touch tank, and revel in the 80-degree warmth of the butterfly garden. There are more than 800 free-flying butterflies that flit among lush, lovely flowers, including the stunning blue morpho. It's open 10 a.m. to 6 p.m. Mon through Sat and 11 a.m. to 5 p.m. Sun Memorial Day through Labor Day and 10 a.m. to 4 p.m. Mon through Sat and 1 to 4 p.m. Sun the rest of the year (605-334-9466; sertomabutterfly house.org).

Country Apple Orchard, 4 miles south of Sioux Falls on Minnesota Avenue, lets autumn enthusiasts score their favorite sweet and crunchy apples or pick their own during one of the most treasured rites of the season. You can hop on a tractor-pulled wagon and jump off when you reach the spot where your favorite variety of apple is grown. Also look for pumpkins here each fall. Call (605) 743-2424 or go to countryappleorchard.com.

Great Bear Recreation Park is a natural for downhill skiing a la East River, with 12 runs nearly 1,500 feet long, a 250-foot vertical drop, chairlifts, and a chalet. A tubing hill, outdoor skating, and a terrain park for snowboarders are also offered at the resort. Great Bear (605-367-4309, greatbearpark.com) is located 3 miles east of Sioux Falls on Rice Street. Ski instruction and rentals for both downhill and cross-country skiing are available. The park is also open for hiking during the summer.

Center presently has a collection of 300 works, including pieces by noted South Dakota artists Oscar Howe, Lova Jones, and Charles Greener. Other artists represented include Signe Stuart and Robert Aldern. The 300-seat Small Theater is available for performances requiring more-intimate space, such as musical ensembles, lectures, poetry readings, experimental theater, and dance and piano recitals. *The Husby Performing Arts Center* brings the best in music, dance, and theater from around the world. The 1,800-seat Great Hall is home to local community groups, as well as the South Dakota Symphony.

If science is more your style, check out the three-story, 45,000-square-foot *Kirby Science Discovery Center,* where you can fly a space shuttle, dig up a dinosaur, try to lift giant blocks of quartzite, watch bees that have

Southeastern Wineries

Like many states across the nation, South Dakota has seen a boom in wineries and microbreweries. Many rely on traditions passed down from their pioneer ancestors who brought recipes from the old country and would make wine with whatever fruit was available: rhubarb, chokecherries, raspberries, buffalo berries, juneberries/serviceberries, plums, currants, and dandelions. They've expanded to include the surge in northern-hardy varieties such as Frontenac, Le Crescent, and Valiant grapes that have been developed by Minnesota and South Dakota universities. In most cases, they offer a sweet and festive excuse to hit the road and find a rural winery.

You can download a *wine trail* brochure at southeastsouthdakota.com/what-to-do/winery-trail or call (888) 353-7382. More information also can be found through the South Dakota Wine Growers Association, (888) 353-7382, sdwinegrowers.com.

Prairie Berry East Bank
Prairie Berry expanded its Hill City success to 322 E. 8th St. in Sioux Falls' downtown in 2014, creating a chic gathering place, tasting room, cafe, and marketplace in a restored stone warehouse. While you can do a traditional wine tasting here and buy jams and sauces inspired by their most popular wines (like Red-Ass Rhubarb), most visitors grab a seat, plan to linger, and enjoy flights of wine or their new Miner Brewing Company beers and appetizers (605-496-7175; prairieberry.com/eastbank).

Schade Winery
Like Prairie Berry, Schade Winery has a presence on both sides of the state. Here you can visit its original vineyard in the countryside at 21095 463rd St. (605-627-5545; schadewinery.com) in tiny Volga near Brookings.

a hive just outside the building, or touch a tornado. Science adventure films are shown hourly on the four-story dome screen at the Wells Fargo Cine-Dome Theater. For more information on current events, shows, and exhibits, call (877) 927-4728, or visit washingtonpavilion.org.

The annual *Sidewalk Arts Festival* entertains more than 65,000 visitors each year. The downtown festival along Main and 11th Streets showcases artists and vendors from 15 states. Art Rocks! is the free entertainment stage. The event, which is held the first Saturday after Labor Day, is the annual fund-raiser for the Visual Arts Center at the Washington Pavilion of Arts and Science. Call (605) 977-2002 or visit siouxempireartscouncil.com.

Strawbale Winery

With brightly colored Adirondack chairs, roving chickens, and farm cats, this winery at 47215 257th St. in Renner offers country charm less than 4 miles from the I-29 and I-90 interchange. The wonderful laid-back atmosphere lends itself well to weekly concerts and an annual folk competition. Besides wine by the bottle, on a hot night you can also get frozen drinks made from their black currant wine and may find crisp stone-fired pizza from vendors. Watch for special wine tastings and appetizers during the holidays, followed by helicopter rides over Sioux Falls' Falls Park lit with Christmas lights (605-543-5071; strawbalewinery.com).

Tucker's Walk Vineyard

Look for cold-hardy grape, raspberry, wild plum, and rhubarb wines at this newer vineyard in the countryside at 48332 254th St., in Garretson (605-594-6287).

Valiant Vineyards

The state's first winery opened in 1996 at 1500 W. Main St. in Vermillion on the western edge of town overlooking the Missouri River valley. They host the annual Great Dakota Wine Fest in September and offer winery tours and tastings daily. You can even spend the night here at *Buffalo Run Resort,* which offers 5 elegant guest rooms. The Native American, the USD, the Frontier, the Queen Anne, and the Honeymoon Suite are all uniquely decorated. Call (605) 624-4500; buffalorun winery.com.

Wilde Prairie Winery

This 40-acre vineyard north of Brandon began in 1997. Today *Wilde Prairie Winery* produces about five tons of grapes, which translates into about 2,000 gallons or 10,000 bottles of wine annually. They started out with tomato, rhubarb, and dandelion wine before moving toward northern hardy varietals. The winery's 100-year-old barn serves as a tasting room or special event venue. Call (605) 582-6471; wildeprairiewinery.com.

Near the community of Brandon, just 5 miles east of Sioux Falls on I-90 at exit 406, you'll find two state parks: the *Beaver Creek Nature Area* and the *Big Sioux Recreation Area.*

One of the many treasures at Big Sioux Recreation Area is *Bergeson's Homestead*—the park's very own little house on the prairie—which was built in 1869 by Ole and Soren Bergeson. Ole was one of the first settlers in Split Rock Township. The log frame, which is constructed of hand-hewn cottonwood, was inadvertently discovered in the 20th century during the process of razing the entire old Bergeson homestead. Notice the fine dovetailed notchwork. If you want to spend the night, the park has campsites

Watch for Good Earth

South Dakota's newest park, **Good Earth State Park at Blood Run,** was added in 2012 and encompasses 588 acres about 8 miles southeast of Sioux Falls and along the Big Sioux River near the border with Iowa. It preserves one of the most significant archaeological sites in North America, spanning both sides of the river and known as Blood Run National Historic Landmark. It's considered one of the oldest sites of long-term human habitation in the country with an estimated 10,000 residents. The river, fertile land, availability of pipestone, and protection from prairie winds made it an important gathering place for seasonal ceremonies and as a center of trade from about AD 1300–1700. Most of the early residents were Oneota Tradition Peoples. By the early 1700s, the tribes, including Omaha, Ponca, Ioway, and Otto, were pushed out by other Native Americans who were pushed west by European settlers or they were wiped out by the diseases Europeans brought. While the state park is still in its infancy and only includes trails and guided hikes through the Outdoor Campus, it's considered a sacred place for Native Americans and is destined to become a well-interpreted historic site with a visitor center and joint efforts between South Dakota and Iowa. The park is at 28767 482nd Ave., Canton, SD. Call (605) 987-2263 or go to gfp.sd.gov for updates on the park's development.

and basic camping cabins that come with heat, air conditioning, and electricity that would have looked luxurious to Ole and Soren Bergeson in the 1860s.

The *Valley of the Giants Trail* at Big Sioux is a 1.5-mile hiking trail that passes some of the oldest trees in the state. The cottonwood and ash trees provide a heavy cover, almost blocking out the sun. It's a pleasant hike around a little lake. There are 7 more miles of trails in the park, 1.5 miles of paved biking trails, a disc golf course, archery range, equestrian trails, and access to the Big Sioux River Canoe Trail. Call (605) 582-7243.

Brandon's Hometown Days is an annual festival in McHardy Park each July. The three-day event attracts a wide variety of artists and food vendors. There are also games for the kids, musical entertainment, and a tractor pull.

The annual *Homesteader Day Harvest Festival* at *Beaver Creek Nature Area* (5 miles southeast of Brandon) offers a glimpse into what life on the prairie was like for the pioneers. First, turn back the clock to the year 1869: John and Anna Samuelson, both Swedish immigrants, were new-lyweds, and John bought his bride a 160-acre homestead east of present-day Sioux Falls. For the first three years, they made their home in a dugout carved from a nearby hill. They later moved to a log cabin, which is now the centerpiece of the Homesteader Day Harvest Festival every September. An interpretive shelter tells the story of the Samuelsons' cabin. As part of the festival, volunteers demonstrate candle making, sheep shearing, tatting, butter churning, wheat grinding, and more. Visitors can try their hand at rope making and can sample fresh-squeezed apple juice made in an antique apple press. The festival is held the first Sunday after Labor Day and is free. Call (605) 594-3824.

Vermillion

Vermillion, 56 miles south of Sioux Falls on I-29, best fits the old description of a place where the college is the community. The economy of this town of 10,692 people thrives on the presence of the University of South Dakota (USD), the state's second-largest university, founded in 1862. Vermillion, the seat of Clay County, originally was settled below the bluffs of the Mighty Mo until the flood of 1881 changed the river's course, forcing residents to higher ground. Now it's located in a part of the state that was twice claimed by France and once by Spain before it was sold to the US. As in any college community, there is a vibrant, global energy that students and higher education bring—not to mention an impressive dose of culture.

Start a tour at the campus's **W. H. Over Museum of Natural and Culuture History** (1110 Ratingen St.; 605-677-5228; visit whovermuseum .org), which lacks polish but has plenty to see, including oddities like the bones of an escaped elephant that went on a rampage in South Dakota and an Egyptian mummy. Its strength are Native American exhibits (a life-size diorama of a Teton Dakota village, small replicas of Arikara farming and intricate Lakota beadwork and art), pioneer artifacts, and the Lewis and Clark/Spirit Mound Learning Center that sheds light on the explorers' famous journey, especially through the region. The artifacts include a map drawn in 1806 from Lewis's notations and journal entries. The gift shop includes Dakota beading, pipestone carvings, and star quilts. The museum is free and open from 10 a.m. to 4 p.m. Mon through Sat.

South Dakota's Musical Treasure

On the University of South Dakota campus, you will find more than 15,000 musical instruments from all over the globe in the world-renowned **National Music Museum** (414 E. Clark St.). Exhibits include a 1693 Stradivarius violin, a 9-foot-tall slit drum from the South Pacific, Civil War band instruments, Elizabethan ivory lutes, and a 1785 French harpsichord. A guitar autographed by B. B. King is displayed here as well. The museum also is the only place in the world where you can find two 18th-century grand pianos with the specific type of action conceived by the piano's inventor, Bartolomeo Cristofori. One of these, built in 1767 by Manuel Antunes of Lisbon, is the earliest signed and dated piano by a maker native to Portugal; the other, built by Louis Bas in Villeneuve les Avignon in 1781, is the earliest extant French grand piano.

This is a must-see museum that continues to expand, with such stellar acquisitions as two guitars and a banjo from the Johnny and June Carter Cash estate. The 1971 Martin D-28 guitar, known as the Bon Aqua, was kept at Johnny's 100-acre farm near Bon Aqua, Tennessee, outside Nashville. Returning from extensive tours in the US and abroad, Johnny would go there alone, as he wrote in his autobiography, "to cook my own food, read my own books, tend my own garden, water my own land, and think, write, compose, rest, and reflect in peace." As such, the guitar, which Johnny used while writing songs during the last 30 years of his life, was more intimately connected with him than the hundreds of other guitars that came and went through his hands on the road.

The National Music Museum also acquired the 1967 Gibson "Hummingbird" guitar that was one of June Carter Cash's favorite guitars, according to Marshall Grant, bass player with Johnny's show from 1955 to 1980. She was still playing it when she posed for the September 18–24, 1999, issue of *TV Guide*. The third acquisition is a 1980 Gibson five-string banjo that was given to Johnny by Earl Scruggs, the bluegrass legend, who wrote on the head of the banjo, "To my friend Johnny Cash/Earl Scruggs." Johnny and Scruggs collaborated often throughout their careers.

This one-of-a-kind facility is open daily, and suggested donations are $10 for adults, $8 for seniors, and free for anyone under 18, USD students, and faculty. Admission is free for active military and up to 5 family members between Memorial Day and Labor Day or $8 the rest of the year. Admission includes a self-guided multimedia tour that you can check out at the front desk. Metered one-hour parking can be found in the lot on the museum's east side, or find a free space on the streets south of the museum. Call (605) 677-5306; usd.edu/nmm.

Another worthy stop for history buffs is the ***Austin–Whittemore House,*** an impressive Italian villa–style structure that also houses the ***Clay County Historical Society Museum*** at 15 Austin St. The museum, built in 1882 on a riverside bluff overlooking Vermillion, is best known for its Victorian displays and settings. Call (605) 624-8266 or visit historicclay county.org.

The campus of the ***University of South Dakota*** (usd.edu) is a stately one, with historic buildings and grand shade trees. The Dakota Dome sports facility includes an indoor football stadium, where the USD Coyotes meet other colleges for competition. The school's strongest rival is the South Dakota State University Jackrabbits. USD, whose alumni include former NBC news anchor Tom Brokaw, is considered one of the best liberal arts colleges in the state. Accordingly, there are fine productions to see on campus, including dance, theater, and fine arts. Slagle Auditorium is often home to concerts by the USD Chamber Singers and Chamber Orchestra and the USD Men's and Women's Chorus Concert. You also can see a play at the Fine Arts Building theater, or enjoy a piano concert at the Colton Recital Hall. Events are listed at calendar.usd.edu.

If you work up an appetite, head to Vermillion's historic downtown with ***Cafe Brule*** at 24 W. Main St. It has built a huge fan base since it opened in 2011 with food such as smoky red pepper gouda soup, a croque-monsieur with ham and gruyère on their own brioche bread, pot roast on a baguette, salad with mango vinaigrette, limoncello chicken, or smoked pork chops. Get a side order of their famously creamy, four-cheesy potatoes brulé that can alone be a meal (and a steal at $3.50). Be sure to leave room for dessert—***Cakes by Monica*** with sumptuous choices such as champagne cake layered with raspberries or drunken berry compote, white chocolate mousse, and buttercream frosting. They're open 7 a.m. to 9 p.m. daily. Call (605) 624-2945 or go to cafebrule.com for more details and a full menu.

About 8 miles north of Vermillion on Route 19, you can walk off the calories and walk in the footsteps of Lewis and Clark, who came through this area with its conical ***Spirit Mound,*** on August 25, 1804. Native legends claimed there were 18-inch devils with big heads on the mound, which also is one of the highest places in the county, but they were undaunted and claimed it to be a "most butifull landscape." It's a wide-open prairie hike dotted with fragrant wild roses, deep-purple spiderwort, and lavender penstemon in early summer and swaying with native grasses later in the season. The reward for reaching the summit—about a three-quarter mile from the parking lot—is a view that unfurls for miles and a peaceful silence occasionally interrupted by the honk of a pheasant. For more information on Spirit Mound Historic Prairie, go to gfp.sd.gov.

Like North Dakota, South Dakota takes great pride in its close relation to explorers Meriwether Lewis and William Clark, who set out to explore America's newest land acquisition—the Louisiana Purchase—in 1804.

Southeastern South Dakota Parks and Birding

Union Grove State Park, located 11 miles south of Beresford off I-29, offers hiking and bridle trails, picnicking, camping, and a playground on 500 beautiful acres. Call (605) 987-2263.

Newton Hills State Park, just 6 miles south of Canton on CR 135, is a wooded oasis where plants and animals thrive. This southern tip of the Coteau des Prairies was spared the plow, and its grassy knolls and wooded ravines today shelter deer, wild turkey, and more than 200 species of birds. Explorers can make their way along several hiking trails, while horse riders and all-terrain bikers can enjoy a 6-mile multiuse trail. To add a little excitement, hike those trails by candlelight during FestiFall the first Saturday of October. The annual Sioux River Folk Festival (fotm.org) attracts music aficionados from all over and is held the first weekend in August. Call (605) 987-2263.

Adams Homestead and Nature Preserve, located 2 miles southwest of McCook Lake (take exit 4 off I-29), includes 1,500 acres that encompass several restored buildings, including the Adams homestead, and 10 miles of hiking and biking trails. The town of McCook was the first homesteader settlement in the state, and the McCook Cemetery, plotted and registered in 1869, is regarded as the first homesteader cemetery. The visitor center is open from 8 a.m. to 4:30 p.m. Mon through Fri and from 10 a.m. to 6 p.m. Sat and Sun. Call (605) 232-0873.

South Dakota Birding Festival, at Fort Randall on Lake Francis Case, is a weekend-long event in early May brings together birding experts and speakers and offers guided field trips to look for the thousands of birds that migrate along the Missouri River flyway. Call (888) 353-7382 or go to southeastsouthdakota .com for more details.

Edgar's Ol' Fashioned Soda Fountain

Every once in a while you can find vintage soda fountains nicely preserved in America's small towns. It's easy to reach this little gem in Elk Point 20 miles north of Sioux City. Use Highway 16 or 18 from I-29 and head downtown. The soda fountain debuted in 1906 in Centerville and was then abandoned in the early 1960s. Pioneer Drug owners Kevin and Barb Wurtz rediscovered and rescued it, adding the soda fountain to their business. The toughest part may be deciding what to order: a Rocket (a vertical banana split), Green River and cherry cola phosphates, or classic floats, sundaes, sodas, and cookies. Call (605) 356-3336 or go to edgarssoda.com.

The Lewis and Clark National Historic Trail follows Highways 1804 and 1806, which hug the Missouri River and trace the route that Lewis and Clark traveled. Indeed, some parts of the vast Missouri shoreline remain as wild and breathtaking as they were in the explorers' days.

The South Dakota Tourism Department has put together a helpful Lewis and Clark brochure that includes a map of the explorers' journey highlighting 15 significant sites, excerpts from their journal, and a complete list of campgrounds along the way. You can find it at visitor centers or download it at travelsd.com/TravelSD/media/PDF/Guides/LCguide_2014.pdf.

Yankton

Long before railways and interstates—and even the Dakota Territory—the fastest way to the Dakotas was along the Missouri River. The river enters the state at North Sioux City, winds its way to Vermillion, then less than 30 miles to **Yankton.** In this once-bustling capital of the Dakota Territory from the 1860s through 1889, you can see a **Dakota Territorial Capitol Replica,** a simple white structure in Yankton's Riverside Park, as a reminder of those ambitious beginnings before the title went to the more centrally located city of Pierre.

Yankton and its 14,591 residents are still closely tied to the river that constantly flows by, bringing boaters, paddlers, and migrating birds by the thousands and offering a serene view of the chalky white bluffs that rise from the Nebraska shoreline.

If you want to get a feel for the river's expanse without renting a boat or picking up a paddle, park near Walnut Street and take a stroll along Yankton's unique double-decker *Meridian Bridge.* Closed to vehicle traffic in 2008, it reopened for foot and bike traffic in November 2011. It was originally built in 1924 and is considered the longest pedestrian bridge connecting two states. You can choose whether to walk on the top level or the lower level. It links to more than 30 miles of riding in the Meridian Trail System that connects Yankton and the Lewis and Clark Recreational Area.

hickok's killer hanged

One of the most famous events to take place here was the trial of Jack "Crooked Nose" McCall, who shot Wild Bill Hickok in Deadwood, South Dakota. The trial was held in late 1876 in what is now the **Charles Gurney Hotel** (corner of 3rd and Capital Streets), and he was hanged on March 1, 1877—the first legal execution in the Dakota Territory. McCall is buried in the Yankton Cemetery. A historic marker in the parking lot at the corner of US 81 and SD 50 marks the spot of the hanging.

If you want to learn about the area's history, check out the *Dakota Territorial Museum* at 610 Summit St. The Yankton County Historical Society has lovingly preserved and displayed rare memorabilia from early Yankton and Dakota Territory days, including a rural schoolhouse, a blacksmith shop, a Burlington Northern caboose, an American LaFrance fire engine, and artifacts such as vintage boat motors and fishing equipment and the musical instruments from General Custer's 7th Cavalry band. Free admission. Call (605) 665-3898 or go to dakotaterritorial museum.org.

Yankton boasts some of the finest historical homes in the Midwest. The Architectural Walking and Auto Tour of Historic Yankton Homes offers visitors at least a curbside glimpse at the exteriors of some homes, most of which are clustered on Douglas, Capital, Pine, and Mulberry Streets, between 5th and 6th Streets. Pick up brochures at the Yankton Chamber office at 803 E. 4th St. or at the Dakota Territorial Museum.

The *Cramer Kenyon Heritage Home* and *Dorothy Jencks Memorial Garden* at 509 Pine St. are an outstanding example of Queen Anne architecture. The home, erected in 1886, is open to the public from Memorial Day to Labor Day from 1 to 5 p.m. Wed through Sun and by appointment year-round. Admission is $5 adults; $2 for children. Call (605) 665-7470 or go to cramer-kenyon.webs.com.

If you want to pick your own berries in South Dakota, head for **Hebda Family Produce and Prairie Gardens,** an orchard and berry farm just 7.5 miles northeast of Yankton. Pluck strawberries or raspberries, pick apples or pumpkins, or buy fresh vegetables and jams, jellies, pies, and other South Dakota products. Fall visitors can take hayrack rides or challenge themselves with the corn maze. Call (605) 665-2806 or go to hebdaproduce.com.

thelawrence welklegend

In 1928 a young accordionist and his novelty band from Strasburg, North Dakota, arrived in Yankton, South Dakota, and asked a new radio station, WNAX, if they could perform. Audience reaction was so tremendous that the manager offered to add the band to the station's roster of entertainers. That brief stop lasted almost nine years and began the career of the great Lawrence Welk.

Missouri National Recreational River

Most visitors to Yankton head 4 miles west of downtown and settle into a spot along the river. There are two stretches of the 2,341-mile Missouri River that are protected as a National Recreational River, and Yankton sits ideally located on the upriver end of a 59-mile section that runs from the Gavins Point Dam east past Vermillion to Ponca State Park in Nebraska.

How beloved is this area? If you don't plan ahead on summer weekends (especially holidays), you'll find that the more than 400 campsites plus camping cabins book quickly at the **Lewis and Clark State Recreation Area** along US 52. You'll find all the amenities here—from hot showers and electric hookups to paved pads that stretch along Lewis and Clark Lake, created by Gavins Point Dam.

If you want to be in a more tucked-away area, there are more than 200 additional sites at **Chief White Crane Recreation Area** and **Pierson Ranch Recreation Area,** which are behind the dam and along the smaller Lake Yankton. Those campgrounds are accessed via Crest Road (or Toe Road), which crosses the dam and the Missouri River. Sites for all the campgrounds can be reserved by calling (800) 710-2267 or visiting campsd.com.

While it's technically in Crofton, Nebraska, across the dam and on the opposite shore of the Missouri River, you'll want to check out the **Lewis and Clark Visitor Center** that overlooks the river. It tells a little about the famed Lewis and Clark expedition but is more focused on the area's geology and natural history, the river, and the landmark 1944 Pick-Sloan Plan Flood Control Act that sought to tame and control the country's biggest rivers after disastrous 1930s droughts and massive flooding in the early 1940s. For more information, call (402) 667-2546.

calumetbluff

The Lewis and Clark Visitor Center sits on Calumet Bluff across the river from Yankton. It's where Lewis and Clark hosted a Grand Council with the Yankton Sioux in late August 1804. You can read a copy of Lewis's speech at the center.

Gavins Point Dam, completed in 1957 at a cost of $51 million, created Lewis and Clark Lake, a reservoir that stretches for 30 miles upriver. It brims with large- and smallmouth bass and offers postcard-perfect opportunities for sailing. If you like engineering and are intrigued by the colossal effort needed to build a dam, you can stop by the **Gavins Point Powerplant.** Free tours are given daily Memorial Day through Labor Day. During the 30-minute tour, visitors can examine such areas as the control room, generator housing, and high-voltage cable areas. IDs are required for anyone 17 and older, and no cameras, phones, or bags are allowed. For more information call (402) 667-2546.

If you have kids with you or are camping nearby, be sure to swing into the **Gavins Point National Fish Hatchery and Aquarium** 3 miles west of Yankton on Highway 52. It's free and offers a quick introduction to what's beneath the water. You can see fossils from when the area was a prehistoric inland sea, gawk at Oscar, an albino catfish, watch turtles, and see the bizarre contraband (think cowboy boots made from turtles) confiscated by the US Fish and Wildlife Service. You also can see the endangered paddlefish and pallid sturgeon. The

gavinspoint dam

Gavins Point Dam is one of 6 main dams and reservoirs along the Upper Missouri River Basin, stretching through both Dakotas.

Archery Central

Yankton is home to the *National Field Archery Association (NFAA) Head-quarters and Museum.* The largest archery association in the world had been in Redland, California, for more than 60 years, but a combination of high real estate prices in California, the low cost of living in South Dakota, and the presence of the Easton Aluminum Company in Yankton, which makes arrows, resulted in the headquarters moving here in 2008. The property is 20 acres and includes 28 stations outside and 17 stations inside, appropriate for hosting world-class tournaments.

But you don't have to be a competitive archer to enjoy this center. For $10, you can come in and shoot at targets all day ($5 for NFAA members). There's also a museum on the history of archery, which is surprisingly interesting. It includes, among other items, artifacts from the Battle of the Little Big Horn and souvenirs from major movie sets. There also are classrooms, a fitness studio, and an art studio here, so you could find yourself taking classes in woodblock prints and Raku pottery or belly dancing and tae kwon do. The center is just east of town at 800 Archery Ln. Call (605) 260-9279 and check upcoming classes at yankton archerycomplex.org.

hatchery harvests their eggs, nurtures the small fry, and releases these fish into the river. Open 10 a.m. to 5 p.m. Apr through Sept. Call (605) 665-3352 or go to fws.gov/gavinspoint.

Anchoring the area's water sports is *Lewis and Clark Marina,* on the lake's northeast corner. The marina is home to more than 400 boats from April through October. Slips are available by the night, week, or season, and boats, pontoons, and personal watercraft can be rented. A boat-up gas dock, convenience store, and full-service dealer will keep you well provisioned. Call (605) 665-3111 or go to lewisandclarkmarina.com. You can also dine at *The Marina Grill* and enjoy some of the area's best views.

If you want to stay somewhere with a river view but prefer not to camp, you have a few options. *Lewis and Clark Resort,* located by the marina, offers 24 moderately priced motel rooms and 17 two- and three-bedroom cabins. There's an outdoor pool, along with easy river access. A six-bedroom lodge built in 2012 sleeps 28 people and can be ideal for special occasions and reunions. Call (605) 665-2680 or visit lewisandclarkpark.com.

Take a Hike or Paddle

Stop at the interpretive center at the Lewis and Clark Recreational Area or the Yankton Visitor Center for a list of the many hiking trails along Lewis and Clark Lake. The 1.2-mile Gavins Point Nature Trail that loops through the west end of the park has about 10 interpretive stops with information on Native Americans' use of local plants, views of the Nebraska cliffs, a spot to look for some of the 414 species that migrate through the area, and how to identify animal tracks. If you're intrigued by the Nebraska cliffs, look at the interpretive center for examples of fossils found there.

Leisurely paddlers can find kayaks and canoes to rent in the area, but for a true adventure, there's the 79-mile Missouri National Recreational Water Trail that runs from below Gavins Point dam to North Sioux City. Go to mnrrwatertrail.com for more information. For details on all the area's trails, go to seeyanktonsd.com.

About 21 miles west of Yankton near Springfield, there's another option for staying along the river at the ***Cogan House Bed and Breakfast.*** If you're not competing with sportsmen for prime hunting weekends, it's a peaceful place to soak up sweeping views of the river and an excellent spot for bird watching. The log home was built new in 2009, but owners Greg and Diana and their son, Grant, are tapping some of South Dakota's deepest roots in hospitality. Their ancestors built the original Cogan House in 1869 and fed guests ranging from Sitting Bull to General Custer. If you're lucky, they might be serving pancakes and homemade chokecherry syrup for breakfast. Call (605) 464-0238 or go to thecoganhouse.com for more information.

Mitchell

Located 60 miles west of Sioux Falls on I-90, ***Mitchell*** (population 15,539) has been synonymous with its iconic ***Corn Palace*** since it was first built in 1892. More than 750,000 people from around the world stop by each year to gawk at this "world's only" marvel at 604 N. Main St.

The effect is supersized seed art meets the Taj Mahal of the Great Plains. This ode to agriculture was dreamed up by city founders to debut with Mitchell's first Corn Belt Exposition. It was part of a big-wow trend in the late 1800s when farm communities were seeking to make a name for themselves. Aberdeen had the Grain Palace, and Rapid City had an Alfalfa Palace, and more than 20 other towns had palaces across the Midwest, but only Mitchell's has survived for more than 100 years. Work is under way on what's being called Next Generation Corn Palace with a walkout balcony, new lobby, illuminated exterior sign, larger murals, color-changing domes, and wind turbines.

The Corn Palace is open year-round with free tours from Memorial Day through Labor Day. Throughout the building, you'll also find plenty of vintage photos showing past corn palace themes and designs and many fun, interactive exhibits about corn geared toward families. Hours are 8 a.m. to 9 p.m. Memorial Day through Labor Day, daily 8 a.m. to 5 p.m. Apr and May and Sept through Nov, and 8 a.m. to 5 p.m. Mon to Sat from Dec through Mar. Call (605) 996-6223 or go to cornpalace.org

The Corn Palace also serves as a multiuse center for the community and region with stage shows as well as sports events in its arena. Every third weekend in July, thousands of people gather here to attend the nightly PRCA rodeo performances, as well as other activities throughout ***Rodeo Week.***

The corn craze peaks in late August with the ***Corn Palace Festival,*** a weeklong celebration with marching bands, country music concerts, a polka fest, and carnival rides. The highlight comes when the new mural is officially presented. Most years, themes are agricultural or nature related, although previous designs have celebrated the space race, the youth of America, patriotism, nostalgia, and the Internet.

Not surprisingly, the Corn Palace makes a mighty fine bird feeder. After Corn Palace Week ends and winter arrives, local pigeons and squirrels devour the murals. The area around the Corn Palace can be touristy, but

acloserlook atthecorn palace

Farmers plant 12 different colors of corn for the murals, which require about 275,000 ears that are sliced in half and nailed to the Corn Palace walls. Cherie Ramsdell creates the designs, which are accented with other locally grown grains and grasses that include: bundles of ryegrass and sour dock, bromegrass and bluegrass, wild oats, rye, straw, and wheat.

don't brush off Mitchell as a one-attraction town. It's worth at least a full day of exploring.

Mitchell's *Dakota Wesleyan University* campus houses the *Dakota Discovery Museum* at 1300 McGovern Ave. More than 100,000 Native American and pioneer artifacts are displayed in the building complex. Sites include a restored 1886 Victorian home, built for the cofounder of the Corn Palace; the 1909 Farwell Methodist Church; the Sheldon School, an 1885 one-room territorial school; and a 1914 railroad depot. The *Case Art Gallery* is best known for its display of the oil painting *Dakota Woman,* by Harvey Dunn. Over the years this classic of plains art, depicting a young woman basking in the sunshine in an open field while her baby rests under a parasol, has become synonymous with prairie life and prairie people.

Three other art galleries (Oscar Howe, Charles Hargens, and one for changing exhibits) feature original works by Howe, Dunn, and Hargens, James Earle Fraser, Gutzon Borglum (the sculptor for Mount Rushmore), and others. The changing exhibits gallery features one-person shows, emphasizing American Indian artists of the Northern Plains.

Oscar Howe in particular was one of South Dakota's most revered artists and a graduate of Dakota Wesleyan University. Howe was born on the Crow Creek Indian Reservation in South Dakota. In 1940 the painter was commissioned to create the dome mural, *Sun and Rain Clouds Over Hills,* for the *Mitchell Public Library* as a WPA project. He also did many of the Corn Palace's early murals. In 1972 Howe was widely recognized as one of America's preeminent Native American artists. The Howe Gallery boasts a collection of drawings and paintings that traces the history of Howe's development as an artist from when he was a student of the Santa Fe Indian School. His later work reflects a highly stylized interpretation of his heritage, using the formal elements of line, color, and space to create vivid, abstract designs.

The *Hargens Gallery* includes an intriguing replica of his studio, which is packed with saddles, vintage furniture, pen nibs, easels, cowboy hats, and other props he used for painting characters and lively scenes that graced western novels and magazines for decades.

Kids will love *DiscoveryLand,* an interactive center that allows children to experience life on the prairie from a number of different perspectives.

They can grab a scavenger hunt list and feel a full sense of history with impressive exhibits and vivid murals. The gallery's gift shop features the work of area artists and artisans, including original works on canvas and paper, sculpture, pottery and ceramics, quilts, jewelry, and reproductions. Admission is $7 for adults, $6 for senior citizens, $3 for youth, and free for children 5 and under. Hours vary by season, and it may be closed one or two days a week. Call (605) 996-2122 or visit dakotadiscovery.com for details.

Other prominent alumni of Dakota Wesleyan University were 1972 presidential candidate George McGovern and his wife, Eleanor. The *McGovern Legacy Museum* at 1201 McGovern Ave. tells the story of their years at the university, followed by his service in World War II, the 22 years he represented South Dakota in Congress, and his work to end world hunger as an ambassador to the United Nations. Hours follow the campus schedule, so call ahead for details at (605) 995-2935 or go to mcgoverncenter.com. Free admission.

Mitchell's Ancient History

A student from Dakota Wesleyan University first discovered evidence of ancient villages along the lake just north of Mitchell in 1910, and the *Mitchell Prehistoric Indian Village* has been an ongoing project since then and the state's only National Archaeological Landmark. An estimated 200 people lived here about 1,100 years ago along the Firesteel Creek growing crops such as corn, beans, squash, sunflowers, and amaranth. A video and exhibits at the visitor center offer insight into this prehistoric community. You can then take a short walk to the *Thomsen Center Archeodome,* where you can watch excavations in progress. A group of students comes from England each summer to help with the work, and there are hands-on areas where you can see if you have an eye for significant fragments. Children also can dig for an arrowhead and try to throw an ancient weapon called an atlatl. The site is open from 8 a.m. to 7 p.m. Mon through Sat and 10 a.m. to 6 p.m. Sun Memorial Day through Labor Day. It's also open 9 a.m. to 6 p.m. Mon through Sat and 10 a.m. to 6 p.m. Sun in Apr, May, Sept, and Oct. Admission is $6 for adults; $5 for seniors; $4 for those between 6 and 18 years old. Call (605) 996-5473 or visit mitchell indianvillage.org.

A drive through the hinterlands of South Dakota may seem lonely at first, but it can be the best way to see a generous slice of Americana. That's why it's worth a trek up SD 37 from Mitchell to find the epicenter of South Dakota's beloved *Forestburg* melons. Some people say it's the rich bottomlands of the James River Valley between Mitchell and Huron that makes these such stellar fruits, while others say sandy soil helps sweeten them. No matter what theory makes sense, you'll find a juicy bonanza from mid-August through the end of October, when old-fashioned produce stands overflow with watermelons, pumpkins, squash, Indian corn, sweet corn, and gourds. Apparently the local melon rage began in the grim 1930s, when Ernie Schwemle and Harold Smith planted a few seeds and sparked the tradition of an annual melon harvest.

From Forestburg, travel west on SD 34 to Wessington Springs and step back in time to the Renaissance and the enchanting *Shakespeare Garden and Anne Hathaway Cottage* in Wessington Springs. Shakespeare and Anne Hathaway in rural South Dakota? In 1926, Mrs. Emma Shay, English teacher at Wessington Springs Seminary, borrowed $1,000 to travel throughout England. Her purpose was to increase her knowledge and ability to teach English literature. By the next year, on the April 23 birthday of England's most famous playwright, construction began for a Shakespeare Garden in an alfalfa patch on campus. The work was done by Professor and Mrs. Shay, other faculty, and students. Shrubs, trees, and flowers of all kinds were donated by the city, the May Seed Company, Henry Field Company, and private citizens. The summer house was built by the boys of the English department, and the sophomore class of 1928 made the lily pond. A sundial and gazing globe were also donated. By the end of 1928, the Shakespeare Garden, South Dakota's first, was a noted attraction with many visitors. The Shays then built the Anne Hathaway Cottage when they retired in 1932 and were inspired by a postcard of the original at Stratford-on-Avon. In observance of the state's centennial in 1989, the Shakespeare Garden Society of Wessington Springs purchased the Shakespeare Garden and Anne Hathaway Cottage. Listed on the National Register of Historic Places, Anne Hathaway Cottage is the only thatched-roof building in South Dakota.

The cottage and garden host teas, tours, a Maypole dance, one-act plays, Christmas events, and weddings. Located at 501 Alene Ave. North, the garden is open during daylight hours and the cottage is open daily 1:30 to

4:30 p.m. Wed, Sat, and Sun during the summer months or by appointment. Admission is free. Tours and English tea reservations can be made at (605) 539-1529 or visit shakespearegarden.blogspot.com.

Wessington Springs also is fabled for its excellent pheasant hunting in the fall. The town is located in the draws of the Wessington Hills, surrounded by wooded gulches, fertile farmland, and rolling prairie. Two large springs that still provide water for the town first attracted native tribes, French fur traders, and settlers.

Where to Stay in Southeastern South Dakota

SIOUX FALLS

ClubHouse Hotel and Suites
2320 S. Louise Ave.
(605) 361-8700
siouxfalls.clubhouseinn
.com
Moderate

Country Inn & Suites
200 E. 8th St.
(605) 373-0153
countryinn.com/
siouxfallssd_central
Moderate

Courtyard by Marriott
4300 Empire Place
(605) 444-4300
marriott.com/fsdcy
Moderate

Dakotah Lodge
3200 W. Russell St.
(605) 332-2000
dakotahlodge.com
Inexpensive

Holiday Inn City Centre
100 W. 8th St.
(605) 339-2000
sfcchotel.com
Moderate

Steever House Bed and Breakfast
46850 276th St.
Lennox, SD
(10 miles south of Sioux Falls)
(605) 647-5055
steeverhouse.com
Inexpensive

VERMILLION

Buffalo Run Resort
(at Valiant Vineyards)
1500 W. Main St.
(605) 624-4500
Moderate

Prairie Inn
916 N. Dakota
(605) 624-2824
prairieinnusd.com
Inexpensive

YANKTON

Best Western Kelly Inn
1607 E. Hwy. 50
(605) 665-2906
bestwestern.com
Moderate

Riverfront Event Center
(Formerly the River Rose Hotel)
121 W. 3rd St.
(605) 664-0120
theriverfrontevent
center.com
Moderate

SOUTHEAST SD CHAMBERS OF COMMERCE

Southeast South Dakota Tourism
1101 Broadway St.
Yankton 57078
(605) 665-2435
SoutheastSouthDakota.com

Mitchell Convention and Visitors Bureau
601 N. Main St.
Mitchell 57301
(605) 996-6223
visitmitchell.com

Sioux Falls Convention and Visitors Bureau
200 N. Phillips Ave.
Suite 102
Sioux Falls 57104
(605) 336-1620
visitsiouxfalls.com

Vermillion Area Chamber of Commerce
116 Market St.
Vermillion 57069
(605) 624-5571
vermillioncvb.com

Yankton Convention and Visitors Bureau
803 E. 4th St.
Yankton 57078
(605) 665-3636
visityanktonsd.com

Where to Eat in Southeastern South Dakota

MITCHELL

Cafe Teresa
312 N. Main
(605) 990-2233
mitchellcafeteresa.com
Inexpensive

Chef Louie's
601 E. Havens St.
(605) 996-7565
Moderate to expensive

Crazy About Cupcakes
417 Main St.
Suite 104
(605) 990-9866
Inexpensive

The Depot Pub & Grill
210 S. Main St.
(605) 996-9417
mitchelldepot.com
Moderate

SIOUX FALLS

Bob's on 12th
1312 W. 12th St.
(605) 336-7260
bobscarryout.com
Inexpensive

Chedd's Gourmet Grilled Cheese
323 S. Phillips Ave.
(605) 274-7676
chedds.com
Inexpensive

Crawford's Bar and Grill
214 S. Phillips Ave.
(605) 332-5333
crawfordssf.com
Moderate

Grille 26
1716 S. Western Ave.
(605) 444-1716
grille26.com
Moderate

Kaladi's Coffee Legend and Bistro
200 S. Phillips Ave.
(605) 977-0888
kaladisbistro.com
Moderate

Oh My Cupcakes!
524 Main Ave. N
Suite 106
(605) 310-6742
ohmycupcakes.com
Inexpensive

Wild Sage Grille
300 N. Cherapa Place
(605) 274-1667
wildsagegrille.com
Moderate

VERMILLION

Red Steakhouse
1 E. Main St.
(605) 624-0079
theredsteakhouse.com
Moderate to expensive

Silk Road Cafe
12 W. Main St.
(605) 658-1923
Moderate

YANKTON

Bella's Restaurant
(at Riverfront Event
Center)
121 W. 3rd
(605) 689-3333
bellasrestaurantyankton
.com
Moderate to expensive

Ben's Brewing Company
222 W. 3rd St.
(605) 260-4844
bensbrewing.com
Inexpensive

Charlie's Pizza House
804 Summit St.
(605) 665-2212
Moderate

Tastee Treet Drive-In
413 W. 4th St.
(605) 665-7512
Inexpensive

The Landing
104 Capitol
(605) 664-2779
thelandingyankton.com
Moderate to expensive

Along the Missouri River

For sheer wanderlust and a love of the outdoors, travel the **Missouri River** section of South Dakota. It's a hunting and fishing paradise, rich in water, wildlife refuges, and parks. Beyond the capital, there are few communities along this central strip—except those of Old World and Native American heritage that proudly share their culture. The Missouri River winds through central South Dakota for 453 miles, offering not only a spectacular ribbon of blue water but also shore land rich in history, mystery, and adventure. Sliding past forts, monuments, ruins, reservations, and pioneer towns in South Dakota, the Missouri River ultimately flows into the Mississippi River and then to the Gulf of Mexico.

The powerful Missouri neatly divides the state into two dissimilar geographic and cultural regions. Along the west side of the river, wide stretches of prairie are broken by low hills and cut by ravines. Trees are sparse, and great cattle ranches fill the expanse of land. In the extreme west rise the forested Black Hills, one of the primary sources of the nation's gold. Fertile farmlands stretch out east of the Missouri River. Culturally speaking, East River is the well-heeled cousin who needs to be sent away to the spirited West River

NORTH DAKOTA
SOUTH DAKOTA

THE NORTH-CENTRAL
RESERVATIONS AND
LAKE OAHE

Lake
Oahe

Eureka

PIONEERS
AND
WALLEYES

Mobridge

Missouri R.

Gettysburg

THE CAPITAL

Pierre

THE CENTRAL
RESERVATIONS

Chamberlain

N

Winner

LAKE FRANCIS
CASE

0   30 mi
0   30 km

SOUTH DAKOTA
NEBRASKA

The Oyate Trail

The concept of a scenic route to the Black Hills of South Dakota has been around since before the Missouri River was dammed and before Mount Rushmore was even finished. Since the day the state could boast of having a "fully improved road" along its southern border, South Dakotans have been promoting this 388-mile stretch of highway as an educational alternative to the interstate. Travelers will discover diverse geography, as well as the cultural and historical contributions of both the Sioux Nation and European immigrants.

The Oyate Trail of today turns off I-29 at Vermillion and heads west on SD 50 and US 18 to Edgemont near the Wyoming border. For local attractions along the way and suggested itineraries, call the Southeast Tourism Association, (888) 353-7382, or visit oyatetrail.com.

once in a while to get a good grasp of terra firma in his hand and in his soul. Likewise, West River could head east to mellow out the wildness and soak up some culture.

The Mighty Mo, as residents like to call the river, served as the first highway into the region at a time when fur trappers pulled keelboats up the river by hand. Later, fur traders arrived in steamboats, beginning with the arrival of the *Yellowstone* in 1831. They sang the now-familiar folk song "Oh, Shenandoah," and you can almost hear the strain of ". . . across the wide Missouri."

River traffic became a thing of the past as the railroad reached the area at the turn of the 20th century, and the number of settlements increased rapidly thereafter. The river in those days was known as the Muddy Mo, and the standard joke was that a person didn't know whether to plow it or drink it. Jokers had their last laugh when the construction of four dams across the Missouri River created Lewis and Clark Lake, Lake Francis Case, Lake Sharpe, and Lake Oahe. These reservoirs have transformed Old Muddy into a series of crystalline blue lakes that have become popular recreation areas for South Dakotans and nonresidents alike.

Today life along the Missouri River isn't as bustling as life in East River or as animated as that in West River, but the beauty of wildlife, the grandeur of the bluffs, and the peaceful flow of the river make the Mighty Mo a magical place to be.

Lake Francis Case

The first lake you'll reach after exploring southeastern South Dakota and heading west is 120-mile-long **Lake Francis Case.** While it feels more open and remote than the Lewis and Clark Recreational area, this lake, **Pickstown** (population 215), and the Fort Randall Dam have their share of boating, fishing (catfish, walleye, bass, and pike), camping, and birding.

Start at the **Fort Randall Dam Visitor Center** for an overview of the area's history, including its time as a frontier fort and the creation of the 165-foot-high dam that was begun in 1946. Tours of the dam are offered three times a day Memorial Day through Labor Day. Call (605) 487-7845 for details.

You also can get directions and a self-guided tour for exploring the fort's cemetery, the original site of the 1856 **Fort Randall Military Post** with remaining building foundations and salvaged ruins of the fort's church. The fort's visitors list reads like a Who's Who in Great Plains history: George Custer, Philip Sheridan, and Hunkpapa Sioux leader Sitting Bull (who was held prisoner at the fort for two years). Call (605) 487-7847 for more information.

Birders should also check out the area's national wildlife refuges. **Lake Andes National Wildlife Refuge Complex** includes **Karl E. Mundt National Wildlife Refuge** near **Randall Creek Recreation Area** on the south side of the river. It's considered one of the country's most important habitats for bald eagles. Up to 300 of them roost here in the winter months, and some nest in cottonwoods along the shore. Call (605) 487-7603 for more information or go to fws.gov/refuge/karl_e_mundt.

lewisandclark

Near Greenwood in the south-central part of the state, Lewis and Clark wrapped a newborn Sioux in a US flag and predicted the babe would always be a friend of the whites. The child grew up to become Struck by the Ree, chief of the Yankton Sioux.

To get the best access to regional birding areas (not to mention the expertise to spot birds), attend the **South Dakota Birding Festival** in early May. In addition to speakers and workshops, participants get a guided glimpse of the more than 300 species following the Missouri River to breeding and nesting grounds. Check with southeastsouthdakota.com for details.

If you continue traveling west, crossing the Missouri River and staying on Highway 18, you'll reach **Gregory County** and the town of Gregory, where a large artificial pheasant greets visitors arriving from the west. Thousands of hunters flock to this area every year, making hunting the second-largest industry in the county, behind agriculture.

Circle H Ranch, located 8 miles south of Gregory, is a working ranch known throughout the region for its fine crops, superb grassland, and excellent natural game habitat. In 1992, the ranch was opened as a private retreat to accommodate hunters and guests for business retreats and vacations. The quiet serenity, along with the breathtaking natural beauty of the land, makes a visit to the Circle H Ranch a perfect getaway. Lodging options include a guest house with 5 rooms or a renovated pioneer church with 6 bedrooms (605-731-5050; circlehranch.com).

If you want to travel across the longest bridge this side of the Mississippi, connect to eastbound SD 44 and cross the Missouri River on a bridge that's just over a mile long.

The Central Reservations

Continue traveling north along SD 50 (the Lewis and Clark Trail) until you reach I-90. Go one exit west, and you'll reach the Chamberlain-Oacoma community. Its beautiful, undulating bluffs that flank the Missouri River make quite a statement and create what feels like a gateway to the Old West.

Chamberlain, population 2,444, was named for Selah Chamberlain, who was director of the Milwaukee railroad in 1880, when the town was started. Rumor has it that, before 1880, natives called Chamberlain *Makah Tepee,* or "mud house," because a hermit had a dugout there.

When traveling from the Black Hills to Sioux Falls (or vice versa), one of the most popular stops is **Al's Oasis,** off exit 260 on I-90. A great almost-halfway-there point (or over-halfway-there, depending on which way you're traveling), the restaurant has been a respite for weary travelers for more than 80 years. They come for the homemade pie, buffalo burgers, and 5-cent coffee. Owners Albert and Veda Mueller moved the Oasis to its present location in the 1950s when it was a grocery store and 10-stool lunch counter.

Since then Al's Oasis has expanded into a full-menu, 325-seat restaurant and lounge with moderate prices. The Oasis Trading Post and General Store has anything and everything you forgot or need on your trip—from food and toiletries to men's, women's, and children's clothing, and cowboy boots—as well as a campground and an 86-room inn if you need to crash for the night (605-234-6051; alsoasis.com).

The **Cedar Shore Resort** (605-734-6376; cedarshore.com) is the first resort erected on the shores of the Missouri River. The 80,000-square-foot facility on 164 acres features a marina breakwater, a 99-room hotel, a day spa, a full-service convention center, and a 200-seat restaurant with lounge, art gallery, and more. The marina facility is one of a kind, with 100 boat slips and a floating concession. The interior design centers on themes indigenous to the area such as buckskin, the pasqueflower, yucca, coyotes, horses, and prairie wind.

The Oacoma-Chamberlain area offers one of the state's best places to appreciate Native American culture with **St. Joseph's Indian School** and its impressive **Akta Lakota Museum and Cultural Center.** The museum rightly lives up to its name, which means "to honor the people," with exhibits and art that represent the past and present Lakota way of life.

On display at the museum are extraordinary hand-painted winter "counts," which provided a record of history. For generations, Plains Indians drew pictographs to document their daily experiences and to record time. A historian appointed by the tribal community drew one pictograph on a buffalo or deer hide at the end of each winter season. The pictograph represented a significant event that happened within that year.

A new wing of the museum with heartfelt and creative multimedia displays offers a poignant glimpse into the often challenging life at an Indian School. St. Joseph's, founded by the Priests of the Sacred Heart in 1927, was among the many boarding schools where Native American children were sent in an effort to make them more like Europeans. St. Joseph's eventually changed that mission, embraced and celebrated Native American culture, and continues to aid the spiritual and educational growth of more than 200 Lakota and Dakota Indian children and young adults of all religious backgrounds. The school uses the concept of *tiospaye,* or "extended family," in its four communities. The campus also includes a new Medicine Wheel Garden and an extensive gift shop filled with Native American art and products.

Summer hours are 8 a.m. to 6 p.m. Mon through Sat and 9 a.m. to 5 p.m. Sun, and 8 a.m. to 5 p.m. Mon through Fri from Nov through Apr. Admission is free, but donations are encouraged. You can also take a self-guided tour of the campus. For information on the school or museum, call (800) 798-3452 or visit stjo.org.

Driving north on SD 50, you'll reach both the **Crow Creek and Lower Brule Indian Reservations,** which flank both sides of the Missouri between Chamberlain and Pierre. This is **Lake Sharpe** country as well, a looping reservoir created by the Big Bend Dam in the early 1960s.

With the side-by-side reservations, this area also is a handy place to test your luck at casinos.

The **Lode Star Casino** in **Fort Thompson** is accessible from the Native American Loop just north of Chamberlain. Owned by the Crow Creek Sioux tribe, the Lode Star boasts 250 slot machines, 6 game tables, and bingo. A 50-room hotel and restaurant also are on-site (605-245-6000; lodestarcasino .com). To reach the **Golden Buffalo Casino,** cross the river at Fort Thompson and head northwest on Highway 10/1806 until you reach **Lower Brule.** Slot machines and live blackjack and poker in the 9,000-square-foot casino keep the adrenaline flowing. The 38-room resort motel and convention center, restaurant, lounge, and gift shop overlook Lake Sharpe. Call (605) 473-5577 or go to thegoldenbuffalocasino.com for more information.

While driving in the area, keep an eye out for the **Lower Brule buffalo herd** of about 300 spread across 6,200 acres. If you're yearning to learn more about South Dakota's most iconic mammal and to get a closer look, stop in at the Buffalo Interpretive Center, 29349 Hwy. 1806, 7 miles east of Fort Pierre. The center includes videos and hands-on exhibits about the importance of buffalo to the plains culture. For more information, call (605) 223-2260 or go to lbst.org.

The Capital

The easiest way South Dakotans can spot a newcomer is by how he or she pronounces **Pierre,** the state capital. French class will be no help. Here, they say *pier.* The ruggedly autonomous forefathers were perhaps trying to downplay the *très français* beginnings of the state, but it was indeed a Frenchman who started South Dakota's first permanent white settlement in

1832. American Fur Company agent Pierre Chouteau Jr. piloted his steamboat, the *Yellowstone,* to the mouth of the Bad River and established Fort Pierre Chouteau. Representatives from nine Sioux tribes brought their furs to trade, principally buffalo, which were valued at the time from $3 to $4 per hide. An average of 17,000 buffalo robes were traded each year. The site of the settlement is now a designated landmark on the National Register of Historic Places. Pierre is the nation's second-smallest capital, with a population of 14,000, but its central location in the middle of the state makes it neutral when it comes to East River–West River favoritism.

The **Oahe Dam,** 4 miles north of Pierre on SD 1806, is the nation's largest rolled-earth dam. It creates the fourth-largest man-made reservoir in the US, running 231 miles from Pierre to Bismarck. With 2,250 miles of shoreline, it claims a longer coast than the state of California and boasts 51 recreational areas. The power plant, dedicated by President John F. Kennedy in 1962, houses seven of the world's largest generators. If you want to tour the plant, go to the Oahe Visitor Center at 20207 SD 1804 to sign up and show your ID. Tours are offered three times a day Memorial Day through Labor Day. Call (605) 224-5862 or go to recreation.gov.

Overlooking the Oahe Reservoir, the Oahe Visitor Center offers information on anything from recreation to local hotels and restaurants. The center has numerous informational displays, which include Lewis and Clark, the Oahe Chapel, Oahe intake structures, and a Kid's Korner. The center is open from Memorial Day through Labor Day.

The lake takes its name from the Oahe Mission, started in 1874 by the Reverend Thomas L. Riggs, a Congregational minister, and his wife, Cornelia Margaret Foster, to serve the Dakota Indians. The mission was originally located on the site of an old Arikara Indian village, about 5 miles from the location of the modern-day chapel.

In the 1950s, when it became evident that the completion of the Oahe Dam would flood the mission location, the chapel was given to the South Dakota Historical Society. In 1964 it was relocated at the eastern end of Oahe Dam, where it stands today. Nondenominational Sunday services start at 8 a.m. Memorial Day through Labor Day. The chapel is also a popular wedding location.

Fishing on Lake Oahe or Lake Sharpe is legendary. The Walleye Capital of the World also is known for its trophy northern pike. Chinook salmon, white and smallmouth bass, brown and rainbow trout, and catfish also are caught here. Eminent filmmaker Ken Burns, creator of the popular PBS documentaries *Baseball* and *The Civil War,* made a documentary of the Lewis and Clark expedition along the Missouri River system. His crews visited Pierre in the summer of 1995 to capture sections of the river and to film buffalo near the Lower Brule Indian Reservation. "We're looking for stretches of river that represent how it really was," Burns told the *Lincoln* (Nebraska) *Star Journal.* "We want to see it as [Lewis and Clark] might have seen it."

The French connection is underscored at the ***Vérendrye Monument*** in Fort Pierre, just off US 83 across the Missouri River. The two French brothers Vérendrye were the first white people to set foot in South Dakota in 1743. They buried a lead plate on a bluff that overlooks Fort Pierre to claim the area for King Louis XV of France. A monument in Fort Pierre marks the spot where the plate was discovered after being covered by dirt for generations. Schoolchildren accidentally unearthed it in February 1913. Now the artifact is on display at the ***South Dakota Cultural Heritage Center,*** 900 Governors Dr., a must-see during a visit to Pierre. The free museum uses award-winning displays and hands-on activities to explain the state's heritage of northern plains tribes, trappers, soldiers, pioneers, ruthless gold-diggers, and Old West scoundrels. *Oyate Tawicoh'an* ("The Ways of the People"), a permanent exhibit at the center, showcases Native American history with more than 300 Native American artifacts, including an eagle feather headdress, a full-size tipi, and a mounted buffalo. It's open from 9 a.m. to 4:30 p.m. Mon through Sat and 1 to 4:30 p.m. Sun year-round. Hours extend until 6:30 p.m. Mon through Sat from Memorial Day through Labor Day. Admission is $4 for adults, $3 for seniors, and free for children under 17. All visitors can get in free on the first Sunday of every month. Call (605) 773-3458 or go to history .sd.gov for more details.

During the Thanksgiving and Christmas seasons, the Capitol Rotunda at 500 E. Capitol Ave. is awash in the lights and color of beautifully hand-decorated trees. The annual ***Christmas at the Capitol*** event began more than 25 years ago after Dottie Howe and her friends couldn't find a perfect tree to display in the rotunda. The group took a dozen or so and bunched them together—kind of like an exaggerated version of Charlie Brown's Christmas tree. Now the display has grown to include close to 100 trees—Black Hills spruce, pine, and other evergreens—that are decorated with a holiday theme. See a teddy bear tree, a Victorian Christmas tree, a music tree, even a pheasant tree. More than 50,000 people visit the striking display each year. **Capitol Christmas Trees** is open 8 a.m. to 10 p.m. daily the week of Thanksgiving until just after Christmas. For more details, call (605) 773-4010.

South Dakota's State Capitol, which more than casually resembles the Capitol in Washington, DC, looks dazzling. You can see for yourself by scheduling tours with volunteer guides or taking your own self-guided tour between 8 a.m. and 7 p.m. Mon through Fri or 8 a.m. to 5 p.m. weekends. Call (605) 773-3688 or stop by the Capitol Lake Visitor Center for more information.

Built on a foundation of South Dakota granite, the graceful building features terrazzo floors, coolly elegant marble staircases, stained-glass skylights, and a solid copper dome. This striking limestone structure, which looks much as it did when it was completed in 1910, is one of the most fully restored capitols in the US. The state seal, which bears the motto "Under God the People Rule," symbolizes the way of life in South Dakota and the resources that keep it vital: farming, ranching, industries, lumbering, manufacturing, and mining. The seal was adopted in 1885, four years before the state was admitted to the union, and it is repeated on the state flag. A blazing sun encircles the seal, and the state's motto encircles the sun.

Fed by a warm artesian well, **Capitol Lake** never entirely freezes. It has become a winter haven for Canada geese, mallards, wood ducks, and many other varieties of migratory waterfowl. The **Flaming Fountain** perpetually glows as a memorial to all veterans while the **South Dakota Korean & Vietnam War Memorial** stands as a tribute to the valiant South Dakotans who lost their lives in those two wars. The names of these slain veterans are carved in granite next to the Flaming Fountain.

Pierre also has a long military history from the Civil War to the Iraq War. You can learn more about it

trivia

A reproduction of Korczak Ziolkowski's **Fighting Stallions** also stands on the capitol grounds. It was erected in remembrance of the late governor George S. Mickelson and seven staff members and state leaders who died in a plane crash in 1993.

Pierre Celebrations

The Lewis and Clark *Goosefest,* held every September at Steamboat Park, celebrates both the journey of Lewis and Clark and the return of migrating geese to the Pierre area. The three-day event celebrates crisp autumn days, South Dakota Arts Showcase, craft booths, children's activities, and live entertainment along the shores of the Missouri River. Vendors also sell a variety of unique products, including South Dakota honey, Arikara-style pottery, dried flower arrangements, and Indian tacos. Entertainment in the park's band shell ranges from goose-calling demonstrations to folk music. August visitors can join in the three-day *Riverfest* with a water-ski show, car and air shows, a Kiddie Parade, kids carnival and fishing events, a buffalo chip flip, and paddleboat and kayak rides along the Mighty Mo. Call (800) 962-2034 for details on either event.

and get up close to a Sherman tank, General Custer's sword, a Civil War horse-drawn gun, and an A-7D jet fighter at the **South Dakota National Guard Museum,** 301 E. Dakota St. It's open 9 a.m. to 4 p.m. Mon through Fri. Tours can be arranged by calling (605) 224-9991. There is no admission charge.

While the goings-on of state government present a busy and intriguing scene in Pierre, this town has more to offer than just politics.

Another popular Pierre stop is the **South Dakota Discovery Center and Aquarium** (805 W. Sioux Ave.), a former Pierre power plant that now houses hands-on science and technology exhibits and much more. Three aquariums feature native species of fish. Visitors can experience the universe through astronomy in the Sky Lab planetarium or test their reflex skills in the reactionary car. The center is open Sun through Fri 1 to 5 p.m. and Sat 10 a.m. to 5 p.m. Summer hours are from 10 a.m. to 5 p.m. Mon through Sat, 1 to 5 p.m. Sun. Admission is $4 for adults and $3 for children 3 and older (605-224-8295; sd-discovery.com).

If you've worked up an appetite, settle into **La Minestra,** in a restored 1886 tavern at 106 E. Dakota, with wainscoting and original pressed metal walls and ceiling. You might wish the walls could talk: The building has been a funeral parlor, a pool hall and card room, and a country-western bar. As a popular Italian restaurant, it's now known for freshly made pasta dishes and hand-cut steaks (605-224-8090; laminestra.com).

Fort Pierre was the stomping ground of rodeo legend **Casey Tibbs,** who was born in a log cabin on the family homestead outside Fort Pierre in 1929. A life-size statue of Casey, riding the famous bronc "Necktie," is on display at the Fort Pierre community park and historical turnout. By 15, he was in nationwide competitions, and in 1949, at age 19, Casey became the youngest man ever to win the national saddle bronc-riding crown. Between 1949 and 1955, he won a total of six PRCA saddle-bronc-riding champion-ships, a record still unchallenged, plus two all-around cowboy champion-ships and one bareback-riding championship. You can learn more about his colorful, spirited life (including a couple of movies and stunt work) and celebrate South Dakota's rich rodeo history at the **Casey Tibbs Rodeo Center** overlooking Pierre and Fort Pierre at 210 Verendrye Dr. Exhibits spotlight the work of Mattie Goff Newcombe, a spectacular trick rider of the 1920s, and the work of rodeo clowns, cowboys, entertainers, and rodeo queens. Hours are 9 a.m. to 5 p.m. Mon through Fri, 10 a.m. to 4 p.m. Sat, and noon to 5 p.m. Sun June through Aug and 10 a.m. to 5 p.m. Tues through Fri, 10 a.m. to 3 p.m. Sat, and 1 to 4 p.m. Sun the rest of the year. Admission is $6 adults, $5 seniors, and $4 kids 6 to 18 (605-494-1094; caseytibbs.com).

About 8 miles south of Pierre is the **Fort Pierre National Grassland**, 200 undulating square miles of grasslands bisected by US 83. It's a hotspot for birders who come to see the greater prairie chicken, burrowing owls, and raptors, which are especially easy to see during the winter months. This is part of the national grassland that ranges across Nebraska and central and western South Dakota. Call (308) 432-0300 for more information.

On Lake Oahe

South Dakota's most northern stretch of the Missouri River snakes its way from North Dakota to Pierre, much of it a lonely stretch with few towns and Standing Rock and Cheyenne River Reservations expanding west from the river. The largest city, **Mobridge** (population 3,524), enjoys the prosperity that the river has afforded. Mobridge calls itself the Walleye Capital of the World, and no one is likely to dispute that moniker, since both the Missouri and the Oahe Reservoir envelop this town. In 1906 the Milwaukee Railroad built the first bridge to cross the Missouri River in South Dakota, at what was

Site Selection

Founded in 1901, Pollock, northeast of Mobridge in Campbell County, thrived until the early 1950s, when construction of the Oahe Dam threatened to leave the town underwater. For several years the people of Pollock struggled with whether to move, abandon their town, or consolidate with nearby Herreid. After much consideration the town decided to move. But in what direction? A vote was held and ballots cast, some with a touch of humor. One vote called for Pollock to be put even deeper under the waters of Lake Oahe. Groundbreaking ceremonies for the "new" town were held on June 4, 1955. Today Pollock is surrounded on three sides by water and enjoys its reputation as one of South Dakota's most mobile cities.

formerly the site of an Arikara and Sioux village. A telegraph operator used the contraction *Mobridge* to indicate his location, and the name has stuck.

Lake Oahe, with a shoreline of more than 2,250 miles, is the longest lake on the main stream of the Missouri River, stretching 231 miles from Pierre to Bismarck, North Dakota. Begun in 1948, it is the largest of the four impoundments. The shoreline is virtually devoid of trees, making it a curious earthbound moonscape. The lake's azure waters and native stands of grass on the bluff, however, make it appealingly endless and warm.

The genuinely down-to-earth people of Mobridge are eager to accommodate the visitors who flock to the town during hunting, fishing, and boating seasons. The choices in lodging are appropriate for both the serious-minded and casual sportsperson.

The sparsely furnished but clean rooms of the **Mo-Rest Motel** on US 12 are perfect for no-frills fishermen who appreciate special amenities for anglers such as aerial river maps. The motel is across the street from two bait shops with boat repair, and you can easily find a guide for on-the-water instruction using the latest fishing techniques and boat control. Call the motel at (605) 845-3668.

History buffs will find a profusion of items to marvel at in the **Scherr Howe Arena,** or the city auditorium, on Main Street. Colorful murals by the late Oscar Howe, a highly esteemed Dakota Indian and art professor at the University of South Dakota, depict both the history and ceremonies of Native Americans. Each mural measures about 16 feet high by 20 feet wide.

For instance, one mural depicts the Social Dance, a prenuptial ceremony common among the Sioux. Custom prescribed a well-established routine for courtship and marriage, but the marital relationship was mostly the result of an agreement between the parties. Since marriage involved being taken into the families of the contracting parties, there were usually group meetings of the relatives with feasting, dancing, and ceremonies that sometimes lasted four or five days. Members of the family wishing to pay tribute to the bride and groom brought appropriate gifts. The bride was suitably honored, her hair combed and braided, and she was given face paints and beautiful garments. Earthenware vessels and other household goods also were common wedding presents.

The groom's father also brought gifts that he bestowed upon his son. Spirited horses and weapons used in the chase and in battle were among the gifts given to honor the new union. Songs of praise about the newlyweds were sung, and small gifts were distributed to the elderly and needy people of the camp. Admission to the center is free. Call (605) 845-2387 for more information.

For more history on the Arikara and Sioux Indians, head 2 miles west on US 12 to the *Klein Museum* at 1820 W. Grand Crossing. Arikara and Sioux artifacts share space with relics of the pioneer past, such as old farm machinery and a restored schoolhouse. This museum was the dream of an early homesteader, Jake Klein, long before the building was ever designed. His goal was to have a top-notch museum that would represent the counties of Campbell, Corson, Dewey, and Walworth, where he traded, homesteaded, and finally retired.

The museum building, with its native stone front, was Klein's gift to Mobridge and the surrounding area with the help of a $15,000 grant from the South Dakota Bicentennial Commission. The museum displays focus on prairie and Native American artifacts. More than 20 pictures of Sitting Bull are featured, along with stone and bone artifacts. The culture of the Sioux and Arikara Indians is reflected in the many articles of clothing, beadwork, pottery, tools, and implements that are on display. The daily tasks of the early pioneers also come alive through the room scenes. For instance, the 1900s pre-electric kitchen features a wood/coal stove, large doughmaker, berry press, kraut cutter, and wooden icebox. A one-room schoolhouse and the original Glencross post office are also located on the museum grounds.

Mobridge's Mystical Stones

One of the biggest mysteries in Mobridge can be found in City Park on N. Main Street. It's here that what was called the Conqueror's Stones were discovered. No one knows why or when they were put here on the north side of the park, platted in 1910. The original inscription once said:

NOTE THE GROOVES

ACCORDING TO TRADITION, DEFEATED INDIAN WARRIORS WERE REQUIRED TO PLACE THEIR HANDS IN THESE GROOVES AS A SIGN OF SUBMISSION

SHETAK CAPTIVES RESCUED HERE
NOVEMBER, 1862
BY FOOL SOLDIER BAND

Continued research revealed a more hopeful meaning. The stones were commonly referred to as prayer rocks. Native Americans would place their hands in the grooves in the rocks when taking an oath as part of initiation ceremonies. Some believe the grooves are the handprints of the Thunderheads, the powerful gods displayed on totem poles. According to this belief, by putting their hands in the prints before they died, the Indians would be taken to the Sky World, or heaven.

The museum is open 9 a.m. to noon and 1 to 5 p.m. Mon through Fri, and 1 to 5 p.m. Sat and Sun April 15 through October 15. It's closed Tues in Apr, May, and October. Admission is $3 for adults, $2 for students (605-845-7243; mobridgekleinmuseum.com).

The **_Fool Soldier Band Monument_** is located at the Klein Museum. On August 20–22, 1862, a group of Santee Indians fled west with a group of white captives as part of the US-Dakota War that started in the Minnesota River Valley. A group of young Teton Sioux negotiated for the release of the white captives and returned them to their families in Minnesota. They expected no rewards or reimbursement, and their actions seemed to be motivated by purely humanitarian concerns. This act of heroism took place in what is now Walworth County.

In Mobridge the Missouri River and Lake Oahe are the center of outdoor leisure. Fishing isn't the only sport in town; the Mobridge area is also a hunter's paradise, with open seasons on pheasant, grouse, turkey, deer, and antelope. Water-skiing, swimming, boating, or just soaking up the brilliant South Dakota sun can easily fill an afternoon.

Indian Creek Recreation Area (located 2 miles east on US 12, then 1 mile south) on the Oahe Reservoir offers fishing and water sports, along with picnicking, playgrounds, and tent and trailer sites. For more information call (605) 845-7112.

Sitting Bull Monument, in Dakota Memorial Park, west of Mobridge on US 12, marks the burial site of the famous Hunkpapa medicine man. Like many chapters in the collective Plains Indian story, Sitting Bull's is one of a fascinating, enigmatic man who met an untimely death. Sitting Bull was born in 1834 on the Grand River, a few miles west of Mobridge, and his tragic demise years later occurred in the same place. The last known leader of the *Cante Tizna,* an elite warrior society, Sitting Bull also helped to defeat General George Custer's troops in 1876 at the Battle of the Little Big Horn. Sitting Bull met his own death, however, after he was arrested and then shot at his camp on the Standing Rock agency near Fort Yates in North Dakota.

trivia

Some 135 million years ago, the area around Mobridge was covered by a great shallow sea, teeming with marine mollusks and shellfish. Clues to their prehistoric existence have turned up along the shores of Lake Oahe in the form of fossil ammonites, baculites, and belemnites that range from 1 to 6 inches long. If you look hard enough, you might find one of the ancient treasures.

Native South Dakota

After the US-Dakota War in 1862, most of Minnesota's Dakota tribes were banished west to reservations in South Dakota. Today there are nine tribes in South Dakota, representing about 62,000 residents and operating as sovereign nations. They speak three dialects: Dakota, Lakota, and Nakota. They include:

Cheyenne River Sioux

Crow Creek Sioux

Flandreau Santee Sioux

Lower Brule Sioux

Oglala Sioux

Rosebud Sioux

Sisseton-Wahpeton Sioux

Standing Rock Sioux

Yankton Sioux

The bodies of Sitting Bull and his men were buried in the corner of a post cemetery at Fort Yates. On April 8, 1953, descendants, with the help of the Dakota Memorial Association, moved Sitting Bull's remains to the present location and dedicated the memorial.

The giant granite bust of Sitting Bull was carved by Korczak Ziolkowski, who also started the Crazy Horse Memorial in the Black Hills. The marker today seems desolate and rather forgotten. Sitting Bull's remains, encased in a steel vault, are embedded in a 20-ton block of concrete on which the monument stands. The grave site is open to the public free of charge.

Adjacent to the Sitting Bull Monument on the west bank of the Missouri River is the *Cheyenne River Tribe's Grand River Casino & Resort,* with more than 15,000 square feet of gambling fun, as well as a lounge, an outdoor amphitheater, and a restaurant, perched high on a bluff overlooking Lake Oahe. The Grand River casino, owned by the Standing Rock Sioux

Powwow Etiquette

With numerous tribes throughout South Dakota, you can find *wacipis* (powwows) throughout the year. These celebratory, spiritual, and often public events offer non–Native Americans a chance to learn about the culture. They can last anywhere from a few hours to several days and frequently include craft displays, rodeos, ethnic foods, cultural exhibits, and the marvelous drumming, singing, dancing, and vibrant regalia.

To be a courteous guest at a powwow, here are a few tips:

- It's generally acceptable to take photos or videos, but check beforehand.
- Ask permission before taking someone's photo outside of the dance circle.
- Stand at the "Grand Entry" to pay respect to the dancers. Remain standing for the Great Sioux Nation's national anthem.
- The dance area is considered sacred; don't enter it unless invited.
- Many powwows lack seating, so bring along a lawn chair or blanket and make yourself comfortable.

To find out about upcoming powwows, check with sites such as sdtribalrelations .com or drumhop.com.

TOP HITS ALONG THE MISSOURI RIVER

Akta Lakota Museum

Grand River Casino & Resort

Karl E. Mundt National Wildlife Refuge

Oahe Dam

Scherr Howe Arena

Sitting Bull Monument

South Dakota Cultural Heritage Center

South Dakota Discovery Center and Aquarium

West Whitlock Recreation Area

tribe, features slots, blackjack, and poker. The casino walls are decorated with the artwork of Del Iron Cloud. The casino is located 2.5 miles west of Mobridge on US 12. For more information call (605) 845-7104 or go to grandrivercasino.com.

It is also fitting that a memorial to Sakakawea (an alternate spelling of Sacagawea), the indomitable guide of Lewis and Clark, is located near the Sitting Bull Monument. Sakakawea, or Bird Woman, was a Shoshone Indian princess of the Big Horn Mountains of Montana. She was captured and taken to North Dakota. There she married a French fur trader, and together they were hired by Lewis and Clark for their first trip west in 1804.

Sakakawea guided the expedition over seemingly insurmountable obstacles. Much of the credit for the venture's success is given to her. She died later of "putrid fever," in 1812, at the age of 25, at Fort Manuel, a short distance north of Mobridge. In 1929 Mobridge schoolchildren donated pennies to erect a monument to honor this illustrious Indian woman. On September 27, 1929, a graceful cement shaft with a bronze plaque was erected at the Dakota Memorial Park in her memory.

The North-Central Reservations

Two of the state's more sparsely populated Indian reservations abut Mobridge to the west. The **Standing Rock Indian Reservation** covers 562,366 acres in South Dakota (it extends into south-central North Dakota).

South Dakota Mixtape

Liven up a long road trip with downloads, audio books, and compact discs from South Dakota authors and artists:

- *Dakota: A Spiritual Geography* by Kathleen Norris

- *Little House on the Prairie* by Laura Ingalls Wilder

- *A Long Way from Home: Growing up in the American Heartland, The Greatest Generation,* and *Album of Memories* from longtime *NBC Nightly News* anchor Tom Brokaw

- *The Wizard of Oz,* by L. Frank Baum, who was apparently inspired by a tornado he saw in Aberdeen

- "A Few Small Repairs" or "Fat City" from singer/songwriter Shawn Colvin

- "We the People" or other recordings by Brule, one of the nation's best-known and most award-winning Native American musical groups

The ***Cheyenne River Indian Reservation*** covers 1.4 million acres, making it the second-largest reservation in the state.

In Eagle Butte southwest of Mobridge, the ***H. V. Johnston Cultural Center*** (605-964-2542) displays traditional beadwork and murals that depict the Lakota way of life. You also can buy beadwork and paintings by contemporary artists here. The center is located on US 212 near SD 63 on the Cheyenne River Indian Reservation. Free admission.

One of the area's more famous residents is Arvol Looking Horse, a 19th-generation keeper of the Sacred Pipe of the Great Sioux Nation. In this position he cares for the Sacred Pipe, presented by the White Buffalo Calf Woman many years ago. Looking Horse leads the annual Sacred Pipestone Run, which was formed to stop the sale of sacred pipestone. He holds an honorary degree from the University of South Dakota and has been profiled many times by local and national media. Looking Horse also is featured in the book of portraiture, *Visions Quest,* the story of contemporary Lakotas, Dakotas, and Nakotas who have chosen to carry on the traditions and culture of their people.

Pioneers and Walleyes

While Native American history swells from the central plains of the state, the tiny town of **Eureka** (eurekasd.com), northeast of Mobridge on SD 10, shows the Old World's contribution to America's melting pot. For more than 100 years, beginning in the late 1700s, German colonists had been permitted to live in Russia and retain their culture, customs, and language; then, in 1871, Czar Alexander II revoked the agreement, which spurred a mass exodus. Thousands of German-Russian immigrants made their way to Dakota Territory, and eventually to Eureka. You can find German influences throughout Eureka. Many of the 1,101 residents still speak German, often slipping between English and German without a thought. The Lutheran church had two pastors—one English-speaking and one German-speaking—well into the 1960s. Appropriately, the town celebrates its heritage with the annual **German-Russian Schmeckfest** during the third weekend in September. It's an ideal opportunity to enjoy the local cuisine, from savory sausages to the famed state dessert—**kuchen.** The town even has a kuchen factory, so you're sure to find a wide variety of the sweet, custardy dessert.

You can learn more about the area's German-Russian roots and its frontier past at the **Eureka Pioneer Museum of McPherson County** on SD 10 at the west edge of town. Open Wed through Sun April 15 to November 1, its exhibits encompass military memorabilia, furniture, household items, and antique farm machinery. There is no admission charge, but donations are always appreciated. Call (605) 284-2711 for hours.

Neuharth is a common name in this part of the country, and it's also the last name of Al Neuharth, one of its most famous natives. Founder of Gannett Newspapers, Al Neuharth recalls his impoverished youth in his book, *Confessions of an S.O.B.* The town's information booth on the west edge of town is dedicated to Al Neuharth's father, Daniel J. Neuharth.

To see one of South Dakota's more intriguing pieces of history, take US 212 east for just a few miles to **Gettysburg** (population 1,201), located in the Whitlock Bay area on the eastern shore of Lake Oahe. Gettysburg was settled in 1883 by 211 veterans of the famous Civil War battle after which the town was named. Many of the streets, townships, and communities in the area share names intrinsically associated with the Civil War. The town's most popular historic exhibit is the mysterious 40-ton Medicine Rock on display at the **Dakota Sunset Museum,** 205 W. Commercial St. The rock—considered sacred by local Native Americans—is embedded with footprints believed to have been made by the Great Spirit. The museum also includes a Civil War exhibit, big game exhibition, and a painting of the Battle of Shiloh. The local historical society also takes care of the **G. L. Stocker Blacksmith Shop,** which served as the Grand Army of the Republic Hall during the post–Civil War years and later became a blacksmith shop. Renovated to its original condition from the early part of the 20th century, it includes an interpretive center. Dakota Sunset museum is open 1 to 5 p.m. daily during summer months and Tues through Sat the rest of the year. For more information call (605) 765-9480.

wheatkings

From 1887 to 1902, Eureka was known as the greatest primary wheat market in the world. As many as 32 grain buyers worked day and night, storing and shipping wheat brought in by horses and oxen. In 1892, 3,330 freight-car loads of wheat were shipped from the town.

If you like camping, Gettysburg offers free sites in its city park, and you'll find both state-run and privately operated camping facilities nearby. One of the most popular destinations for campers, boaters, and anglers is **West Whitlock Recreation Area** with its 105 sites and 2 camping cabins (800-710-2267; campsd.com). Just 15 minutes west of Gettysburg on US 212, its beautiful setting on giant Lake Oahe began as a campsite for the Arikara and Mandan people. The replica of an Arikara earth lodge found in the park is a reminder of the many lodges that the Lewis and Clark expedition saw as they traveled this area. Each lodge, made of cottonwood logs, willow branches, and grass, could house up to 20 people. The Arikara people were farmers and grew crops such as corn, beans, squash, sunflowers, and tobacco.

When the area became a park, it was named for Mrs. J. F. Whitlock, whose pioneering family once owned the land. Whitlock Crossing was the name given to a small settlement that operated a ferry across the river near the area. Although a 36-pound northern pike was caught from shore in 1993, the main sport fish here is walleye. The annual **Whitlock Bay Walleye Tournament,** which is held each summer, offers competitors big prizes and lots of action. The reservoir's newest sport fish is the Chinook salmon. Each year thousands of eggs are taken from adult salmon at **Whitlock Spawning and Imprinting Station;** after hatching, fingerling salmon are returned to the lake. When adult salmon return in the fall, these fast and furious swimmers will test the skills of even the most avid fishermen. West Whitlock is open year-round. Call (605) 765-9410 or go to sdgfp.info for more information. Daily admission is $4 per person or $6 per vehicle or $30 for an annual permit.

Hunters will feel right at home on the 10,000-acre **Paul Nelson Farm.** Half the acreage is dedicated to pheasant hunting. They offer different hunting packages, corporate retreats, shooting schools, fly-fishing schools, and more. For more information, call (605) 765-2469 or visit paulnelsonfarm.com.

fishingrules

You can download a copy of the current *South Dakota Fishing Handbook* by visiting the website at sdgfp.info/publications/fishing handbook.pdf. Or request the *South Dakota Hunting and Fishing Guide* by logging on to travelsd .com.

SELECTED CHAMBERS OF COMMERCE

Chamberlain–Oacoma Area Chamber of Commerce
112 N. Main St.
Chamberlain 57325
(605) 734-4416
chamberlainsd.org

Mobridge Chamber of Commerce
103 N. Main St.
Mobridge 57601
(605) 845-2387
mobridge.org

Pierre Convention and Visitors Bureau
800 W. Dakota Ave.
Pierre 57501
(605) 224-7361
pierre.org

South Dakota Missouri River Tourism
(888) 386-4617
sdmissouririver.com

Where to Stay Along the Missouri River

CHAMBERLAIN-OACOMA

Howard Johnson Inn and Suites
203 E. Hwy. 16
(605) 234-4222
hojo.com
Moderate

Quality Inn
100 Hwy. 16
(605) 734-5593
qualityinn.com
Moderate

EUREKA

Lakeview Motel
1307 J. Ave., Hwy. 10
(605) 284-2400
motellakeview.com
Inexpensive

MOBRIDGE

Wrangler Inn
820 W. Grand Crossing
(605) 845-3641
wranglerinn.com
Inexpensive

PIERRE/FT. PIERRE

Best Western Ramkota
920 W. Sioux Ave.
(605) 224-6877
pierre.ramkota.com
Moderate

Comfort Inn
410 W. Sioux Ave.
(605) 224-0377
comfortinn.com
Moderate

Eagle's View Bed & Breakfast
710 Verendrye Dr.
(605) 224-4053
eaglesview.org
Inexpensive to moderate

Governor's Inn
700 W. Sioux Ave.
(605) 224-4200
govinn.com
Moderate

Where to Eat Along the Missouri River

CHAMBERLAIN/OACOMA

Bridges Restaurant & Lounge
(at Cedar Shore Resort)
1500 Shoreline Dr.
(605) 734-6376
cedarshore.com

Busted Nut Bar and Grille
309 Glen Ave.
(605) 234-3000
Moderate

Indulge Bakery and Bistro
121 Main St. #2
(605) 234-0196
Inexpensive

MOBRIDGE

Grand Oasis Restaurant
906 W. Grand Crossing
(605) 845-7474
Inexpensive to Moderate

PIERRE

Big Tom's Diner
1415 E. Wells Ave.
(605) 224-7600
Inexpensive

Cattleman's Club Steakhouse
29608 Hwy. 34
(605) 224-9774
cattlemansclublodge.com
Moderate to expensive

RedRossa Italian Grill
808 W. Sioux Ave.
Suite 20
(605) 494-2599
redrossa.com
Moderate

Zesto Shop
213 W. Capitol
(605) 224-4681
Moderate

Western South Dakota

While glaciers flattened the eastern half of South Dakota, the west kept its ruggedness in more than just geography. Strength and a sense of individualism thrives in the lifestyles of its residents, from its early visionaries, explorers, and miners to modern cowboys and Plains Indians who also embrace centuries-old traditions. This is a land so rich in natural wonders, you'll find something fresh to experience no matter how many times you visit. There are few other places where you can go deep into a jeweled cave and enjoy top-of-the-world views in the same day. No wonder there's a tangible spirit here in this often sacred landscape known as *Paha Sapa*, or Black Hills.

That diverse topography and spirit also make a trip here one of America's most beloved road trips, from wide-open grasslands and the eerie moonscape of the Badlands to the patriotic pride of Mount Rushmore and fragrant, thick pine forests. The Black Hills in particular buzz with activity from Memorial Day to Labor Day as seasonal shops and attractions hit full swing. Visitors stream in from across the globe, especially for the famed Sturgis bike rally. It's surprisingly easy, though, to dodge crowds and find overlooked places

or fresh ways to experience favorite attractions. Give yourself time for quiet hikes along the Black Hills' glittering trails where you can hear the wind singing through the pines. Or walk across wide-open prairies to imagine the lives of Native Americans more than a century ago.

Southwestern Reservations

To truly get off the beaten path, explore some of South Dakota's reservations where towns are few and far between, but history and tradition remain deeply rooted in the rolling hills and grasslands. Nine federally recognized tribes call South Dakota home. Rosebud Reservation, home of the Rosebud Sioux, and Pine Ridge Reservation, home of the Oglala Sioux, are among the largest. Far away from the noise of more prominent attractions, their towns and other Dakota reservations offer an authentic glimpse at the state's Native American culture, both its past and its present.

siouxordakota?

The term *Sioux,* short for *nadoues-sioux,* or "little snakes," actually came from the Chippewa, a longtime foe. The people of the Great Sioux Nation, however, prefer to be called *Dakota, Nakota,* or *Lakota,* according to their language group. (*Dakota* means "friends" or "allies.")

Start at **Rosebud Indian Reservation** in south-central South Dakota. The state's most populated reservation, with about 20,000 residents, covers 882,416 acres with headquarters in Rosebud. Most visitors head to St. Francis, home of the **Buechel Memorial Lakota Museum** (350 S. Oak St.). The museum displays many Lakota items, ranging from traditional dress to hunting tools, as well as historic photographs of Sicangu Sioux Chief Spotted Tail, who strove for peace between Native Americans and the white settlers during the turbulent 1800s. Spotted Tail selected this land for his people in 1877.

The museum was named for another spiritual leader of the times, although he was not a Sioux. Father Buechel was a Jesuit priest assigned to the St. Francis Mission. Intrigued by the native culture, he collected photographs and artifacts and wrote several books in Lakota. His collection is the heart of the museum. Located on the grounds of the St. Francis Mission (which was built in 1916), the museum is open 8 a.m. to 5 p.m. Mon through

Sat and 9 a.m. to 4 p.m. Sun Memorial Day through Labor Day. Admission is free. You may be able to visit in the off-season by making an appointment Call (605) 747-2745 for more information or visit sfmission.org.

If you drive about two hours west of the Rosebud Reservation, following US 18, you'll reach the heart of Pine Ridge Indian Reservation, the second-largest reservation in the country.

Pine Ridge is most famous for the tragedy of **Wounded Knee,** a massacre of innocents in the winter of 1890. Chief Big Foot and his Minniconjou band had set out for Pine Ridge following the death of spiritual leader Sitting Bull on December 15. They were intercepted by the 7th Cavalry and were brought, under a white flag of truce, to Wounded Knee. On the morning of December 29, soldiers prepared to search the band for weapons. A rifle was fired, setting off intense shooting that killed more than 250 natives, most of them unarmed. Bodies of women and children were found as far as 3 miles from the site, apparently shot as they fled into the plains.

If you know the story and don't mind the extra driving, you can visit the **Wounded Knee National Historic Landmark,** which is 8 miles east of the town of Pine Ridge on US 18, then 7 miles north on an unnumbered paved road. While bits of prayer fabric tied to the chain-link fence riffle in the wind, it's a sad site that doesn't seem to have the care and dignity you'd

Famous Sons

The late **Ben Reifel,** a five-term US congressman, was born near Parmelee on the Rosebud Reservation in 1906. During his lifetime he worked for the Bureau of Indian Affairs, served in the US Army, and received a doctoral degree from Harvard University. Reifel ran for office in 1960 and served until his retirement in 1971. He died in 1990. The Badlands Visitors Center is named for him.

White Eagle, a member of the Rosebud Sioux tribe, was the first Native American to sing leading tenor roles in American musical theater and opera. He graduated from the prestigious Merola Opera program at the San Francisco Opera and performed with the Pennsylvania Opera Theatre, Florentine Opera, and Cleveland Opera, among others.

Among the most famous members of the Pine Ridge Indian Reservation is runner **Billy Mills,** who won the 1964 Olympic gold for the 10,000-meter race, becoming the first American to win it.

TOP ANNUAL EVENTS

Black Hills Powwow and Art Expo
Rapid City, October

Buffalo Roundup
Custer State Park, late September

Central States Fair
Rapid City, every August

Days Of '76 (Rodeo and Parade)
Deadwood, first full weekend in August

Gold Discovery Days
Custer, late July

Native American Day
Crazy Horse Memorial, October

expect for a national historic landmark and tragedy of this size. A solitary stone monument stands on the mass grave site.

Residents of Pine Ridge Reservation struggle with the highest level of poverty in the US with up to 80 percent unemployment. The culture and traditions are rich, though, and you can learn more about the tribe by heading north toward Kyle, where you'll find a visitor center (at 7900 Lakota Prairie Dr.) and *Oglala Lakota College Historical Center* about 7 miles southwest of Kyle. The historical center depicts their story from the early 1800s through the Wounded Knee Massacre. Call (605) 455-6000 for details or go to olc.edu.

The *Heritage Center at Red Cloud Indian School* (100 Mission Dr.; 605-867-1105; redcloudschool.org) features a Native American art collection that is considered one of the finest in the Northern Plains. It includes more than 2,000 graphics, paintings, and sculptures from the annual Red Cloud Indian Arts show, a large national competition for native artists from all over North America. The show runs from June through mid-Aug and attracts more than 11,000 visitors who enjoy discovering up-and-coming Native American artists. Leave time to browse the gift shop with its locally crafted star quilts, bead and quill work, Dakota dictionaries, pottery, and music recordings. Purchases help support the community. The Heritage Center is open from 8 a.m. to 6 p.m. Mon through Sat and from 10 a.m. to 5 p.m. Sun during the summer, and 9 a.m. to 6 p.m. Tues through Sat Labor Day through Memorial Day. Free admission.

For more information on the Pine Ridge community and its attractions, including tours, horseback rides, and events, check with the Pine Ridge Area Chamber of Commerce at (605) 455-2685 or pineridgechamber.com.

About 120,000 acres of the Pine Ridge Indian Reservation lie within ***Badlands National Park.*** Farther from the interstate, this less-crowded South Unit was added to the park in 1976. Oglala Sioux Parks and Recreation Authority runs the White River Visitor Center here, open 10 a.m. to 4 p.m. from June 1 through mid-Sept. It includes cultural exhibits and a videotape program on Oglala history. Call (605) 455-2878 for more information.

Heading into the Badlands

If you're approaching the ***Badlands*** from the east, take exit 131 off I-90 and look for the new visitor center at the ***Minuteman Missile National Historic Site*** that opened on the north side of the exit in November 2014. The historic site itself opened to the public in 2004, and a 12-minute film will get you oriented to South Dakota's Minuteman Missile Field that included 150 silos and cost $56 million in the early 1960s. By today's dollars, the Cold War national defense would be well over $9 billion.

Visitors can look through a glass enclosure at the Delta-09 missile silo, catch a ranger talk, or choose a cell-phone or self-guided brochure tour.

AUTHOR'S FAVORITES IN WESTERN SOUTH DAKOTA

Badlands National Park
(605) 433-5361
nps.gov/badl

Black Hills National Forest
(605) 673-9200
fs.fed.us/bhnf

Crazy Horse Memorial
(605) 673-4681
crazyhorsememorial.org

Custer State Park
(605) 255-4464
gfp.sd.gov/state-parks/directory/custer

Jewel Cave National Monument
(605) 673-2288
nps.gov/jeca

Mammoth Site
Hot Springs
(605) 745-6017
mammothsite.org

Mount Rushmore National Memorial
(605) 574-2523

Rapid City Downtown
(800) 487-3223
downtownrapidcity.com

The best option, though, is to plan ahead and get a coveted spot on the in-depth 90-minute tours that go into Delta-09 and the Delta-01 launch control facilities. South Dakota's missiles were decommissioned after a 1991 treaty.

Due to confines within the missile areas, only six spots are available and can be reserved up to three months in advance. The site is now open year-round, with spring and fall the ideal times to secure a tour. Call (605) 433-5552 or go to nps.gov/mimi for more information. As of publication time, admission and tours were still both free.

From the missile site exit, head south on SD 240 toward Badlands National Park and its east entrance. On the way you'll pass **Prairie Homestead Historic Site,** with one of the only original sod buildings on public display in South Dakota. It is furnished in the style of the original homesteaders, and letters and photographs of the original homesteader's family and neighbors offer riveting insight into the hardships they endured. Many of the early homes on the plains and prairies of the Dakotas were built of sod. The homes were efficient—cool in the summer and warm in the winter—but also dark, dirty, and often infested with mice, bedbugs, and other unsavory houseguests. It is open daily, sunrise to sunset, from May through September. For more information call (605) 433-5400 or go to prairiehomestead.com. Admission is $7 for adults; $6 for youth 10–17.

Badlands National Park (605-433-5361; nps.gov/badl) is as oth-erworldly as land can be; soft clays and sandstones were deposited as sediments 26 million to 37 million years ago by streams from the Black Hills that left vast plains. This once rich landscape attracted a commu-nity of ancient creatures. Remains

fifteenminutes offame

Scenes from *Starship Troopers,* the Paul Verhoeven movie based on Robert A. Heinlein's classic 1959 science-fiction novel, were filmed in the Badlands. Although the movie didn't win an Oscar for best acting or script writing, it gets two thumbs-up for best natural location that is as otherworldly as it gets.

of three-toed horses, dog-sized camels, and saber-toothed cats have been discovered here in the Oligocene beds. They're considered some of the world's richest vertebrate fossil sites. More than 250,000 of the discovered fossils have been collected by the Museum of Geology in Rapid City while others have gone on to museums such as the Smithsonian. Protecting these fossils from the golden age of mammals was one reason the park expanded to include the White River unit that's part of the Pine Ridge Indian Reservation.

Eventually humans stumbled upon this seemingly hostile land. Upon arriving in the Badlands, native tribes called it *mako sica,* meaning "land bad." French Canadian trappers who traveled through its rugged terrain in the early 1800s dubbed it *les mauvaises terres à traverser,* or "bad lands to travel across." But that doesn't mean they're barren. Keep your eyes peeled and binoculars handy, and you may spot Rocky Mountain bighorn sheep, antelope, mule deer, prairie dogs, bison, and the reintroduced black-footed ferret and swift fox living among the Badlands. At a minimum, most visitors drive the stunning 32-mile *Badlands Loop,* which begins at exit 131 off I-90. Leave plenty of time to stop at numerous scenic points for photos and hikes. The Badlands may look stark from the highway, but a closer look lets you see some of the 200 kinds of wildflowers and 50 grasses.

As you wind down the road, you'll pass the *Ben Reifel Visitor Center,* which offers the best all-around introduction to the park from 8 a.m. to as late as 7 p.m. in peak season. Check out the exhibits and cool off in the air-conditioned theater that shows "Land of Stone and Light."

Even if you've seen the Badlands once or several times, they're always worth another look. Like a fine wine, they improve with time as every rainstorm and windstorm gnaws at the sediments and accentuates each ravine and ragged pinnacle. Shifting light constantly repaints the landscape in new colors. If you're lucky enough to see the Badlands when heat lightning crackles up from the horizon or when a rainbow follows a sultry storm, it's a sight you'll never forget. The same goes for staying in the park and enjoying the sunset and moonrise. You'll see rabbits coming out at twilight and hear nocturnal birds and insects cue their evening song. Sunrise, too, can be spectacular with its extra dose of golden light blanketing the buttes and peaks. Favorite hikes include the Fossil Trail, Castle Trail, Door Trail, and Notch Trail.

You can camp in the park's Cedar Pass Campground or the primitive Sage Creek Campground or check into the nearby four-season *Cedar Pass Lodge* cabins. With porches facing the Badlands, small refrigerators, microwaves, and hand-built log beds as part of a major renovation and rebuild, they offer a good reason to stay for a night or more (605-433-5460; cedarpasslodge.com). You can also head to the *Badlands Inn* a few miles away near the small town of Interior. If you need a place to dine, stop at the Cedar Pass Lodge restaurant, which includes Indian fry bread buffalo tacos as its signature item, along with lovely views and a gift shop with handmade Oglala Dakota jewelry and crafts, benches made from wagon wheels, local wine, and some groceries.

As you leave the Badlands at exit 110, you might be parched. The Hustead family built its iconic, campy *Wall Drug* complex banking on that theory and first luring Depression-era travelers with free ice water. Curiosity is the other draw after seeing countless hyped-up billboards spool past on the interstate. It's the kind of place where people playfully pose with statues of cowboys and showgirls perched on benches or sitting atop the famous 6-foot jackalope. My kids barely give it any notice—not with a snarling, roaring, smoke-snorting animatronic T-Rex that comes to life about every 15 minutes. There's also a water show with jumping jets of water that tempt kids to get playfully soaked. Beyond the gimmicks

A Rock Hound's Paradise

South Dakota's Badlands and Black Hills region ranks among the top five places in the US for its variety of minerals and rocks. The Black Hills are obviously famous for gold, but also copper, silver, iron, lead, tin, zinc, feldspar, spodumene, and more than 140 other minerals. Expansive surface outcroppings of all three major rock types—igneous, metamorphic, and sedimentary—yield not only rock specimens, but embedded crystals, ores, and fossils. Beds of alluvial outwash on the perimeter of the Black Hills offer a colorful mix of all kinds of stones.

While it's a no-no for rock hounds to go collecting at Badlands National Park, the surrounding public lands—*Buffalo Gap National Grasslands*—hold some fine rock beds that produce Fairburn agates, funny eye, gay prairie, and bubblegum agates, red jasper, blue chalcedony, and petrified wood. You can stop by the *National Grasslands Visitor Center* at 708 Main St. in Wall to learn more about four main ecosystems of the High Plains and learn more about one of the country's largest protected mixed-grass prairies. Kids can earn one of the national park service's junior ranger badges, and you can get maps and advice for the best areas to find rocks (605-279-2125; fs.usda.gov/nebraska).

and souvenirs, the tale of this sprawling 72,000-square-foot emporium and how it became famous is in itself interesting. You also can enjoy displays with more than 600 cattle brands, hundreds of historical pictures, and a collection of Native American artifacts. The cafe still serves 5-cent coffee. You might want a homemade donut or hot beef sandwich to eat with it. Wall Drug Store is open year-round. Call or go online for current hours (605-279-2175; walldrug.com).

Just a minute away from Wall Drug Store, *Wounded Knee Museum* (605-279-2573; woundedkneemuseum.org) shares harrowing and heart-breaking details of the Wounded Knee Massacre through vivid graphics and photographs. Indian gifts, jewelry, books, and T-shirts are also sold here.

As the Badlands disappear into the rearview mirror, it's just an hour to Rapid City and the foothills of the Black Hills National Forest. About 7 miles before you reach the city, you'll hit exit 66 and the Ellsworth Air Force Base. It's home to the *South Dakota Air & Space Museum* (605-385-5189; sdairandspacemuseum.com) at 2890 Rushmore Rd. The free museum includes historic bombers, fighters, missiles, and utility aircraft, as well as many indoor exhibits of aviation memorabilia June 1 through early September. Here you can see a three-fifths-scale model of the Honda Stealth bomber and General Eisenhower's personal Mitchell B-25 bomber. Ellsworth is home to the 28th Bomb Wing and B-1B bombers, and it's not uncommon to see the sleek, low-level bomber graze the skyline. The museum is open 7 days a week from 8:30 a.m. to 4:30 p.m., with expanded hours until 6 p.m. during the summer. Visitors can also take an official 50-minute bus tour of the base and a Minuteman Missile silo for $5 to $8 per person mid-May through mid-Sept. Identification is required for anyone over 18.

Once you hit the Hills, the number of places to go and things to do can be overwhelming. Head to the *Black Hills Visitor Information Center* to get oriented to the vast region and to get help with must-have maps, on-site trip counseling, free Wi-Fi, and brochures galore. Exhibits and displays preview national parks, state parks, and every community in the Black Hills and Badlands region. To reach the center, take exit 61 (Elk Vale Road) north off I-90. Open year-round from 8 a.m. to 5 p.m. daily, with extended hours from May through Sept. Call (605) 355-3700 for more information or go to blackhillsbadlands.com.

Rapid City

To "lay out a Denver" was what the city founders—a group of unlucky miners—had in mind for **Rapid City,** founded in 1876. With a population of 70,812, South Dakota's second-largest city didn't reach the same size as Colorado's capital, but you won't hear anyone complaining. Growth has been steady, downtown is thriving, and Rapid City is large enough to lure a variety of cultural attractions while remaining laid-back and welcoming.

Rapid City's most remarkable museum, **The Journey,** at 222 New York St., blends local history with the nature of the universe. Its excursion through time unifies collections from five sources: the Museum of Geology, the South Dakota State Archaeological Research Center, the Sioux Indian Museum, the Minnilusa Pioneer Museum Collection, and the Duhamel Collection. The museum tour begins with a 20-minute video, which details pioneer and Native American history. The self-guided tour begins with 1,000 points of light that represent the immense nature of a universe deep in space and time. The time line takes you from the formation of the Black Hills billions

Dinos, Fossils, and Rocks

Head to the *Museum of Geology* at the *South Dakota School of Mines and Technology,* 501 E. St. Joseph St., on the third floor of the O'Harra Building, and you'll understand why folks from Rapid City are so crazy about dinosaurs. This gem of a museum exhibits some of the best local fossils, giant fish, prehistoric mammals, and dinosaurs, including the state's official dinosaur, a triceratops skeleton found in Harding County in 1927. The school boasts the largest paleontology program in the country. It's no wonder with major digs and discoveries in western South Dakota and eastern Wyoming.

Dioramas tell the story of the Badlands and the strange and wild creatures that once lived there. Rock hounds can find a collection of minerals, ores, and local agates, including the state gemstone: the beautiful Fairburn agate. Hours are 9 a.m. to 5 p.m. Mon through Fri; until 6 p.m. on Sat, and noon to 5 p.m. Sun during the summer. From Labor Day through Memorial Day it's open 9 a.m. to 4 p.m. Mon through Fri and 10 a.m. to 4 p.m. Sat. Call (605) 394-2467 or go to museum.sdsmt.edu for details and special programs, including hands-on paleo trips for families or adults during the summer. Admission is free, but donations are appreciated.

tip

You can see more than 700 dancers in full regalia, hear the jingle of skirts, and feel the drums each October at the **Black Hills Powwow.** Plains Indians from nearly 60 tribes attend this annual event at the Rushmore Plaza Civic Center (605-341-0925; blackhillspowwow .com).

of years ago to the present day. Visitors are given sound sticks so they can listen to historical stories and descriptions at each exhibit. Open daily from 9 a.m. to 6 p.m. during the summer, and 10 a.m. to 5 p.m. during winter, except Sun, when hours are 1 to 5 p.m. Admission is $10 for adults, $8 for seniors, $7 for children 6 to 17. Call (605) 394-6923 or go to journey museum.org for updates on the Storyteller Series, Family Fun Days, teas, and other events that bring to life the colorful and sometimes infamous characters of the Dakota past.

Downtown Rapid City

Don't miss **Rapid City's historic downtown** district, especially if you haven't seen it in a few years. With the **Main Street Square** project that creates a lively gathering place, fountains, and events, there's new energy humming along its pretty blocks, and you'll want at least a few hours to explore and enjoy it. What else will you need? Bring an appetite for the tasty temptations down every block, tucked between galleries and boutiques and offering date-night dinners, kick-back lunches, and cold beers. At a minimum, grab an ice-cream cone or frothy coffee and take a seat at Main Street Square to watch kids playing in the fountains on sunny summer days or skating in the winter.

If it's summer, grab a seat in the shady courtyard outside **Firehouse Brewing Co.**, 610 Main St. If you traveled from the east, you probably saw their red attention-grabbing fire engines along the interstate, because, yes, this is in an honest-to-goodness 1915 firehouse, complete with historic photos and memorabilia. It was the first brewpub in the state and has beers ranging from Chukkar Ale and Smoke Jumper Stout to seasonal chocolate mint porter and apple cider ale. They expanded in 2014 to include the **Firehouse Wine Cellars** with 16 wines. The restaurant is popular for English pub foods such as beer-battered fish and chips and bangers, gorgonzola ale soup and beer bread, gumbo, and ribs. Call (605) 348-1915 or go to firehousebrewing.com.

At the sleek **Tally's Silver Spoon,** 530 6th St., Chef Benjamin Klinkel's focus is on food, with duck confit and foie gras or biscuits and gravy for breakfast, buffalo hanger steak on a baguette or pulled pork with a pickled beet slaw for lunch, or a mocha-rubbed tenderloin with rhubarb-artichoke butter and roasted vegetables. Leave room for desserts such as reverse cobbler with seasonal fruit and homemade strawberry-basil ice cream with pistachio shortbread. Call (605) 342-7621 or go to tallyssilverspoon.com for more details.

Enigma also has drawn praise. While it's located in the Radisson at Main Street and Mount Rushmore Road, it doesn't feel anything like a typical hotel restaurant. Diners slide into dark-wood booths beneath blue pendant lights and choose from menu items that may include berry-and-balsamic salad, slow-braised bison short ribs, elk tenderloin with blackberry demi-glace, and Colorado lamb with lavender, blackberry, and raspberry chutney. Desserts might include crème crepes, panna cotta, and amaretto tiramisu. If you're in the mood for a drink, its 445 Lounge serves more than 50 types of martinis plus specialty drinks (605-716-0600; enigmarestaurant.com).

Looming over downtown, you'll see the stately **Hotel Alex Johnson** (605-342-1210; alexjohnson.com) at 523 6th St. Built in 1925 and on the National Register of Historic Places, the impressive yet manly lobby has hosted countless celebrities and politicians over the years. It's also one of the city's grandest places to stay, after extensive renovations in the late 2000s. If you need an excuse to wander the lobby, head to its **Chubby Chipmunk** shop for a taste of haute chocolates and fancy truffles.

Less than a block away you'll find downtown's No. 1 don't-miss destina-tion: **Prairie Edge Trading Co. and Galleries** (800-541-2388; prairieedge .com) at 606 Main St. It's jaw-dropping to see the vast arrangement of American Indian art, much of it Smithsonian quality. You might be lucky enough to catch a demonstration of native flute playing, see an astonish-ingly detailed wall-sized homemade paper casting of a powwow or buffalo hunt scene, admire handmade beaded cradleboards and drums, and wander through an airy, high-ceilinged room full of Native American work. The multilevel store continues upstairs and sideways, with new rooms and col-lections around every corner: modern paintings and a music collection with

Art Alley

If you prefer wilder art than you'll find at galleries, check out the vibrant, often-surprising street art that covers Rapid City's Art Alley. The alley, which runs behind the buildings that border Main and St. Joseph Streets between 6th and 7th Streets, is packed with cultural icons from Homer Simpson to Bob Marley, thought-provoking statements, and deep thoughts. The visual jungle of color covers everything, even electrical transformers and Dumpsters. Our kids were so wowed by it and willing to pose near their favorite graphics that this graffiti-filled alley provided a memorable and fun backdrop for one of our all-time favorite (and unexpected) family photo shoots.

more than 500 Native American titles, an impressive bookstore, wool and buffalo leather clothing and accessories, a glass bead museum in the loft, and even a Native American trading post with bundles of sage and every adornment used to make powwow regalia. Think of this store as more like a museum than an art gallery and give yourself the luxury of time to savor what it offers. You're sure to leave impressed.

You'll spot a few sculptures, such as the Dakota woman and child, in front of the Prairie's Edge Gallery, but Rapid City is first and foremost the *City of Presidents.* Ronald Reagan in his cowboy hat beams from one street corner while Jimmy Carter waves a big hello from another. John F. Kennedy smiles down at his young son, and polio survivor Franklin D. Roosevelt stands tall with the help of a podium. Every president is represented up until Barack Obama, who will be the next addition. All the presidents were cast in bronze and designed to be life-size, which can be a fun lesson for kids by pointing out eras when people were smaller but could still have a supersize impact on America for generations to come. For more details and to find out where specific presidents are located, go to CityofPresidents.com.

At 512 6th St., the 1911 Elks lodge and opera house—now the *Elks Theatre*—offers the grandest, cushiest spot to nuzzle next to a date over a bucket of popcorn, especially if you're in the balcony with the most sweeping view of the state's largest movie screen. Movies start at just $5 (605-343-7888; elkstheatre.com).

A few blocks away, at the corner of 7th and Quincy Streets, the *Dahl Fine Arts Center* (605-394-4101; thedahl.org) is another great place to admire local talent and art. It houses 3 galleries, including one that brings in world-class artists; the Cyclorama Gallery, a unique 180-foot oil-on-canvas panorama spanning 200 years of US history; and an interactive children's area. The Dahl Theater Black Hills Community Theatre stages five productions in the 170-seat theater during the fall and winter. The Dahl is open 10 a.m. to 6 p.m. Mon through Fri, and 10 a.m. to 5 p.m. Sat. Admission is by donation ($5 per person is suggested).

If you travel south on **West Boulevard,** you'll see the grand homes of this residential historic district with turn-of-the-20th-century grandeur. Tudor revival, neoclassical, Queen Anne, federal revival, and many more styles are represented on this street. Residents take great pride in their homes, and it shows through their vigilant upkeep of the properties and some fantastic flower gardens. If you're here in wintertime, take a slow drive up and down the boulevard to see some ornate Christmas-light displays that make the area shine like an enchanted village.

Chocoholics can't miss **Mostly Chocolates** (1919 Mount Rushmore Rd.). The charming store features more than 23 kinds of truffles. The fudge is equally tempting, especially in such seasonal themes as pumpkin pie and fresh strawberry. To keep the sugar buzz going on steamy summer days,

Rapid City Park Sampler

Memorial Park & Garden, north of downtown along Omaha Street, is dedicated to the 239 people who died in the devastating flood of 1972. Stroll fragrant rose gardens, catch a concert at the band shell, and see one of America's largest sections of the Berlin Wall.

Dinosaur Park, along Skyline Drive, geographically divides the town in half and offers some of the city's finest scenic views. Let yours kids loose among 7 life-size replicas of dinosaurs, including a triceratops and a Tyrannosaurus rex, all on the National Register of Historic Places.

Storybook Island, 1301 Sheridan Lake Rd., is another nostalgic (and free) family favorite.

The Rapid City Urban Mountain Park encompasses 390 acres of land, including Hanson-Larsen Memorial Park with 12 miles of mountain biking, hiking, and running trails and the Skyline Drive Wilderness Area with fantastic views.

Take a Spin Through the Hills

Biking has soared in popularity in the Black Hills. Rapid City has a 13.5-mile bike-way along Rapid Creek, but most riding is done on the area's wide-shouldered highways. Some of the favorite routes are Rapid City to Mount Rushmore, the Needles Highway, Iron Mountain Road, Spearfish Canyon, and the Badlands Loop Road. All feature some steep grades and long climbs, but the spectacular scenery along the way makes the effort worth it.

Mountain bikers can explore 6,000 miles of fire trails, logging roads, and aban-doned railroad grades that crisscross the backcountry ridges, wind down can-yons, and climb to mountaintops. Or they can join the fun at the annual *Black Hills Fat Tire Festival* (bhfattirefestival.com).

you can also try the frozen yogurt bar. For more information call (605) 341-2264 or go to bhchocolates.com.

Located 5 miles west of the downtown district at 3788 Chapel Ln. is *Chapel in the Hills* (605-342-8281; chapel-in-the-hills.org). Stavkirke, as it also is known, is an exact replica of the famous 12th-century Borgund Church in Norway. Wood carvings, Christian symbols, and Norse dragon heads adorn the building, which features pegged construction. It's a favorite and most romantic place for couples to exchange their wedding vows. Eve-ning services are at 7:30 p.m. daily during the summer months and last about 30 minutes. The chapel itself is open dawn to dusk May 1 to September 30. While you're there, check out the nearby *Norwegian Log Cabin Museum.* Admission is free; donations are welcome.

For the most part, western South Dakota has taken advantage of its handsome surroundings, and tourism is vital. The tourist trappings are evi-dent in Rapid City—sometimes upscale, sometimes cheesy—but to get a true snapshot of what makes this part of the country so magical, just get in the car, drive, and go wherever the wind takes you.

Heading into the Black Hills

If you take US 16 west, you'll find tourist attractions and small towns threaded throughout the *Black Hills National Forest.* Actually a domed mountain region, the **Black Hills** extend about 6,000 square miles. They often are described as intimate because they don't loom above you like the Rockies and other mountain ranges. Ingenious scenic roads and hiking and biking trails all tug you into the landscape, threading through thick pine forests, tunneling through rocks, ambling along cold, clear streams or through prairie wildflowers. Round out your adventures with fishing, camping, skiing, mountain climbing, rock hunting, and daydreaming, and you have an outdoors-lover's menu for magic. Where else can you hike across trails where mica sparkles like glitter beneath your feet and hillsides are studded with pink quartz?

Mount Rushmore and Keystone Area

Making their way from Rapid City toward Mount Rushmore on US 16, families may find themselves happily distracted by two of the area's venerable attractions. **Reptile Gardens** has been fascinating visitors since it started in 1937. Even if you aren't fans of creatures that slither, there's a botanical garden with exotic birds and blooms, an 11-foot alligator named "Gus" (short for "humongous"), and an even more bafflingly large 22-foot saltwater crocodile named Maniac. Look closely at exhibits, which show off founder Earl Brockelsby's museum-worthy collection of rocks and crystals. You may see a 180-pound 15-foot yellow python snaking across a giant amethyst formation and using the spiky crystals to shed its skin. Blue arrow frogs from the Amazon perch on the lip of a water bowl that's a beautifully polished agate. Outdoor exhibits let kids pet giant land tortoises. The vast gift shop features plenty for rock and fossil fans, and a large collection of crafts from Papau New Guinea. Admission is $16.50 for adults, $14.50 for seniors, and $11 for children 5–12 from Memorial Day through Labor Day. Prices drop $3–$4 if you go during the spring or fall. The site opens in Apr and closes in late Nov. Call (605) 342-5873 or go to reptilegardens.com.

Eight miles from Rapid City and just down the road from Reptile Gardens, you can watch bear, elk, wolves, bighorns, and other North American wildlife from the safety and comfort of your car during a drive through **Bear Country USA.** You'll do the most dawdling at the end, where you can watch bear cubs, wolf pups, and other park offspring in the walk-through Wildlife and Welcome Center at the end of the driving tour. Bear Country is open daily from 8 a.m. to 6 p.m. in the summer months and 9 a.m. to 4 p.m. in May, Sept, and Oct, and 9 a.m. to 3 p.m. in Nov. Tickets are $10 for children, $13 for seniors, $16 for adults (605-343-2290; bearcountryusa.com).

Most travelers beeline from Rapid City to the most famous rock of all: the carved-granite faces upon **Mount Rushmore National Monument.** In this one parking lot, you'll likely see license plates from almost all 50 states—testimony this truly is an all-American road trip. The monument's located 25 miles southwest of Rapid City on US 16A; follow the signs. If you follow Mount Rushmore Road, you'll effortlessly be on US 16A.

You'll hit **Keystone** (population 341) on your way to Mount Rushmore. Its carnival atmosphere will stand out as one of the most raucous and cluttered displays of tourism in the Hills. You either embrace the fudge shops, gem panning, gold-mine tour, old-time photos, ziplines, and other diversions, or you keep driving. Breathing room is just minutes away.

Here's a little secret: Get up and get going at the crack of dawn, and you'll not only skip the crowds and the parking fee as you enter Mount Rushmore National Monument, but you'll be able to get stunning photos of presidents in the rosy glow as the sun rises. The softer morning light shows more details in the carvings and a few sparkles of quartz you might miss in the full light of midday. The downside of an early arrival is needing to kill time before the museum opens, but it's a good opportunity to take the mile-long **Presidential Trail** that loops closer to the presidents and past the sculptor's studio. If you start getting winded climbing all the steps on the way back up to the terrace and museum, imagine the daily commute of the carvers who had to get all the way up the mountain.

Gutzon Borglum designed and led the carving on the 60-foot granite heads of George Washington, Thomas Jefferson, Abraham Lincoln, and Theodore Roosevelt. Mount Rushmore was commissioned as a national memorial by Congress in 1929, although work actually began in 1927. The project was not always looked at favorably. Back east, a newspaper blasted: "Borglum is about to destroy another monument. Thank God it is in South Dakota, where no one will ever see it." Fortunately, Borglum and others had more foresight. When President Calvin Coolidge dedicated the project in 1927, he proclaimed that Mount Rushmore was "decidedly American in its conception, magnitude, and meaning. It is altogether worthy of our country."

Over the next 12 years, Borglum and his crews, using pneumatic drills and dynamite, carved four massive heads out of the mountaintop. Although the sculptor died before the project was finished, his son, Lincoln, made sure his father's vision continued. At present, more than 2 million visitors each year see the Borglums' legacy to America and the four men who inspired it.

A walk down the ***Avenue of the Flags*** with all 50 states plus territories colorfully frames Mount Rushmore as you approach Grandview Terrace and the amphitheater. Go below ground to the ***Lincoln Borglum Museum*** and see what the mountain would have looked like if the sculptors had finished the project down to the presidents' waistlines. Kids and adults love pushing a mock detonator and seeing a virtual blast. Two movies tell tales of the monuments, but you can go even more in-depth with the award-winning audio tour that's considered one of the best in the national parks system. It blends narration, music, sound effects, and historic recordings and runs 30 to 120 minutes. It comes in multiple languages, including Lakota.

One of the park's newer attractions is a ***Lakota, Nakota, and Dakota Heritage Village*** on the first section of the half-mile Presidential Trail loop. It's usually open and staffed from 10 a.m. to 2 p.m. mid-June through mid-Aug. It's also a good place to look for mountain goats. They're not native from the area, but they have thrived here since 1924 when Canada gave six of them to Custer State Park as a gift. You might even spot one on the presidents' heads if you have binoculars handy.

In the ***Sculptor's Studio,*** built in 1939, you'll find winches, jackhammers, and pneumatic drills that date from the time of construction. Borglum's original model of Mount Rushmore also can be viewed here. During summer months, there's also a sculptor-in-residence nearby, creating works using many of the techniques that created Mount Rushmore. You can catch 15-minute ranger talks at the studio or 30-minute talks at Grandview Terrace throughout the day. Check times when you arrive. If you're traveling with children, have them get a junior ranger workbook to make the most of their visit and earn a cool badge before leaving.

Carver's Cafe serves food and drinks with great views of the mountain, plus the chance to cool off or warm up, depending on the weather. One of the newest treats is ice cream made using a recipe of Thomas Jefferson's.

A patriotically fitting end to a day at Mount Rushmore is watching the 45-minute evening lighting ceremony from the outdoor amphitheater.

Evenings can be downright chilly, so bring a light jacket. The ceremony is held nightly at 9 p.m. late May through mid-Aug and at 8 p.m. through the end of Sept. Mount Rushmore National Memorial is open year-round, and while admission is free, plan on $11 for a parking pass that's good for a year (605-574-2523; nps.gov/moru).

Hill City

Hill City, population 974, has a touristy streak but feels far more genuine and laid-back as a base for Black Hills exploring. It also makes for a great day trip if you're staying elsewhere. As Pennington County's oldest town, Hill City was a bustling region when gold first was discovered in the Palmer Gulch area. Bigger strikes in the Deadwood area left the town almost deserted, but when the Burlington Railroad ran its Hot Springs–Deadwood line through Hill City in 1892, the town reclaimed its place as a gateway to the central Black Hills. It's hard to imagine that the town had a population of 3,000 in the 1890s, but you can close your eyes and imagine that era when the historic *1880s Train* chugs from Keystone to Hill City's depot, wailing its welcome whistle. Round trips that last 2.5 hours run early May through mid-Oct. Look for special events, such as the barbecue with Teddy Roosevelt, the costumes-encouraged Fright Train for adults ages 21 or older on Halloween, or the family-oriented Holiday Express. For more information call (605) 574-2222 or go to 1880train.com.

Modern Hill City boasts an artsy flair with a number of great galleries, a trio of wineries, shops, and cafes. You can't miss its standout sculpture of a horse created by John Lopez. He uses found objects such as gears, silverware, farm tools, and other castoff objects to create incredible details despite using an "I Spy" range of materials.

The statue stands in front of the 200 block of Main Street where you can find Jewels of the West with jewelry, western art, pottery, and more, along with Dakota Nature and Art Gallery. More art can be found at Warrior's Work Studio and Ben West Gallery, Jon Crane Watercolors, Sandy Swallow Art Gallery, and Artforms, which is a member-owned gallery of regional artists.

One of the better-kept secrets in the Black Hills is the *Black Hills Museum of Natural History,* 117 Main St. These are the folks who discovered the famous Tyrannosaurus rex named Sue in Faith, South Dakota, but lost the lengthy court battle to keep her when the Field Museum of Chicago bought her for millions. This museum does, however, have Stan, another stellar South Dakota T. rex find. The original bones are on display in Hill City, but he's been reproduced for the Smithsonian, Oxford University, and 28 other museums worldwide. You'll get a great cross-section of dinosaurs, mammals, birds, minerals, and other fossils here. Their Everything Prehistoric shop is a great place to buy native fossils and minerals, plus resin and bronze casts of dinosaur teeth. Admission is $4 for kids 6–14, $6 for seniors and military folks, and $7.50 for adults (605-574-3919; bhmnh.org).

If you've worked up an appetite, check out the **Alpine Inn Restaurant** (605-574-2749; alpineinnhillcity.com), located in the classic 1886 Harney Peak Hotel, 133 Main St. The lunch menu has a European flair, whereas filet mignon dinners with salad, baked potato, and Texas toast rule the dinner menu. The homemade dessert menu is famous with more than 30 to choose from—including apple cheese strudel. Open Mon through Sat. Moderately priced bed-and-breakfast arrangements also are available.

About two blocks away, at 301 Main St., you can settle in for a meal with charming Old West ambience at **Desperados Cowboy Restaurant** (605-574-2959), which was built around South Dakota's oldest commercial log building dating back to 1885. The food's hearty, too, with big breakfasts, smothered burritos, muleskinner chili, and baked bean skillets with corn bread. Try the walnut pie for dessert.

If you like entertainment with your meal and enjoy the sweet harmonizing of cowboy crooners, head to the **Circle B Chuckwagon,** an almost 40-year-old Black Hills attraction that has relocated to High Country Guest Ranch a few miles out of Hill City. The pre-dinner theatrics—the arrest of the biscuit bandit—get schmaltzy, but you can wander about and watch woodcarving, too. Dinners of hot dogs, chicken, brisket, or buffalo served with beans, biscuits, potatoes, and desserts are eaten indoors where the musicians perform after the meal is cleared. (Tip: If you're bringing kids, it helps to watch *Toy Story 2* to get them into the cowboy mood and to have something they can fidget with if they don't sit still for long.) Tickets are $25–$30 per adult; $5–$15 for kids. Call (605) 574-2129 or go to circle-b -ranch.com for more information.

Black Hills Wine and Beer Trail

As in eastern South Dakota, wines and microbrews are booming in the Black Hills. There's even an official *Black Hills Wine and Beer Trail.* Here's a look at some of the standouts:

Wine lovers will enjoy sipping samples at the stylish, multistory *Prairie Berry Winery,* just 3 miles northeast of Hill City on US 16. The patio offers fabulous views of Harney Peak, making it easy to linger and savor the flavors. Among their 15 wines are Pheasant Reserve, a dry red made with Marechal grapes and wild chokecherries; Blue Suede Shoes, a sweet wine with hints of blueberries; and a semisweet sassily named Red-Ass Rhubarb wine with raspberries that has earned its share of awards. It's also a good and family-friendly lunch stop with flat-grill sandwiches and soups. Prairie Berry also opened a new microbrew, *Miner Brewing Company,* down the hill in late 2013. One of the most popular ways to visit the winery is by boarding the 1880 train for fall's Wine Express weekend. The December Fezziwig Festival also is popular featuring wine, live music, and food prepared with wine, along with self-guided tours of the winery (877-226-9453; prairieberry.com).

Tapping the bawdy side of Black Hills visitors, *Naked Winery* (605-574-3300; nakedwinerysd.com) offers tasting rooms in Hill City and Custer, along with light meals that include pizza, soft pretzels, and sandwiches. Tastings include their wines with names like Tease and Climax Red, the new Sick-n-Twisted microbrews, and even ice cream.

Eastern South Dakota's wineries also have Black Hills' outposts. *Stone Faces Winery* is part of Vermillion's Valiant Vineyards and runs a tasting room at 126

The newest attraction to Hill City is *Brule,* a Native American show with Grammy-award-winning musicians who have toured internationally but built a permanent stage here with the Buffalo Moon Theater in 2012. Nightly summer shows bring together the vivid colors, dances, and pageantry you'd see at powwows, along with rocking music and touching stories. Tickets run $5–$10 for kids ages 5–12; $16–$29 for adults. Call (605) 574-9003 or go to highcountryranch.com/brule for more information.

High Country Guest Ranch also offers 45-minute trail rides with about a dozen horses that head into the surrounding Black Hills National Forest. Groups are small, so reserve early to get your pick of days and times. The wranglers welcome kids as young as 6 to participate, and the ride is gentle

Robins Roost Rd. just off Highway 385 a few miles north of Hill City. It offers a nice variety of whites and reds, but also some dessert wines including a black currant honey wine and a spiced holiday red. Call (605) 574-3600 or go to stonefaces winery.com for more information.

Volga-based **Schadé Winery** has a tasting room at 250 US 14 in Deadwood. It specializes in wines packaged as Black Hills and South Dakota souvenirs with scenic labels and names. Call (605) 627-5545 or go to schadevineyard.com.

Among the bestsellers at **Twisted Pine Winery,** 124 Main St., Hill City, is the Hatch green chile–infused Besito Caliente. This tasting room also includes a variety of gourmet olive oils and vinegars (605-574-9090; twistedpinewinery.com).

Belle Joli Winery has a tasting room for its sparkling wines, traditional wines, and fruit dessert wines at 594 Main St. in Deadwood, but you'll find a more scenic place to try them on the patio overlooking a five-acre vineyard at 3951 Vanocker Canyon Rd. in Sturgis. Call (605) 571-1006 or go to bellejoli.com.

Crow Peak Brewing Co. at 125 W. Hwy. 14 in Spearfish has built a big following with its brews, including a honey-infused Canyon Cream Ale and Pile O' Dirt Porter and seasonal brews such as a fall chili ale. The top sellers come in cans, making them easier than a growler to take home. Call (605) 717-0006 or go to crowpeakbrewing.com.

For more information on regional wineries and breweries, along with tours that provide designated drivers (and unique vehicles that include a modified, oversized Volkswagen bus), check with the Black Hills and Badlands Tourism Association, blackhillsbadlands.com.

enough for first-timers ($32/person; 605-574-9003; highcountryranch.com/trailrides).

Twelve miles north of Hill City off US 385 and on Horseman's Ranch Road, you can taste a little bit of Europe while nestled into the forest. Swiss-born Hanspeter and Christine Streich run **Coyote Blues Village Bed and Breakfast,** a cedar-lodge haven they built more than a decade ago. Guests pick from themed rooms: European Antique, Mediterranean, Turkish, Swiss, Lakota, African, or Celtic. Each is equipped with a deck, a hot tub, and a private bath. There are three smaller rooms as well. Call (605) 574-4477 or go to coyotebluesvillage.com for details on seasonal rates.

Custer and Crazy Horse

Not far from Hill City on US 16A, you can better appreciate the accomplishment of Mount Rushmore by seeing an even larger undertaking—**Crazy Horse Memorial**—painstakingly progressing, blast by blast. The late Korczak Ziolkowski began the project more than 60 years ago when several chiefs asked him to create a sculpture of the famous Oglala Lakota leader. Chief Henry Standing Bear's invitation said, "My fellow chiefs and I would like the white man to know the red man has great heroes, too." Although Ziolkowski died in 1982, and his wife, Ruth, in 2014, their 10 children continue the sculptor's dream, guided by his scale models and detailed plans. The process has been slow but steady and precise; Ziolkowski insisted that no federal or state monies be used to fund the project. The nine-story-high face of Crazy Horse was completed in 1998. The horse's head, which measures 219 feet (or 22 stories), is the focus of current work on the mountain. You can get the most amazing (and rare) up-close view of Crazy Horse by joining in the annual 10K **Volksmarch** in June, which has been so popular they added a September Volksmarch option in 2013. The strenuous two- to four-hour hike up the mountain has drawn up to 15,000 people eager to see the carving face-to-face.

Stay after dark (or return later in the day) to see the evening laser show May through early Oct. They use some of the world's largest lasers and slide projectors for a multimedia blend of Native American music and stories with the mountain providing a 500-foot backdrop.

Beyond the fascinating story of the monument and the work that will be under way for generations to come, the site also is noteworthy for its **Indian Museum of North America and Native American Cultural Center,** the sculptor's studio; and a 40,000-square-foot Orientation Center and theaters. Many Native American artists and craftspeople create their artwork and visit with guests at the memorial during the summer season.

There are two dramatic night blasts scheduled: one to commemorate Ruth's birthday and the Battle of the Little Bighorn in late June, and one to celebrate the death of Crazy Horse and Korczak's birthday over Labor Day weekend. There also is one during early October's Native American Day, a celebration of art, music, dancing, and storytelling, plus free buffalo stew. Crazy Horse is open year-round; admission is $11 per person (children under age 6 free), $28 a carload. Off-season admission is three items for a local foodshelf (605-673-4681; crazyhorse.org).

Heading south on US 16/385, head west at **Custer** and the intersection of US 16A. It's a 13-mile trip to **Jewel Cave National Monument,** the second-longest cave in the world. As of 2014, explorers had mapped 173 miles of passages—many of them beneath just 3 square miles of land. Jewel Cave also is considered one of the country's prettiest caves with calcite crystals glittering along the walls. Guides will point out other formations such as moonmilk, scintillites, and hydromagnesite balloons. Prospectors discovered the cave around 1900 when they heard wind rushing through a hole in the rocks in Hell Canyon. It became part of the National Park System by 1908.

The least strenuous way to see the cave is the 20-minute Discovery Talk with a look at one of the larger caverns. We highly recommend the longer tours, and you'll need to plan ahead and make reservations to guarantee a spot. These include an 80-minute scenic tour and the historic 105-minute Lantern Tours. If you don't mind belly crawling through a few tight spaces while wearing a hard hat and headlamp, the Wild Caving/Spelunking Tour provides a three- to four-hour adventure that's essentially an underground obstacle course with climbing, sliding, and a chance to experience rarer parts of the cave, such as feeling the wind at Hurricane Corner. Go to nps .gov/jeca for full details, schedules of tours, and advice on what to wear. Call (605) 673-8300 to make reservations. The visitor center and trails are free and open year-round. Most of the tours also continue through the off-season, but check the website for current schedules. Tour prices start at $8–$12.

Just west of Custer on US 16, the **National Museum of Woodcarving** celebrates the art in grand fashion. Here, visitors can see the work of nationally recognized woodcarvers and 25 of the nation's top caricature carvers. This unique museum also features the Talking Woodcarvings, more than 30 scenes created by an original Disneyland animator. The museum is open daily May 1 through late Oct. For details call (605) 673-4404 or go to woodcarving.blackhills.com.

Heading back east on US 16, breathe in the local history at the **1881 Custer County Courthouse Museum,** 411 Mount Rushmore Rd. Residents and businesses have lovingly contributed pieces of the past to fill this

Bike Trails Through the Black Hills

One of the best ways to see the spectacular scenery of the Black Hills is pedaling along the 114-mile *George S. Mickelson Trail.* It follows the historic Burlington Railroad line from Deadwood to Edgemont, putting bicyclists right in the heart of the Hills. It's easily accessed in Hill City and Custer. It's $3/day to use the trail, payable at self-service stations.

If you prefer a more rugged journey, the Centennial Trail spans 111 miles from Bear Butte State Park to Wind Cave National Park. For information on either trail, call (605) 584-3896 or go to gfp.sd.gov for more information.

If you need to rent a bike or to hire a shuttle service, or need parts or repairs, contact Rabbit Bicycles and Repair in Hill City (605-574-4302; rabbitbike.com).

commanding brick Italianate building. Visitors see slices of early Custer life, from artifacts of the timber and farming industries, which made the town prosper, to Victorian apparel and furnishings. On the museum grounds, printing equipment from Custer's 1879 first continuously operated newspaper and blacksmith forge and tools are on display. The Custer room depicts photographs of the 1874 Custer expedition when General George A. Custer entered the Black Hills. Custer's epaulets and a first edition of his book, *My Life on the Plains,* are also displayed. Upstairs is the courtroom with the original cherry furniture and judge's chamber. Admission is $6 for adults, $5 for seniors, $1 for students 12 and older, and free for children under 11. Open 9 a.m. to 8 p.m. Mon through Sat, and 1 to 8 p.m. Sun May through Sept (605-673-2443; 1881courthousemuseum.com).

Custer State Park and Norbeck Byway

East of Custer the city you'll enter *Custer State Park,* which at 71,000 acres and packed with fabulous hiking and wildlife, could rival many national parks. Be prepared to spend at least a day or two here, honking through one-way tunnels, circling pigtail bridges, and admiring the amazing rock formations along the Peter Norbeck Scenic Byway. Call (605) 255-4515 for more information.

Hop on the 18-mile **Wildlife Loop Road** early in the morning or close to evening for the best chance to view the park's famed bison herd (one of the largest in the country with about 1,300 animals), along with elk, mule deer, white-tailed deer, pronghorn antelope, burros (that are comically nosy in begging for handouts), and coyotes roaming the prairies. Big- horn sheep and mountain goats can be spotted at the higher elevations, especially near Sylvan Lake or Blue Bell Lodge. Plan at least 45 minutes to an hour and a half to do the drive. Viewing is particularly good in the late spring when animals seek tender roadside grasses as snow melts or in the fall during breeding season.

Entering from the west on US 16A, detour south on SD 87 for two of the park's best scenic views. You can drive up to **Mount Coolidge** (elevation 6,000 feet) to see the fire tower or stop at the peaceful **Heddy Draw overlook** for a picnic. On a sharp, blue-sky day, you can see clear to the Badlands from both. At Mount Coolidge you can also see Mount Rushmore and Crazy Horse. Bring your binoculars or change for the coin-operated ones. On the return to Highway 16A and heading toward Legion Lake, keep an eye out for the Badger Clark Historic Trail on the right. The **Badger Hole** was home of the state's first poet laureate, Charles Badger Clark (1883–1957), whose most popular poem is "A Cowboy's Prayer,"

planearly tocamp

During the summer, the park is so popular its more than 300 camp- sites ($16–$25/night) and camper cabins ($45/night) book up quickly. Plan ahead. Call (800) 710-2267 or go to campsd.com. You can find more than 600 additional camp- sites and a handful of cabins in the Black Hills National Forest's 30 campgrounds. Most have vault toi- lets. Go to recreation.gov for more information.

Custer Resorts

All of Custer State Park's resorts feel steeped in history, especially Sylvan Lake Lodge and the State Game Lodge, which has served as a summer White House. Bluebell Lodge and Legion Lake are more family- and budget-oriented. Check rates and make reservations for all of them at (888) 875-0001; custerresorts.com.

which, incidentally, is frequently misprinted and rarely attributed to its author. After a tour of the four-room cabin where Clark spent most of his literary career, hike the trail and read his poetry at quiet stops amid the pines. The Badger Hole is open from 10 a.m. to 5 p.m. Memorial Day through Labor Day.

tighttunnels

There are a lot of tunnels in the Black Hills, and children will especially love them if you honk the horn while passing through. There are several narrow tunnels you should be aware of, particularly if you're driving a recreational vehicle, camper, truck, or bus. Check details on locations and widths at travelsd.com/Trip-Planner/ Travel-Tips.

The **Black Hills Playhouse,** nestled in Custer State Park, offers top-drawer entertainment but is laid-back enough that you can show up in camping attire. This nonprofit professional summer stock theater has been entertaining Black Hills visitors for seven decades. A visit here can be a fun expedition for the theatergoer, especially kids who will love seeing a chipmunk scurry by or hearing soothing sounds from a nearby stream. The troupe presents five productions each summer, from plays such as *To Kill a Mockingbird* and family-friendly shows such as *Shrek the Musical* to the more adult humor of shows such as *Monty Python's Spamalot.* Shows begin at 7:30 p.m. Tues through Sat with matinees on Wed and Sun at 2 p.m. Tickets are $15 for kids and $32 for adults. Call (605) 255-4141 or visit blackhillsplayhouse.com for more information.

Buffalo Rock Lodge bed-and-breakfast sits between the playhouse and Keystone, 2 miles outside the state park and tucked onto Playhouse Road. Guests can enjoy a distant but clear view of Mount Rushmore while eating a hearty western breakfast on the deck among the pines. Owners Art and

AUTHOR'S FAVORITE HIKES

Harney Peak	Sunday Gulch
Cathedral Spires	Roughlock Falls near Spearfish Canyon
Little Devils Tower	

The Black Hills Rock

My first rock-climbing experience was near the shores of Sylvan Lake in the capable hands of Daryl Stisser, who runs Hill City–based **Sylvan Rocks Climbing School** with his wife, Cheryl. We were there just a few weeks after they had set up camera crews and stunt folks for the dizzying action scenes in National Treasure 2: The Book of Secrets.

The outfitters get their share of adrenaline junkies and people who want multiday trips and the opportunity to climb Devils Tower, but many customers are first-timers. They range in age from preschoolers to gung-ho grannies.

"Most of climbing is from the neck up. It's achievable by many, many people," Daryl Stisser says. "And it's very empowering."

The Hills also are ideal for beginners because the rocks are easy to reach with tapering summits that let you power a climb with leg muscles and balance rather than upper-body strength.

We learned quickly to scrutinize granite grays for tiny toe-holds and bits of quartz and feldspar to gratefully grab onto as we ascended. It was an amazing experience: scary, exhilarating, and surprisingly satisfying to be standing high above ground surrounded by the gentle whoosh of pines. You can find more information about Sylvan Rocks Climbing School & Guide Service at (605) 484-7585 or sylvanrocks.com. If you need gear or maps, check out Granite Sports on Hill City's Main Street (605-574-2121).

Marilyn Daniels trace their family's roots in the Black Hills to Marilyn's grandfather who helped build Custer State Park's State Game Lodge. The fireplace, inset with a variety of local stones they've collected, provides the centerpiece of this spacious yet homey lodge. The three rooms range from $155 to $205 per night, with two large enough for families (888-564-5634; buffalorock.net).

A simple drive through Custer State Park can raise your adrenaline with electrifying spins and knock-your-socks-off views from the 66-mile **Peter Norbeck National Scenic Byway,** easily one of the top scenic drives in the nation. It comprises two brilliantly planned routes: the 14-mile **Needles Highway** and **Iron Mountain Road.** Drivers are meant to drink in the scenery and take their time, so make use of the pullouts, keep a camera handy, and watch for wildlife. (In winter the Needles Highway is closed to allow snowmobiling and cross-country skiing.)

The Other Black Hills

Ninety percent of the Black Hills are in South Dakota, but the mountains also grace Wyoming for 10 to 40 miles. Even though they cross the South Dakota state line, the towns of Devils Tower, Hulett, Upton, Newcastle, and Sundance are very much part of the Black Hills community.

The Wyoming segment of the Black Hills includes a distinct branch known as the Bear Lodge. This is the site of the country's first national monument, Devils Tower. The tower is actually a solitary stump-shaped igneous rock formation that looms 1,267 feet above the Belle Fourche River in northeastern Wyoming like a skyscraper against the rural landscape. The tower is popular with rock climbers and movie makers. Devils Tower was a location for *Close Encounters of the Third Kind.*

If you want to slow down the scenery even more, head to **Sylvan Lake Lodge & Resort** (605-574-2561), one of four historic lodges in the park and a hub for many of the park's best hikes. Guests can choose from cozy lodge rooms for $145–$230/night, or 32 cabins from basic sleeping cabins ($130/night) to a modern three-bedroom housekeeping cabin that goes for $330/night. This magnificent mountain resort overlooks Sylvan Lake and the granite outcroppings of Harney Peak. It's considered Custer State Park's crown jewel and a favorite romantic destination, attracting weddings throughout the summer and anniversary visits ever after. You'll need to book early. Call (888) 875-0001 for reservations.

Sylvan Lake was created in 1881, when Theodore Reder built a dam across Sunday Gulch. By 1895 a Victorian-style hotel opened along its shores and remained popular until it burned to the ground in 1935. The current hotel opened in 1937, and the new wing was added in 1991. The hotel features cozy lodge rooms, a lobby, a lounge, and a restaurant, the Lakota Dining Room, which specializes in native game entrees and seafood and gorgeous views of Harney. If you look closely, you'll just make out the historic stone fire tower on the top.

Feeling adventurous? Hike to **Harney Peak,** which is the state's highest point at 7,242 feet and the highest elevation east of the Rockies. Be prepared, though. This 6-mile trek is a challenge and a workout. The first time

I hiked it, gasping up the last set of stairs, a smiling Kansas dad with kids strapped to his chest and his back put me to shame. The second trek was easier, and both were well worth the chance to gaze across a spectacular 60-mile view of undulating forest and rocky peaks. Stand atop the historic stone fire tower to breathe in the clean, rarefied air and feel it ripple across you. Without question Harney Peak has inspired people of all faiths. When he was only 9 years old, the Oglala holy man Black Elk had his first vision here. "Then I was standing on the highest mountain of them all, and round about beneath me was the whole hoop of the world," he said. Harney Peak is part of the Black Elk Wilderness.

Southern Hills and Hot Springs

If you head south on US 385, you will enter the wonderful wild kingdom of **Hot Springs.** This small town (population 3,514) known for its woolly mammoths, fascinating architecture, a cool cave, and healing springs often ranks as a family favorite. Chalk it up to mammoth bones and the fascination of exploring underground.

You'll reach **Wind Cave National Park** 11 miles before hitting Hot Springs city limits. Keep an eye out for the sprawl of prairie dog towns along the way. While some consider them pests, kids will find them entertaining with the way they pop up and down, call out to others, and play together.

Wind Cave's claims to fame include being the nation's seventh-oldest national park, having one of the country's few intact prairies, and having one of the longest caves in the world with a labyrinth of levels. It also has great examples of boxwork, gridlike formations as delicate as potato chips on the ceiling. Popcorn and frostwork formations also can be seen. Visitors can choose from five tours. Each highlights different sections of the cave and ranges from an easy, quick look to historic candlelight tours and a four-hour wild caving adventure. Tours run $5–$6 for children 8–16 and $10–$12 for adults. Wild cave tours are $30. If you are doing a cave tour, go early in the day or reserve your tickets ahead of time to avoid waits. The tours require admission, but there is no fee to enter the park, check out visitor center exhibits, watch the 18-minute movie on Wind Cave, or explore the several hiking trails threading through the 28,000-acre wildlife preserve above ground. Look for bison, antelope, elk, and deer roaming the grassland

and forests. Park rangers also lead themed hikes that focus on birding and the prairie, a drive to the Sanson Buffalo Jump, or campfire programs at the park's Elk Mountain campground (605-745-4600; nps.gov/wica).

Before European settlers came to Hot Springs, the Lakota named the area Wiwilakahta, or "valley of healing waters." By the late 1800s, Hot Springs and its mineral springs attracted trainloads of wealthy visitors who sought the therapeutic benefits of mineral springs. These days your best bet to experience the springs is a dip in the naturally warm water that flows up through the pebble bottom of *Evan's Plunge,* 1145 North River St. The 87-degree mineral spring water flows at a rate of 5,000 gallons a minute. Anyone seeking extra thrills can slip down the water slides or test their strength with the Tarzan rings. Admission to this giant indoor pool that's open year-round runs $10–$12. Call (605) 745-5165 or go to evansplunge .com for hours.

If you take a stroll on the Fall River Freedom Trail, you can also stick a bare foot into a waterfall and feel the water's warm temperature. It's also a good way to admire downtown's unique Romanesque revival architecture that uses the red, pink, and tan sandstone found on the outer rim of the Black Hills.

You can stay in the heart of downtown and have a pampered getaway at *Red Rock River Resort,* a four-story hotel and spa at 603 N. River St. Rooms are decorated in earth tones, and beds heaped with down comfort-ers. Minnekahta Spa, open to hotel guests and day visitors, offers a full menu of massages and amenities such as Korean-style heat rooms, including one with a four-inch layer of Cheyenne River sand toasted to 115 degrees. New owners were taking over in early 2015, so it's wise to check and see what's new (605-745-4400 or redrockriverresort.com).

History buffs will enjoy the *Fall River County Historical Museum* at 300 N. River St. in an 1893 building that was once a school. Admission is free. The museum is open 9 a.m. to 5 p.m. Mon through Sat May 15 to October 15 (605-745-5147; pioneer-museum.com).

Hot Springs' biggest attraction is mammoth in every sense of the word and packs a wow factor like few places can. More than 26,000 years ago, more than 100 mammoths were trapped and died in a sinkhole on the town's southeastern edge. Mark the *Mammoth Site* as a must-see on your Dakota travel agenda. It was built atop the excavation, which began when a

1974 housing project uncovered the white bones and tusks. Visitors can get a 30-minute guided tour that lets them walk around this mass graveyard and see paleontologists still at work excavating bones or preparing bones and casts in a downstairs laboratory. There also is a great museum with bones of other prehistoric creatures such as camels, short-faced bears, antelope, gray wolves, minks, white-tailed prairie dogs, and frogs.

The Mammoth Site is the only *in situ* (bones left as found) display of fossil mammoths in the US. It's especially exciting for kids ages 4 to 12, who can sign up for the ***Junior Paleontology*** program June 1 to August 15 for $12/person. The 1- to 1.5-hour program lets them experience a simulated dig, excavating casts of different mammoth bones and then trying to identify them. You'll never see a group of kids concentrating this hard and being this quiet anywhere. Digs are popular and limited to 16 participants, so reservations are highly recommended. Additional options include an Advanced Paleontology Program for kids 5 and older who learn excavating along with how to map and jacket a bone ($20/per person). There also is a summer Atlatl Throwing Experience for kids 5 and older who want to learn how to throw this Ice Age hunting weapon ($10/person). Program fees do not include general admission, which is $10 for anyone 13 or older, $9 for seniors 60 or older, and $8 for kids 4–12.

Younger children can do a free dig in the visitor center, using brushes to sweep away sand from casts of mammoth teeth, which look a lot like the bottom of sneakers. The site is open daily 8 a.m. to 8 p.m. mid-May through mid-Aug, 8 a.m. to 6 p.m. mid-Aug to Sept, 9 a.m. to 5 p.m. Sept and Oct, 9 a.m. to 3:30 p.m. Mon through Sat, and 11 a.m. to 3:30 p.m. Sun Nov through Feb, and 9 a.m. to 5 p.m. daily Mar through mid-May. Be sure to show up an hour before closing to catch a tour. Call (605) 745-6017 or go to mammothsite.com for more information.

If you prefer a more recent slice of South Dakota history, fast forward from the Ice Age to when mustangs ran wild and Native American tribes thrived on the prairie. ***Black Hills Wild Horse Sanctuary*** offers a variety of tours through its 11,000-acre private wilderness area where more than 500 horses roam free. Two-hour guided bus tours include a chance to see their horses, along with 10,000-year-old Indian petroglyphs, an authentic Native American Sun Dance site, and the movie sets for *Crazy Horse* (1996) and Disney's *Hidalgo* (2003). Tickets run $50 for adults, $45 for senior citizens,

$15 for teens, and $7.50 for children 5–12. Other tour options range from three to six hours and start at $150/person and go up to $1,500 for three people and two nights in the sanctuary's log cabin. If you simply want to get off the grid, the sanctuary rents its two cabins for two to three people for $137–$150/night for two or more nights. For more information call (605) 745-5955 or visit wildmustangs.com.

The sanctuary is about 15 miles from Hot Springs, following SD 71 south and turning right at Highland Road. Along the way, keep an eye out for the **Cascade Falls Picnic Ground** once you hit the S curve on 71 (about 8 miles south of Hot Springs). It's a good old-fashioned swimming hole along Cascade Creek with a deep pool for adults and strong swimmers and two shallower pools for kids. Cascade Springs pumps out more water than any other natural spring in the Black Hills. It's also home to some rare botanical species. Check fs.fed.us for more information.

If you're craving more water than a mountain stream, head to **Angostura Recreation Area** about 10 miles southeast of Hot Springs via Highway 385. The bluffs offer some of the prettiest campsites in the state with breathtaking views of the reservoir and Cheyenne River Valley. You'll see anglers looking for walleye, bass, and crappie, colorful sailing boats and paddlers on the water, and a sandy beach along the reservoir's 36 miles of shoreline. There are 4 campgrounds with 169 campsites, 10 camping cabins, and additional campsites in nearby **Sheps Canyon Recreational Area.** Privately owned **Angostura Resort** also has 6 rental lodges, an outdoor pool, and a marina. Call (800) 364-8831 for more information. For park reservations, call (800) 710-2267 or go to campsd.com.

If the Wild Horse Sanctuary or the area's scenic hills leave you yearning for a horseback ride, check out **Sage Meadow Ranch,** which offers private trail rides by reservation near Hot Springs. There's a 90-minute option for novices and beginners for $65/person or a three-hour ride for experienced riders at $90/person. Call (605) 745-4866 or go to sagemeadowranchllc.com for more information.

The Northern Hills

The abundant snowfall in the northern Black Hills makes it a winter sports mecca. Snowmobiling, cross-country skiing, and downhill skiing are popular choices, but you can find gambling, entertainment, Old West museums, and enough restaurants to provide something to do year-round—no matter what Mother Nature dishes out.

Sturgis and Fort Meade

Even if you're not into motorcycles, the mass of people and machinery that roll through the Hills during the legendary *Sturgis Motorcycle Rally* offers a spectacle like no other. It's a full-blown, hard-core party during the first full week of August, drawing close to 500,000 attendees to this town of 6,627 people. Even more jaw-dropping: Some folks are predicting close to a million visitors during the rally's 75th anniversary in 2015. The agenda can include anything from AA meetings and Miss Buffalo Chip Beauty Pageants to wine tastings, Harley shows, and live bands. The rally attracts weekend warriors and biker gangs such as the Bandidos, and fuels a few romances as well. In peak years, local officials have issued close to 200 marriage licenses during the rally. Naturally, the legendary event attracts its share of celebrities, too. Peter Fonda, Emilio Estevez, Mickey Rourke, and Neil Diamond are just a handful of the rich and famous cruising into *Sturgis* for this festival of chrome, leather, and heavy-metal thunder.

J. C. "Pappy" Hoel probably never pictured this when he started the Sturgis Rally in 1938 with only nine races and a less-than-capacity grandstand crowd. Sturgis, fortunately, has learned to handle the crowds. There are thousands of campsites available for the event, but anyone planning to travel through the Black Hills that week in August will need to make lodging reservations well in advance, pay up front, and be prepared to hear engines rumbling and echoing through tunnels and along scenic byways. For information about the rally, call (605) 720-0800 or visit sturgismotorcyclerally.com.

You can sample the spirit of the rally without the crush of humanity at *Sturgis Motorcycle Museum & Hall of Fame,* 999 Main St. It blends rally memorabilia, antique motorcycles, unique bikes, and rotating exhibits. It's open 9 a.m. to 5 p.m. Mon through Fri, 9 a.m. to 4 p.m. Sat, and 10 a.m. to 4 p.m. Sun in the summer months. It's open 10 a.m. to 4 p.m. the rest of the year. It pays to bring a friend or two: admission is $10 for one person, $15 for two, or $30 for five people. Call (605) 347-2001 or go to sturgis museum.com.

The normally quiet community of Sturgis also is home to **Fort Meade Museum & Old Post Cemetery,** located 1 mile east of Sturgis on SD 34. Fort Meade was built in the shadows of the majestic Bear Butte, a landmark that made it possible for early-day travelers to find the fort. Cavalry and infantry stationed here beginning in 1878 were assigned to keep the peace in those turbulent years, and so the fort gained the nickname "The Peacekeeper Fort." The site is open daily 9 a.m. to 5 p.m. mid-May through Sept. Admission is $4 for anyone 12 and older. The Fort Meade Back Country Byway winds between Fort Meade near SD 34 and the 120-acre Black Hills National Cemetery near exit 34 on I-90.

trivia

It was on Fort Meade's parade grounds that the "Star-Spangled Banner" was first played in an official capacity in 1892. What later became the national anthem was used during the evening military retreat ceremony.

Colonel Samuel D. Sturgis, a Union general during the Civil War, was commander of the 7th Cavalry and the first permanent post commander at Fort Meade. He was a member of the company that founded the nearby town that bears his name.

The Bureau of Land Management manages approximately 6,700 acres of the former Fort Meade Military Reservation, now the **Fort Meade Recreation Area.** Approximately one-third of this area is on the National Register of Historic Places, due to the numerous historical sites at Fort Meade, mostly remnants of early cavalry life, and the post cemetery. The area accommodates grazing, forestry, wildlife, and a variety of recreational uses that include camping, picnicking, horseback riding, and hiking. The 110-mile multiuse Centennial Trail also winds through this area.

Mato paha (bear mountain) is the name the Indians gave what is now **Bear Butte State Park** (605-347-5240; gfp.sd.gov), an outstanding geological formation located 6 miles northeast of Sturgis. Artifacts from 10,000 years ago have been found here, and the volcanic laccolith is still used today by Native Americans for religious ceremonies and vision quests. Visitors are asked not to disturb the bits of cloth and offerings of tobacco that have been left on trees in prayer. An easy hike will take you around Bear Butte Lake while the Summit Trail offers more of a challenge. The reward for climbing the summit and gaining about 1,000 feet in elevation is an expansive—and inspiring—view of four states and a deep appreciation for why this place is considered sacred. The park and trails are open year-round, and the visitor center is open 9 a.m. to 5 p.m. May 1 through mid-Sept. Because of its natural and historical significance, Bear Butte was designated a National Natural Landmark in 1965.

Spearfish

Eighteen miles northwest of Sturgis, **Spearfish** stands out among the Black Hills communities for its love of the outdoors with scenic drives and stellar hikes, a quieter, more studious pace than nearby Deadwood or Sturgis, and the dose of culture with the High Plains Heritage Center Museum and Black Hills State University.

High Plains Heritage Center Museum honors old west pioneers with art and artifacts from North and South Dakota, Montana, Wyoming, and Nebraska. Outdoor displays include antique implements, a log cabin, a sod dugout, a one-room schoolhouse, live buffalo, longhorns, miniature horses, and an original Spearfish-to-Deadwood stagecoach. You can hear cowboy poetry and music in the 200-seat theater with a view of three states from the upper balcony. The museum is open year-round 9 a.m. to 5 p.m. daily. Admission is $10 for ages 16 and older; $3 for youth 6–16. The center is located at 825 Heritage Dr., off I-90 at exit 14 (605-642-9378; westernheritage center.com).

Back in downtown Spearfish (population 12,000), you can visit the **Matthews Opera House and Art Center** at 614 Main St. Spearfish residents returned it to its original 1906 charm and use it for summer community theater performances and concerts at the 250-seat theater. Productions always have strong support from the college theater department. For a schedule of events and art gallery exhibits, call (605) 642-7973 or visit spearfisharts center.org.

Walk across the footbridge at **Spearfish City Park** to discover the **D. C. Booth Historic National Fish Hatchery and Archives.** It introduced trout to the Black Hills and at one point had coordinated all federal fisheries in the US. The underwater viewing area lets you watch rainbow and brown trout or you can catch a hatchery tour that runs daily from 9 a.m.

to 5 p.m. mid-May through mid-Sept. The museum and grounds, including the historic Booth House where the superintendent lived, are open year-round. It's a must-see place for families, especially with the free admission (605-642-7730; fws.gov/dcbooth).

A 1.7-mile detour southwest of Spearfish to 1920 Christensen Dr. gives you a look at the unique work of artist Dick Termes at ***Termesphere Gallery.*** He paints artwork on spheres using a mathematical process (605-642-4805; termespheres.com). It's also a good excuse to hop onto US 14A and cruise along the ***Spearfish Canyon National Scenic Byway.*** The 19-mile drive is on one of the prettiest, least crowded byways in the Hills. Peak time to go is fall when the vibrant gold of birch and aspen look most striking against the dark green of pine and spruce and the earth tones of the steep canyon walls. Colors usually peak by mid-October.

Thirteen miles south of Spearfish at 10619 Roughlock Falls Rd., ***Spearfish Canyon Lodge*** provides top-of-the-line accommodations in the heart of the canyon. Rates start at $109 in winter and $139 in summer. Suites start at $199. The lodge's ***Latchstring Inn Restaurant & Lounge*** serves meals on the veranda with the fresh scent of pine trees in the air (605-584-3435; spfcanyon.com).

At a 5,760-foot elevation, ***Crow Peak*** has been a northern hills landmark for centuries. If you want to tackle the 7-mile trip there and back, grab a map from the Spearfish Ranger District (605-642-4622). The trail is 7 miles southwest of Spearfish on FR 214, also known as Higgins Gulch Road.

Deadwood

About 14 miles southeast of Spearfish on US 85, ***Deadwood*** buzzes with the colors and energy of a mini Las Vegas teamed with Old West grit and spirit. Walk anywhere in town, and you'll see the flash and hear the blings and dings of slot machines and gaming areas in the town's 26 casinos and gaming halls—many of which operate in Deadwood's historic downtown.

Its gambling habit goes back more than 100 years and helped the town flourish during the Gold Rush. There have been plenty of boom and bust times since then and a clear streak of bawdiness from early days of gunslingers, opium dens, and bordellos. This was one of the last places in the country to outlaw prostitution, in 1980, after more than a century in business.

By 1989 Deadwood (with a current population of 1,288) brought back gambling when the state voted to allow $5 bets. They've since increased those bets to $100, and the number (and size) of casinos grew steadily and rejuvenated the Victorian downtown that's nestled into a valley.

Kevin Costner fans will love the *Midnight Star,* a casino owned by him and his brother, Dan. It's decorated with many costumes and props from his film career—from his never-seen role as the dead friend in *The Big Chill* to the epic filmed-in-South-Dakota *Dances with Wolves.* An elevator sweeps you to the top of the Midnight Star and opens into *Jakes,* one of the most impressive—and romantic—restaurants in the Black Hills. More moderate prices are on the menu at *Diamond Lil's Bar and Grill.* Here the Costners have given their favorite sandwiches and appetizers unique names—those of their family, friends, and favorite movie characters. The main level houses the casino (605-578-3656; themidnightstar.com).

The newer and tucked-away gem, the *Deadwood Social Club,* 657 Main St., is earning rave reviews from its perch on the second floor above the famed Old Style Saloon No. 10. The menu blends northern Italian specialties with South Dakota cuisine for choices such as buffalo ravioli, portabello venison bake, lightly smoked pheasant in a Tuaca cream sauce, and heritage ranch beef. The restaurant also serves more than 200 bottles of wine and 100 kinds of martinis. *Wine Spectator* gave it an Award of Excellence. In the summer you can dine on an outdoor patio (605-578-3346; saloon10.com).

On the main floor, Saloon No. 10 doubles as a lively bar and a museum with old photos, mining and ranching artifacts, and the infamous "death chair," where Wild Bill Hickok was shot and killed in a card game. He was holding a hand of aces and eights, known from then on as "The Deadman's Hand."

The majestic *Silverado Franklin Historic Hotel & Gaming Complex,* 709 Main St., also has a lot of history to bet on. The 1903, 81-room Franklin hotel has been the choice of stars, including luminaries such as President William Taft, President Theodore Roosevelt, John Wayne, Buffalo Bill, Babe Ruth, Pearl Buck, Robert Kennedy Jr., and Mary Hart (a South Dakota girl, too). Call (605) 578-3670 or (800) 584-7005; silveradofranklin.com.

You can learn all about Deadwood's legendary past with gambling and brothels and larger-than-life characters such as Wild Bill and Calamity Jane at the fascinating **Adams Museum,** 54 Sherman St. There's something here to interest everyone, with three levels of artifacts, including a rare plesiosaur dinosaur, folk art, vintage photographs, and the museum's famous Potato Creek Johnny's gold nugget. At 7.75 troy ounces, the nugget ranks as one of the largest ever found in the Black Hills. It was recovered from a sluice on Potato Creek in western Lawrence County in May 1929. The massive chunk of gold was tucked away from public view until 1995, when it was on public display for two days to celebrate the museum's 65th anniversary. It now is safely back in the bank, and a replica of the nugget is on display.

The Adams Museum is open year-round. Admission is $5 for adults; $2 per child 10 and under. It's open from 9 a.m. to 5 p.m. daily May 1 to September 30, 10 a.m. to 4 p.m. Tues through Sat the rest of the year. The home of the museum's founder, W. E. Adams, also has been restored and opened as a museum. The city of Deadwood invested $1.5 million into returning the Victorian Queen Anne–style home at 22 Van Buren St. to its earlier grandeur. It sits in the so-called presidential neighborhood of Deadwood. Admission to the **Historic Adams House** tour is $5 for adults, $2 for children 12 and under, and free to members. Adams House hours are 9 a.m. to 5 p.m. May 1 to September 30, and 10 a.m. to 4 p.m. Tues through Sat the rest of the year. Call (605) 578-1714 or visit deadwoodhistory.org for details on either museum. The Deadwood Historic Preservation Commission also has opened the **Homestake Adams Research and Cultural Center** at 150 Sherman St. (605-920-8444).

Deadwood: The HBO Version

If you want to see a TV version of Deadwood that is far grittier than most fictional accounts of the town, you can rent the HBO series *Deadwood* that aired in 2004–2006. The set looks like Deadwood, but it is actually a $5 million replica on the Gene Autry ranch in California.

The series captures life in Deadwood in 1876, just two weeks after Custer's Last Stand. The settlers, ranging from an ex-lawman to a scheming saloon owner to the legendary Wild Bill Hickok and Calamity Jane, share a restless spirit as they struggle to survive in this frontier town. The Emmy Award–winning show is not for the faint-hearted with an ample amount of profanity, nudity, and violence—but that was part of life in Deadwood.

When you're in the residential area near the Adams House, Deadwood feels like a sliver of San Francisco with steep streets and historic homes. If you follow Lincoln Street uphill, you'll arrive at **Mount Moriah Cemetery,** the final resting spot for some of the Old West's biggest legends, including Wild Bill Hickok, Calamity Jane, and Potato Creek Johnny. Also buried at Mount Moriah, with her parrot and her husband, is madam Dora DuFran, Calamity Jane's gal pal. Dora ran brothels in the Black Hills in the 1920s and 1930s but was known for her humanitarian work as well. Melanie Griffith portrayed Dora in the 1995 made-for-TV movie *Buffalo Girls.* Cemetery admission is $1.

One other place to get a good dose of local history: the **Days of '76 Museum,** which celebrates the area's history, its tribes, its legendary characters, its rodeos and star riders, and its annual community celebration that brings horse-drawn wagons back down main street. There are more than 50 wagons below the museum at 17 Crescent St. Admission is $7 (605-578-2872; daysof76.com).

One mile north of Deadwood on US 85 is **Tatanka: Story of the Bison.** Its centerpiece is the stunning, larger-than-life bronze sculpture by local artist Peggy Detmers, featuring 14 bison being pursued by three Native American horseback riders. The Educational Center depicts the relationship between the bison and the Plains Indians through exhibits and Native American displays. Kevin Costner, who starred in and directed *Dances with Wolves,* founded the attraction, which includes costumes from the movie. Admission is $7.50 for adults, $6.50 for seniors, and $5.50 for kids age 6–11. For more information, call (605) 584-5678 or visit storyofthebison.com.

Lead

Just a few miles from Deadwood is **Lead,** Deadwood's sister city. After seeing the glitzy Deadwood, Lead might look much more bare bones, but you can find eateries, galleries, antique stores, and the Homestake Opera House. Mining was once the mighty force in this town until operations ceased in 2001. You can imagine the glory days, though, with a trip to the **Homestake Gold Mine Visitor Center** to see the largest, deepest, and oldest underground gold mine in the Western Hemisphere. Founded in 1876 by three California investors, including George Hearst, the Homestake mine extends 8,000 feet below the surface of the Black Hills. In addition to the underground mine, Homestake operated the Open Cut surface mine, which was the original site of the Homestake claim. You can tour the Homestake May through Sept. The one-hour guided bus tour goes through the town of Lead before heading underground, taking a peek at surface operations and viewing the 1876 open-cut mine. Guides explain new and old mining technology, and you can learn more about the hoisting, crushing, and milling of gold-bearing ore. After the tour is finished, you will receive a sample of ore that was drilled from the **Homestake Gold Mine.** Tours are $7.50 for adults, $6.75 for seniors, $6.50 for students, and free for children 5 and under. There's also a $25 family rate (605-584-3110; homestakevisitorcenter.com).

For more on the history of mining, the **Black Hills Mining Museum** (605-584-1605) takes a detailed look at mining activity in the Hills during the past 120 years, including a simulated underground level of the Homestake Gold Mine. Count on realism—the simulation was created by more than 140 miners and former mine employees. Open seven days a week during the summer, the museum is at 323 W. Main St. Admission is $8 for adults, $6.50 for seniors, and $5 for students. For more information, visit mining-museum .blackhills.com.

Mystic Miner Ski Resort at Deer Mountain and **Terry Peak Ski Resort** on Lead's southwestern edge take advantage of the 7,000-foot-plus elevation for thrills and maximum snowfall. You'll find 1,200-foot vertical drops, moguls, and snowboarding terrain with jumps, bumps, rails, and half-pipes. There also are plenty of runs gentle enough for beginning and intermediate skiers. For more information on ski packages, sleigh rides, and tubing, call Mystic Miner at (605) 580-1169 or go to skimystic.com. Terry Peak can be reached at (605) 584-2165 or terrypeak.com.

Twenty-one miles south of Lead and Deadwood on US 85 you'll find **Trailshead Lodge,** the most popular pit stop for snowmobilers. They whoosh through powdery snow, wind through deep canyons, and weave through pines on roughly 350 miles of trails throughout the 1.3 million–acre Black Hills National Forest. It's little wonder *Snow Goer* magazine ranks the Black Hills among the top places to sled in the US. Trailshead Lodge offers a convenient stopping point for gas, food, lodging, and a chance to thaw out as needed (605-584-3464; trailsheadlodge.com). You can rent snowmobiles here and at other area resorts and outfitters.

If you prefer quieter winter sports, cross-country skiers and snowshoe enthusiasts will find close to 60 miles of trails to explore, along with national forest lakes for ice-fishing and several open-water streams where fly-fishing is practiced year-round by anyone willing to tolerate the cold for a few good trout.

Northwest South Dakota

The northwestern corner of South Dakota is not as familiar as the Black Hills (even to South Dakotans), but this is a perfect place to get away from it all. Tiny towns occasionally crop up on the plains landscape here, with winsome names such as Promise, Bison, Prairie City, Meadow, Buffalo, and Faith, which gained notoriety when a Tyrannosaurus rex named Sue was found there. Names reflect the ranching spirit and determination of early settlers. This is a place where people tip their hats to fellow drivers, give a friendly finger wave from the steering wheel, or offer a full-blown wave out the window as you pass on the rural roads. These are gestures of warmth you'll never see in a big city. Folks assume they know you, or your kids, parents, employer—you get the idea. The degrees of separation are mighty thin in these big open spaces. It's a fine welcome, no matter how it's delivered.

If you take US 85 north 9 miles from Spearfish, you'll find the western panorama of **Belle Fourche.** It means "pretty fork," honoring the confluence of the Belle Fourche and Redwater Rivers. Dakotans, by the way, say *Bell Foosh*. The town of 4,900 people has two claims to fame. First, there's an official marker and a sheepherder's monument called a "Stone Johnnie" that mark the town's distinction as the geographical center of the US (according to a US Coast and Geodetic Survey). Second is its ranching and cowboy culture. During its profitable era of big cattle drives from the late 1800s through the last roundup in 1902, the region attracted such notables as Butch Cassidy and the Sundance Kid. At the turn of the 20th century, Belle Fourche became known as the largest cattle-shipping point in the world. Today the town claims the largest concentration of sheep in the US and ships more wool from its warehouses than any other city.

You can join in on the community's rough-and-tumble spirit July 3–5 for the annual **Black Hills Roundup Rodeo,** with fireworks, a carnival, and a historic parade. First held in 1918, this rodeo still attracts top Professional

Rodeo Cowboy Association (PRCA) bull riders, bareback bronc riders, steer wrestlers, and other cowboys. Indeed, many Pro Rodeo athletes call Belle Fourche their home, including four-time World Bareback Riding Champion Marvin Garrett.

A handsome addition to the town's tourism offerings is the 4,000-square-foot *Tri-State Museum* (415 5th Ave.), which focuses on the early pioneer, rodeo, and Old West history of western South Dakota, eastern Wyoming, and southeast Montana. The museum houses more than 5,000 artifacts, rodeo memorabilia, historical records, antiques, collectibles, fossils, and an 1876 cabin. For more information, call (605) 723-1200 or go to thetristate museum.com.

Just 9 miles east of Belle Fourche, *Orman Dam* makes a fabulous playground for the water-skiing, boating, camping, fishing, or swimming enthusiast. The yearly Fourth of July fireworks display, too, is legendary, and the surrounding prairies make for the perfect patriotic backdrop.

The world's largest earthen dam, Orman Dam was constructed with the use of horses around the turn of the 20th century to provide irrigation for a huge tract of sugar-beet farms downstream. Although corn, small grains, and alfalfa now dominate the agricultural scene, Orman Dam remains the area's primary dry-season water source. And there is plenty of water to go around: Orman has 185,000 acre-feet of water and 52 miles of shoreline with 13 square miles of water surface.

Continue on US 85 north, and you'll drive through cattle country, where one-pony towns like Redig and Ludlow can be missed with the blink of an eye. The sanctity of space keeps travelers mindful. Just before the town of Buffalo, take SD 20 east to find one of the best-kept secrets in South Dakota. Long before he became president, Theodore Roosevelt hunted bear in the region now known as *Custer National Forest.* (He later established forest reserves in the Cave Hills and Slim Buttes areas.) Custer National Forest is probably the most forgotten forest in the state. Even natives have a puzzled look on their faces when it's mentioned, which is understandable; there's Custer State Park to the southeast, so another Custer moniker seems at first repetitious, but that does not detract from the beauty of this rustic area.

The 73,000 timbered acres in the northwestern part of the state are anomalous to the barren, outlying landscape. Ride and hike, but don't expect a guide or user-friendly visitor center to take you by the hand. You're in the deep forest now, and there are no designated hiking trails.

The *Cave Hills* section of the forest was once a popular hiding place for outlaws. Ludlow Cave, the largest of the caves, sheltered many bandits during the stormy days of the Dakota Territory. Accordingly, ranchers have called this rugged, rough land the "jumping-off spot."

East of the Cave Hills lies the *Slim Buttes* section of forest, where lofty cliffs of limestone are split by dramatic canyons. The Slim Buttes battlefield is nearby, where Sioux veterans of the Custer battle were overtaken by the US Cavalry. The Sioux were taken by surprise in the fall of 1876, but they took shelter high in the hills behind the limestone outcroppings and escaped during the night.

Stay east on SD 20 and you'll eventually run into SD 73. Take SD 73 north, and you'll inch your way toward literature and legend. The first suggested stop on this stretch of highway is *Shadehill Recreation Area* (605-374-5114), one of South Dakota's largest reservoirs with 5,000 surface acres. In addition to the customary sporting opportunities one expects, the reservoir also boasts an intriguing historical marker on the southern shore. The marker describes the legend of Hugh Glass, who survived incredible odds and inspired the book *Lord Grizzly* by Frederick Manfred. In 1823, at the fork of the Grand River, Glass was hunting with the Ashley fur party when he was attacked by a grizzly bear. Horribly maimed, he could not be moved. Two members of the Ashley party were instructed to stay with him,

suethet-rex

The famed Tyrannosaurus rex named Sue was found in Faith, South Dakota, straight south of Lemmon. She's the state's most famous discovery and has a permanent home at Chicago's Field Museum.

but instead they took Glass's weapons and left him for dead. Amazingly, Glass survived on berries and buffalo meat acquired after driving away two wolves from a downed calf. Glass eventually crawled about 190 miles to Fort Kiowa on the Missouri River. Also in the area, the marking left by Custer's 7th Cavalry can be seen on a butte at Shadehill Reservoir.

Lemmon, just 12 miles north on the South Dakota–North Dakota border, is the home of Kathleen Norris, another fine contemporary writer from the state. She captured the essence of small-town life in *Dakota: A Spiritual Geography.* Her collection of poetry, *Little Girls in Church,* also speaks from the heart. Other excellent writers of western South Dakota include Linda Hasselstrom, Virginia Driving Hawk Sneve, and Dan O'Brien. Also writing his way into the annals of history—and by different means—was Ed Lemmon, for whom the town was named. He was one of the first South Dakotans inducted into the prestigious National Cowboy Hall of Fame.

The Lemmon ***Petrified Wood Park and Museum,*** located at 500 Main Ave., five blocks north of US 12, has been around since the early 1930s when Lemmon men under the command of Ole S. Quammen put together this bizarre, yet intriguing blend of petrified wood and fossil sculptures across a city block. It was a labor of love for some and a necessity for others who were unemployed and depended on the project for sustenance during its construction. You can explore the 300-ton castle, a wishing well, a waterfall, and petrified wood cones up to 20 feet. You can envision trolls, or at least gnomes, feeling quite at home in this otherworldly place.

Where to Stay in Western South Dakota

BELLE FOURCHE

AmericInn Lodge and Suites
2312 Dakota Ave.
(605) 892-0900
americinn.com
Inexpensive

CUSTER

Bavarian Inn
855 N. 5th St.
(605) 673-2802
bavarianinnsd.com
Moderate

Rocket Motel
211 Mt. Rushmore Rd.
(605) 673-4401
rocketmotel.com
Inexpensive

Shady Rest Motel
238 Gordon St.
(605) 673-4478
shady-rest-motel.com
Inexpensive

DEADWOOD

Deadwood Gulch Resort
304 Cliff St. (US 85 South)
(605) 578-1294
deadwoodgulchresort
.com
Moderate

Deadwood Mountain Grand
1906 Deadwood
Mountain Dr.
(605) 559-0386
deadwoodmountaingrand
.com
Moderate

SELECTED CHAMBERS OF COMMERCE

Belle Fourche Chamber of Commerce
620 State St.
Belle Fourche 57717
(605) 892-2676
bellefourchechamber.org

Custer Area Chamber of Commerce
615 Washington St.
Custer 57730
(605) 673-2244
custersd.com

Deadwood Chamber of Commerce
767 Main St.
Deadwood 57732
(605) 578-1876
deadwood.com

Hill City Chamber of Commerce
23935 Hwy. 385
Hill City 57745
(605) 574-2368
hillcitysd.com

Hot Springs Area Chamber of Commerce
801 S. 6th St.
Hot Springs 57747
(605) 745-4140
hotsprings-sd.com

Lead Chamber of Commerce
106 W. Main St.
Lead 57754
(605) 584-1100
leadmethere.org

Rapid City Convention & Visitors Bureau
444 Mt. Rushmore Rd. N
Rapid City 57709
(605) 718-8484
visitrapidcity.com

Visit Spearfish
603 N. Main
Spearfish 57783
(605) 717-9294
visitspearfish.com

First Gold Hotel
270 Lower Main St.
(605) 578-9777
firstgold.com
Moderate

Historic Bullock Hotel
633 Main St.
(605) 578-1745
historicbullock.com
Moderate

The Lodge at Deadwood
100 Pine Crest
(877) 393-5634
deadwoodlodge.com
Moderate

Mineral Palace Hotel & Gaming
601 Main St.
(605) 578-2036
mineralpalace.com
Moderate

HILL CITY

Best Western Golden Spike Inn
106 Main St.
(605) 574-2577
bestwestern.com
Moderate

Emerald Pines Refuge B&B
23836 Emerald Pines Dr.
(605) 574-4462
emeraldpinesrefuge.com
Moderate

Mountains to Prairies B&B
200 E. Main St.
(605) 574-2424
mountainstoprairiesbb
.com
Moderate

HOT SPRINGS

FlatIron Historic Sandstone Inn
745 N. River St.
(877) 548-2822
flatiron.biz
Moderate

KEYSTONE

Elk Ridge Bed & Breakfast
12741 Matthew Ct.
(605) 574-2320
erbnb.com
Moderate

K Bar S Lodge
434 Old Hill City Rd.
(866) 522-7724
kbarslodge.com
Moderate

LEAD

Barefoot Resort
21111 Barefoot Loop
(605) 584-1577
barefootresort.com
Moderate

Spearfish Canyon Lodge
10619 Roughlock Falls Rd.
(605) 584-3435
spfcanyon.com
Moderate

RAPID CITY

Adoba Eco Hotel Rapid City
445 Mt. Rushmore Rd.
(605) 348-8300
adobahotelrapidcity.com
Moderate

Backroads Inn and Cabins
13350 Silver Mountain Rd.
(605) 342-2246
cabinsoftheblackhills.com

Black Forest Inn B&B Lodge
23191 Hwy. 385
(800) 888-1607
blackforestinn.net
Moderate

Grand Gateway
1721 N. LaCrosse St.
(877) 742-1300
grandgatewayhotel.com
Inexpensive to moderate

Holiday Inn Rushmore Plaza
505 N. 5th St.
(877) 859-5095
rushmoreplaza.com
Moderate

Summer Creek Inn and Spa
23204 Summer Creek Dr.
(605) 574-4408
summercreekinn.com
Moderate

Willow Springs Cabin B&B
11515 Sheridan Lake Rd.
(605) 342-3665
willowspringscabins.com
Moderate

SPEARFISH

Hampton Inn
240 N. 27th St.
(605) 271-3622
hamptoninn3.hilton.com
Moderate

Orchard Creek Cottages
514 Mason St.
(605) 642-4234
orchardcreekcottages
.com
Moderate

STURGIS

Holiday Inn Express & Suites
2721 Lazelle St.
(605) 347-4140
hiesturgis.com
Moderate

Where to Eat in Western South Dakota

CUSTER

Baker's Bakery & Cafe
541 Mt. Rushmore Rd.
(605) 673-2235
bakersbakerycafe.com
Inexpensive

Bitter Esters Brewhouse
607 Mt. Rushmore Rd.
(605) 673-3433
bitterestersbrewhouse
.com
Moderate

Black Hills Burger and Bun Co.
29 N. 5th St.
(605) 673-3411
blackhillsburgerand
bun.com
Inexpensive

Bobkat's Purple Pie Place
19 Mt. Rushmore Rd.
(605) 673-4070
purplepieplace.com
Inexpensive

Buglin' Bull Restaurant & Sports Bar
511 Mt. Rushmore Rd.
(605) 673-4477
buglinbull.com
Moderate

Sage Creek Grille
611 Mt. Rushmore Rd.
(605) 673-2424
Moderate

Sylvan Lake Lodge
24572 Hwy. 87
(605) 574-2561
custerresorts.com
Moderate to expensive

DEADWOOD

Chubby Chipmunk Chocolates
420 Cliff St.
(605) 722-2447
chubbychipmunk.net
Moderate

Mustang Sally's
634 Main St.
(605) 578-2025
Inexpensive

Pump House Coffee & Deli
73 Sherman St.
(605) 571-1071
Inexpensive

Silverado Grand Buffet
709 Main St.
(605) 578-3670
silveradofranklin.com
Moderate

Tin Lizzie
555 Main St.
(605) 578-1715
tinlizzie.com
Moderate

HILL CITY

Bumpin Buffalo Bar & Grill
245 Main St.
(605) 574-4100
bumpinbuffalo.com
Moderate

Chute Rooster Steak House and Lounge
850 Chute Rooster Dr.
(605) 574-2122
chuterooster.com
Moderate

Slate Creek Grille and Dry Creek Coffee
198 Main St.
(605) 574-9422
slatecreekgrille.com
Moderate

Turtle Town
(Confectionery)
205 Main St.
(605) 574-4124
turtletown.com

KEYSTONE

Powder House Restaurant
PO Box 714
(605) 666-4646
powderhouselodge.com
Moderate

Ruby House Restaurant
124 Winter St.
(605) 666-4404
rubyhouserestaurant.com
Moderate

RAPID CITY

Arnold's Classic 1950s Diner
1940 N. LaCrosse St.
(605) 721-9452
Inexpensive

Black Hills Bagels
913 Mt. Rushmore Rd.
(605) 399-1277
blackhillsbagels.com
Inexpensive

Botticelli's Ristorante Italiano
523 Main St.
(605) 348-0089
botticelliristorante.net
Moderate

Colonial House Restaurant & Bar
2501 Mt. Rushmore Rd.
(605) 342-4640
colonialhousernb.com
Inexpensive

Everest Cuisine
2328 W. Main St.
(605) 343-4444
theeverestcuisine.com
Moderate

**Philly Ted's
Cheesesteaks and Subs**
1415 N. Lacrosse St.
Suite 4
(605) 348-6113
Inexpensive

ROCKERVILLE
The Gaslight
13490 Main St.
(605) 343-9276
Moderate

SPEARFISH
Bay Leaf Cafe
126 W. Hudson St.
(605) 642-5462
bayleafcafe.net
Moderate

**Dough Trader Pizza
Company**
543 W. Jackson Blvd.
(605) 642-2175
doughtrader.com
Moderate

**Green Bean
Coffeehouse**
304 N. Main St.
(605) 717-3636
Inexpensive

**Wide Mouth Frog
Bakery & Wine Bar**
3015 E. Colorado Blvd.
(605) 559-1008
Moderate

Sanford's Grub and Pub
545 W. Jackson Blvd.
(605) 642-3204
Moderate

STURGIS
Jambonz Grill & Pub
2214 Junction Ave.
(605) 561-1100
Inexpensive

**Loud American
Roadhouse**
1305 Main St.
(605) 720-1500
loudamericanroadhouse
.com
Inexpensive

WALL
Red Rock Restaurant
506 Glenn St.
(605) 279-2388
Moderate

Western North Dakota

Wallace Stegner once said that the West is America, only more so. In North Dakota you're privileged to experience an inconceivably huge chunk of the real West. There is no drugstore-cowboy posturing here. Ranchmen and -women work tirelessly, as do the oil industry workers who have come from around the country to work hard and support families back home during a nationwide recession.

The traveler will find long, lonely stretches of land—just like those that the settlers and Plains Indians of the past encountered—west of the Missouri River. Towns steadily grow to accommodate oil industry workers; you might see the flame of a natural gas flare on the horizon, and lightning strikes in the jagged peaks of the Badlands can ignite ancient coal veins that smolder for years.

It serves the soul well to roam over the plains of North Dakota. To feel small. To feel vulnerable. To find strength. To breathe deeply and embrace the wide-open landscape as it ripples to the horizon. The self-reliance espoused by Ralph Waldo Emerson years ago is infectious in North Dakota. As Teddy Roosevelt once said, "My experience when I lived and worked in North Dakota with my fellow

WESTERN NORTH DAKOTA

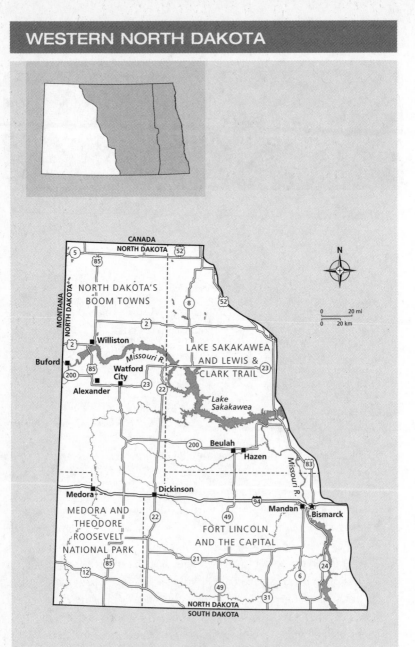

ranchmen, on what was then the frontier, was the most important educational asset of my life."

Medora

South Dakota may have Mount Rushmore and Badlands that look like a galactic moonscape, but when North Dakota pulls out its big guns for tourism promotion, you can be sure that *Medora* will hover at the top of the list. For families, Medora offers a sweet nostalgia trip, a throwback to friendly small towns and tourism from an earlier generation and providing a charming hub for exploring North Dakota's kinder, gentler Badlands. Still rugged and awe-inspiring, the Badlands are also rounder, greener, and filled with more wildlife than what you see in South Dakota's Badlands.

The frontier town of Medora was founded in 1883 and named for the wife of the ambitious Marquis de Mores, a French nobleman whose thirst for adventure was matched only by his intense desire to be the richest financier in the world. When he and his beautiful wife arrived in the tiny, tough railroad town of Little Missouri, he envisioned a unique meat-processing scheme that would process and ship meat—rather than cattle—in refrigerated train cars to the East Coast. Local residents called de Mores "the crazy Frenchman," yet it was Little Missouri that became a deserted pile of splinters when de Mores built his town of Medora and had a population of 251 only a year later. In addition to the meat-packing plant, it boasted a newspaper, a brickyard, several stores and saloons, a hotel, and St. Mary's Catholic Church.

TOP HITS IN WESTERN NORTH DAKOTA

Dakota Dinosaur Museum

Fort Union Trading Post
National Historic Site

Lake Sakakawea

Maltese Cross Cabin

Medora Musical

Theodore Roosevelt National Park

Tobacco Gardens

The marquis often entertained neighbor Theodore Roosevelt at his 26-room chateau that overlooked Medora. De Mores and the man who would be president did not always see eye to eye on everything, but they did agree on socializing over iced champagne. De Mores's dreams proved to be farfetched, however, and he shut down the meat-packing operation in 1886. He and his wife returned to France the following year. Medora became another pale western ghost town when the wicked winter of 1887–1888 wiped out most of the ranchers' herds. The De Mores's home, with its sweeping views of the valley, along with historical exhibits and the towering brick chimney from the slaughtering plant, remind today's visitors of Medora's big dreams and ill-fated beginning.

The elegantly appointed, two-story de Mores chateau is now the *Chateau de Mores State Historic Site.* Lavish furnishings, Oriental carpets, and fine details in this frame house greeted the family when it arrived in 1884. For three years the family occupied the home seasonally, returning to New York during the winter months. The marquis and his wife loved hunting, music, and art. The chateau was given to the state in 1936. The interpretive center and chateau building are open for tours daily from May 16 through September 15. The interpretive center is open Tues through Sat year-round. Tours are $7 for adults, $3 for children 6–15. Call (701) 623-4355 for seasonal hours or visit nd.gov/hist.

Medora's revival began in 1958, when the *Burning Hills Amphitheatre* was built and the drama *Old Four Eyes* was presented to mark Roosevelt's 100th birthday. Four years later, history buff and businessman Harold Schafer reignited de Mores's dream and brought the town back to life, this time as a premier vacation destination. In 1986 the Schafer family donated its holding in Medora to the Theodore Roosevelt Medora Foundation, a public, nonprofit organization that operates the public attractions and provides a one-stop spot for visitors (701-623-4444; medora.com).

In the summer of 1995, the *Harold Schafer Heritage Center,* 335 4th St., opened to tell the story of Schafer's engaging life at his Gold Seal Company (which sold Mr. Bubble bubble bath, Glass Wax, and Snowy Bleach worldwide) and as the promoter of Medora, the state's leading tourist attraction. The center's *Sheila Schafer Gallery* shows art exhibits each year.

The biggest ticket around is still the *Medora Musical,* which hit its 50th anniversary in 2014 and still serves up a rollicking song-and-dance variety show peppered with patriotism, a few special effects, cowboys on real horses, aw-shucks humor, history, and North Dakota pride. It might look a little schmaltzy at first glance, but the spirit of it pulls you in, especially in its jaw-dropping setting carefully nestled into the Badlands. The dramatic escalator ride into the 2,900-seat amphitheater alone can trip its share of "wow"s from first-time visitors.

If you're a seasoned musical-goer, consider adding on a behind-the-scenes tour that starts at 6:30 before the show. Tour tickets are $5 for adults; $2 for students. Tours begin at the *Medora Musical Welcome Center* and last about 40 minutes. Tickets to the musical are $31-$35 for adults; $14-$16 for students 7-17. Preschoolers are always free, and kids are free Wed and Sun.

Showtime is 8:30 p.m. nightly in the *Burning Hills Amphitheatre,* with performances running mid-June through Labor Day weekend.

It's easy to make a full evening of a musical outing. You can start by watching chefs plunge steaks speared by pitchforks into vats of boiling oil—a pitchfork fondue—before dining on the nearby Tjaden Terrace with some of the most scenic views anywhere.

If you're craving a more intimate date-night kind of dinner, head to the *Rough Riders Hotel,* 301 3rd Ave. You can start with drinks in the saloon with a pressed-tin ceiling, then head to dinner in the dining room, which serves walleye, duck, and buffalo rib eye.

What's in a Name?

On March 2, 1861, President James Buchanan signed the bill creating the Dakota Territory. It originally included the area covered today by both Dakotas as well as Montana and Wyoming. The word *Dakota* means "friend" in the Dakota (Sioux) Indian language.

Beginning about 1887, efforts were made to bring Dakota into the Union as both a single state and as two states. The latter was successful, and on November 2, 1889, both North Dakota and South Dakota were admitted.

Since President Benjamin Harrison went to great lengths to obscure the order in which the statehood proclamations were signed, the exact order in which the states entered is unknown. However, because of the alphabetical position, North Dakota is often considered the 39th state.

Once a cozy nine-room seasonal hotel, Rough Riders underwent a major expansion with 68 new rooms and a conference center in the early 2010s that allows it to stay open year-round. Despite the new construction, the hotel kept its Victorian western look (oak armoires, shower tiles with Teddy Roosevelt's ranch brand) while adding the modern comforts of pillow-top beds and flat-screen TVs. If you want the best room, ask for No. 501, a king corner suite with seven windows facing the Badlands. Or try No. 503 with a balcony where you can pretend you're Theodore Roosevelt giving his presidential pitch in 1900.

The biggest winter event is the *Old-Fashioned Cowboy Christmas* the first weekend in December, with most of the events taking place in the community center. The highlight is sleigh or hay rides, but the event also includes an antiques and crafts show, as well as a Christmas quilt show, a family Christmas dance, ice skating, a cowboy poker game, cowboy poetry, and a Best of the West doll show. The kids are entertained with a children's story hour and a chalk-art drawing session. To round off the activities, the chamber hosts a traditional Christmas supper, Western Parade of Lights, and a cowboy Christmas jamboree. In conjunction with all the holiday wonderment, the chamber honors a veteran each year.

trivia

The highest point in the state of North Dakota is straight south of the national park near the tiny town of Amidon. White Butte, south of town and east of US 85, rises to 3,506 feet. You can pitch a tent about 16 miles south of it at Butte View State Campground.

Just about everything in Medora sits within easy walking distance, including a handful of shops ranging from candy stores and a bookshop to western wear.

Rough Riders Gift Shop features jewelry, including Landstrom's original Black Hills gold and sterling silver. And you must certainly visit the good folks at Corner Corral to dress up right in Medora. The store is filled with outerwear and sharp-looking western wear for men, women, and children.

Look for Teddy Roosevelt's historic *Maltese Cross Cabin* at 315 2nd Ave. by the national park's visitor center. When Roosevelt first came to the Badlands, he was an asthmatic young man who scoured the wild ravines—in bad weather for two weeks—until he finally found and shot a bison. The adventure thrilled Roosevelt so much that before he left he bought a cattle ranch about 7 miles south of Medora and renamed it the Maltese Cross Ranch near the Little Missouri River.

At Roosevelt's request, ranch managers built a 1½-story cabin complete with shingle roof and cellar. In its day the cabin was considered a mansion, for it had wooden floors and three separate rooms. The steeply pitched roof, an anomaly on the Dakota plains, provided an upstairs sleeping loft for ranch hands. You can see the desk at which Teddy wrote his book *Hunting Trips of the Ranchman,* which he completed between 1884 and 1885. The rocking chair in the living room was his favorite piece of furniture. During the Roosevelt presidency the Maltese Cross Cabin was exhibited in Portland, Oregon, and St. Louis, Missouri. It was then moved to the capitol grounds in Bismarck and finally relocated to its present site and renovated in 1959.

When Roosevelt returned to North Dakota for the second year after the buffalo hunt, it was for far grimmer reasons. His wife and mother had died within hours of each other, and Roosevelt was inconsolably grief-stricken. In a move to further isolate himself from civilization and his own pain, he bought another cattle operation, the **Elkhorn Ranch,** 35 miles north of Medora. The ranch buildings no longer exist but interpretive signs tell

Riding Tall in the Saddle

When in Theodore Roosevelt National Park, do as Teddy did—go on horseback. The South Unit of the park features more than 80 miles of marked horse trails, and endless unmarked trails carved by the park's buffalo herd. Riders are permitted in all areas of the park except for the camping and picnicking areas and nature trails. A group horse campground is available in the South Unit by reservation, and backcountry horse camping is allowed. The Peaceful Valley Ranch offers horse rentals and guided trail rides. Popular riding areas include Petrified Forest, Peaceful Valley Ranch, Halliday Wells, and Painted Canyon. Be on the lookout for bison, wild horses, long-horned cattle, elk, and deer.

Call the Peaceful Valley Ranch (701-623-4568; ctctel.com/peacefulvalley) for trail rides May 1 to October 1. A variety of rides and trails are available: You can ride across the high plateaus to the largest outcropping of petrified stumps in the forest or see trails used by the pioneers to cross the Badlands. Medora Riding Stables also offers rides, but they fill fast, so reservations are recommended (800-633-6721; medora.com).

TOP ANNUAL EVENTS

Cowboy Poetry Gathering
Medora
(701) 623-4910

The Fort Union Trading Post
Rendezvous held annually in June
(701) 572-9083

Frontier Army Days
Every summer in Fort Abraham Lincoln
Park, Mandan
(701) 667-6340

Old-Fashioned Cowboy Christmas
Early December
Medora
(701) 623-4910

The Roughrider Days Rodeo
Held over the Fourth of July weekend
Dickinson
(800) HELLO-ND

where the house and outbuildings were. You can visit the ranch, but be forewarned that it can be reached only on rough dirt roads. Call the visitor center at (701) 623-4466 for conditions before attempting the trip.

Teddy's cattle ranches during the late 1800s let him practice and nurture his philosophy of practical conservation. He also was aware of the problems of the West and possessed the rugged spirit of its settlers, an enviable asset when he became president in 1901. His time in North Dakota greatly shaped his groundbreaking conservation efforts that helped national parks and the nation's wildlife thrive in the 20th century.

Theodore Roosevelt National Park

"It was still the Wild West in those days . . . and ours was the glory of work and the joy of living," Theodore Roosevelt said of North Dakota. The former president knew the Badlands intimately, and his passion for these endless buttes and clay-streaked bluffs inextricably pulses throughout the region. You'll start to understand it with that first sweeping glance across *Theodore Roosevelt National Park's Painted Canyon* overlook and rest area just off I-94. To truly appreciate the landscape, you need to enter the park, hike its buttes, watch bison take a dirt bath in a wallow, and photograph majestic wild horses as they trot alongside a curve in the Little Missouri River.

The park is divided into three distinctly different units: the South Unit (accessible from Medora via I-94), the Elkhorn Ranch site, and the North Unit, which can be reached via US 85 near **Watford City.** Although the park is open year-round, some portions of the road system may be closed during winter. The park includes 110 square miles of Badlands and is considered one of the nation's least crowded gems. Since the withdrawal of an ancient salt sea 130 million years ago, rain, wind, and the Little Missouri River have shaped a curious, mystical landscape in the Badlands. Exposed seams of lignite coal create a band of black below one ridge. On another butte, clay is baked into red scoria, the result of smoldering lignite, ignited by lightning strikes or prairie fires. The burning of lignite beds through the ages has helped lend color as well as shape to the Badlands, as the baked rocks become more resistant to erosion than the neighboring layers. Painted canyons, ash coulees, and broad cottonwood river bends are breathtaking.

Hit the Maah Daah Hey Trail

My first taste of mountain biking was on a section of the 140-mile **Maah Daah Hey Trail** near Medora. It took almost 30 minutes to ease the death grip I had on the brakes. When I finally relaxed and let myself speed down the hills and let momentum carry me up new ones, it was an exhilarating breakthrough. I've been hooked ever since. Dakota Cyclery (701-623-4808; dakotacyclery.com) offers great introductory experiences for beginners and families, along with bike rentals, shuttles, and anything an expert will need, from repair parts to having your gear waiting at your campsite when you're ready for an epic ride. They're open from 9 a.m. to 6 p.m. daily May through Oct. People come from across the nation to tackle this trail, following the iconic posts marked with the simple outline of a turtle. In the Mandan language, *maah daah hey* means a place that will be around for a long time. We can only hope so. While the scenery isn't as colorfully intense as the red rock in the Moab, Utah, mountain biking mecca, North Dakota makes up for it with solitude and only slightly more muted colors in this gorgeous and challenging terrain. One section, "The Deuce," climbs buttes and zig-zags through switchbacks in the 30-mile extension south from Sully's Creek State Park to the US Forest Service's Burning Coal Vein Campground. The trail also is popular with horseback riders. The trail extends north to the USDA Forest Service CCC Campground in McKenzie County 20 miles south of Watford City. For maps or more information, contact the US Forest Service at (701) 250-4443 or fs.fed.us, or the Maah Daah Hey Trail Association at mdhta.com.

North Dakotans like to call the park Rough Rider Country, and no doubt it was the rough-and-tumble lifestyle of the West and the starkness of the North Dakota Badlands that primed the young Roosevelt for a much larger role later in his life, that of a Rough Rider leading his men to battle in Cuba. The *Medora South Unit Visitor Center* (701-623-4466; nps.gov/thro) at 315 2nd Ave. in Medora will formally introduce you to Teddy, and if you haven't already fallen madly in love with the former president, you certainly will here. While the presidential history is fascinating, the highlight for most visitors is the national park's awe-inspiring 36-mile scenic loop drive through the wide expanse of the park's South Unit.

Along this paved road you will see panoramic views of the Badlands with plenty of opportunities to get out and hike through this 46,158-acre section. A word to the wise: Drive carefully and make sure you're not in a hurry. On my first visit to the park, a herd of bison took its sweet time crossing the road. A few shaggy males rumbled so close to our vehicle and seemed so huge, it was like we were in a sardine tin. Don't even think about getting out to shoot a photo unless it's from the car or a good distance away with a telephoto lens. They look tame (and even slow) until you see a National Park Service clip of ignorant tourists getting swiftly head-butted like a game-winning field goal.

You'll likely see elk and deer in the park, as well, especially during early morning or late afternoon drives when wildlife are most active. Park rangers can clue you in on where the wild horses were recently spotted and show you where to watch for prairie dog towns. The prairie dogs are especially entertaining as they interact and pop up and down in their intricate towns. They may seem cute and timid, but do keep your distance to avoid

Vibrant Souvenirs

Pottery lovers head 25 miles west of the national park on I-94 to visit the studio of Tama Smith at 127 E. Main St. in the tiny border town of Beach. A self-proclaimed "fire potter," Smith's most distinctive palette of colors is prairie fire. The mix of brilliant red, rich ochre, and earthy browns graces her pots, vases, mugs, and other practical works of art. Her studio is open 8 a.m. to 6 p.m. daily through the summer and 9 a.m. to 5 p.m. Mon through Sat Oct through Dec. Call (888) 229-9496 for winter hours; prairiefirepottery.com.

painful bites or disease. Also be on the watch for prairie rattlesnakes, which might strike if surprised on the trails.

The North Dakota Game and Fish Department urges people not to touch wildlife, especially baby animals that appear to be abandoned. It is illegal to take wild animals home, and captive animals returned to the wild will lack the necessary survival skills. Motorists also should watch for deer along roadways throughout the entire region—not just the park. June and November are the peak months for deer-vehicle accidents when deer are more on the move.

If you take US 85 north from Belfield, you're well on your way to the **North Unit of Theodore Roosevelt National Park.** The highway first will take you through **Grassy Butte,** where you can find the **Old Sod Post Office.** Construction materials were scarce in 1912, so the Grassy Butte Post Office was built of logs and sod. The building was used until 1964. Now listed on the National Register of Historic Places as a historic site, the building serves as a museum that is filled with sundry antiques and relics from the 1800s and early 1900s. The museum is open 9 a.m. to 4 p.m. July 1 through Labor Day, and weekends in May and June. Admission is free. Call (701) 863-6604 for more information.

In the less-visited North Unit of Theodore Roosevelt National Park, the buttes are taller and certain areas are heavily forested. Squaw Creek (1.1 miles) and Caprock Coulee (1.5 miles) nature trails are self-guided and interpret the Badlands, coulees, and breaks. Upper Caprock Coulee, Achenbach, and Buckhorn trails will take you into the backcountry. A 14-mile scenic drive has turnouts with spectacular views and interpretive sites.

North Dakota's Boom Towns

Oil has boomed in northwestern North Dakota. The epicenter? Williston, which fittingly dubs itself "Boomtown." This is the fastest-growing community in America's fastest-growing state, according to CNN Money reports. In this once-sleepy farm community, new fracking technology has made it possible to tap the Bakken formation that stretches below much of northwestern North Dakota with an estimated 24 billion barrels of oil.

Williston grew 10.7 percent between July 2012 and July 2013 (about 2,500 new residents), according to US Census reports, and that kind of growth is rippling across the state. Dickinson is No. 2 right behind Williston—both considered "micropolitans"—and Minot ranked No. 5 nationwide for micro growth in 2013. It's affecting the big cities, too, with Fargo-Moorhead and Bismarck-Mandan ranked as the No. 4 and No. 5 fastest-growing metropolitan areas in the country in 2013.

After some tough years of trying to meet the high demand for housing as workers flooded to oil fields from across a nation stalled with a recession, housing is catching up. For travelers, that means it's possible to get a hotel room again. The roads and fields may look a little more crowded with oil trucks and equipment, but you'll also find more places to eat and more things to do as the entire region grows. And the natural beauty of national wildlife refuges, state parks, Lake Sakakawea, private ranches, and quirky attractions endure and beckon people to explore oil country.

Watford City, which bills itself as a slice of the New Old West, provides a gateway to the northern section of Theodore Roosevelt National Park and to the Bakken oil field as it sprawls west and north. You can get a feel for the grit and masculinity of the area with a hand-cut steak, western-themed food, and a slice of community history through old photos on display at *Outlaws' Bar and Grill* and Six Shooters' Showhall. The historic theme includes a coatroom jail cell (701-842-6859; outlawsbarngrill.com).

You can see North Dakota's largest fossil at *Long X Visitor Center and Museum* in Watford City (100 2nd St. SW; 701-444-5804). The petrified bald cypress tree stump is estimated at 17,000 pounds and measures about 6 feet in diameter and 8 feet tall. The 60-million-year-old fossil was discovered in the Badlands south of Watford City during an archaeological dig in 2001. You'll also find tourist information and the Pioneer Museum of McKenzie County, which has added an oil exhibit. The new exhibit, which pays homage to North Dakota's jump to No. 2 in US oil production, includes a replica of an oil rig, industry information, and replicas of drilling bits. Hours are 9 a.m. to 9 p.m. Mon through Sat year-round and 1 to 5 p.m. Sun from Memorial Day through Labor Day. No admission fee.

Swing into the *McKenzie County Heritage Park* for a look at how hunters, trappers, and pioneers survived life on the northern plains. Or follow US 85 back south to some of the state's best modern hunting and fishing grounds. Mourning dove, sharp-tailed grouse, Hungarian partridge, and ring-necked pheasant are just some of the upland bird-hunting opportunities.

Wing-shooters take to the fields and prairie water holes on the first of September, as mourning dove hunting traditionally kicks off North Dakota's shotgun season. Drive almost anywhere among the rolling green grasslands, and you'll be sure to see and hear the honk of pheasants.

Belfield, some 18 miles east of Medora and the Badlands south unit, is a magnet for weary travelers and hunters with ***Trapper's Kettle*** (701-575-8585) restaurant and gift shop. It incorporates the hunting/ trapping theme throughout its decor and menu. Authentic traps serve as door pulls in the restaurant, and the

hunting101

For more information on resident and nonresident hunting requirements and licenses, call the North Dakota Game and Fish Department at (701) 328-6300 or check out the website at gf.nd.gov.

cedar dining tables have inlaid traps. Examples of taxidermy of almost every animal imaginable seem to stare vacantly in the dining areas. The hearty and well-prepared food is stick-to-your-ribs good here; the thick and beefy chili is served in a crock with grated cheese—perfect winter fare. Pan-fry dishes and mini-kettle soups also hit the spot. Prices are moderate.

Bright orange is the fall fashion color of choice in these parts as hunters remind their buddies to reset watches to mountain standard time and team up to land the biggest bucks. White-tailed deer are found almost everywhere, but the mule deer tend to cluster in the jagged country of the Badlands and other broken terrain. Lightning-swift antelope inhabit the western borders of the region, and the regal white elk and bighorn sheep confine themselves primarily to the Badlands and the Killdeer Mountains.

Dickinson

Dickinson (19 miles west of Belfield off I-94) has surged from 17,787 people in about 2010 to 20,836 by 2013. It still hangs onto its cowboy and cowgirl personality, and considers itself the rodeo capital of North Dakota with one of the state's biggest events—***Roughrider Days Rodeo***—and additional festivities during the Fourth of July weekend.

Dickinson's biggest claim to fame for most visitors is its ***Dakota Dinosaur Museum*** (701-225-3466; dakotadino.com), a fantastic earth science

Catch a Rodeo

About 50 rodeos throughout the state attract hundreds of cowboys each year. The word *rodeo* is actually derived from a Spanish word meaning "roundup." The history of the rodeo traces back to the 1800s when most ranches had untamed horses (or broncos). Cattle outfits often challenged one another to bronc-riding contests in which cowboys could prove their mettle. Eventually someone reckoned there would be good money to be made if there was an admission charge to see the battle between the bronc and the cowboy.

Rodeos remain a popular, breathtaking event in both North Dakota and South Dakota. Basically there are four types of rodeo: high school, college, amateur, and professional. For a listing of rodeos in North Dakota, check the North Dakota Rodeo Association's website at ndrodeo.com.

museum that features dinosaur bones found in North Dakota, including a complete triceratops, which lived in the Badlands when they were a swampy and warm area, and a duck-billed edmontosaurus. Ten other full-scale dinosaurs, a complete fossil rhino, and rocks and minerals are impressive displays as well. Located right on I-94 at 200 E. Museum Dr., it's attached to the Joachim Regional Museum complex. It is open 9 a.m. to 5 p.m. daily May 1 through Labor Day. Admission is $8 for adults, $5 for children 3–12.

The dinosaur museum is adjacent to the ***Joachim Regional Museum and Prairie Outpost Park*** (dickinsonmuseumcenter.org), where through a self-guided tour you get an idea of how rugged pioneers settled southwestern North Dakota. The museum offers tours of a Norwegian *stabbur* (storage house), a Germans-from-Russia homestead house, a one-room schoolhouse, a railroad depot, a church, and other buildings that reflect the area's ethnic and immigrant past. For more information call (701) 456-6225.

If you travel 3 miles west on I-94, then 1 mile south, you'll be at ***Patterson Reservoir*** (701-225-2074), ideal for swimming, fishing, boating, camping, and picnicking during the summer. The reservoir is part of the Missouri River Valley reclamation project. The park is open daily June through Aug.

Back on the interstate, two exits east of the Enchanted Highway is ***Richardton,*** population 625. The twin spires of its historic **St. Mary's Catholic Church** on 418 3rd Ave. W are quiet testaments to the faith that has steadfastly guided Dakotans through lean and prosperous times.

Benedictine monks built this stunning structure a century ago on what's known as Russian Ridge, which stretches for dozens of miles and divides the Heart River basin in the south from the Knife River basin in the north. The original church and its immovable central altar are the focal point amid the vaulted ceilings, original medallion paintings, ornate altars, and more than 50 stained-glass windows. St. Mary's is a wonderful example of Bavarian-Romanesque–style architecture. Today the church is lovingly tended by about 35 resident monks living in the Assumption Abbey, which is connected to the church. They warmly welcome visitors. Be sure to see

Enchanted Highway

About 20 miles east of Dickinson at exit 72, a 110-foot-tall sculpture of Canada geese looms over the interstate, dwarfing the cars that pull over to admire it and drawing attention to one of America's most interesting, quirky, and endearing stretches of roadside art: the 32-mile *Enchanted Highway.* This ribbon of rural road stretches from the freeway to tiny *Regent* with North Dakota–inspired sculptures pulling you forward as they rise from the wide-open rolling landscape about every 10 to 15 miles.

Former teacher and school principal Gary Greff—with no welding or art training—was worried his hometown of Regent (population 200) would disappear like so many other farm-dependent towns. One day he saw drivers pulling over to snap pictures of a giant figure of a man created out of hay bales. He then dreamed up the idea of metal sculptures. In 1991, he finished the first sculpture of a tin family made from used farm equipment and erected it a few miles out of Regent. He has built and put up seven more in the years since with each getting more complex, more artsy, and less folksy. Look for Teddy Roosevelt, pheasants, deer, Canada geese, and the delightful "Fisherman's Dream," featuring a lively group of fish made from recycled scrap metal, oil well pipes, drums, and tanks. Go ahead and ham it up beneath the 40-foot-tall grasshoppers, which represent one of the Midwest's most devastating plagues. You can lighten the mood with a B-movie moment, looking miniature and posing with mock looks of terror beneath Godzilla-size grasshoppers.

Despite the allure of the Enchanted Highway, Regent remains a tiny town but nudges up in charm and appeal with a Metal Magic gift shop and Greff's newest creation: the Enchanted Castle hotel, Excalibur Steakhouse, and Medievals Tavern that transformed the town's former brick school at 601 Main St. Call (701) 563-4858 for more information and to make a reservation.

The Great Survivor

As many as 60 million bison once roamed over one-third of the entire land mass of North America. It was not unusual for a herd to contain 4 million animals and cover an area 50 miles long and 20 miles wide.

On the Dakota prairies, bison provided food, clothing, shelter, arrow points, ropes, and ornaments for the Plains Indians. As late as 1866 a huge herd of bison estimated at 100,000 was sighted 18 miles north of Fargo. Often mistakenly called buffalo, bison are not related to the true buffalo of Africa and Asia. Their ancestors, wild cattle that found their way across the now-vanished land bridge from Siberia to Alaska, came to North America during the Pleistocene era.

Prized for their meat and hides and as trophies, bison were hunted almost to extinction; by 1891 the US bison population had been reduced to a mere 541 animals. The species was saved from annihilation by concerned conservationists, ranchers, and lovers of the outdoors who protected the remaining bison, gradually replenishing their number and building today's herds.

their gift shop, printing facility, wine cellar, church, and library. Nuns of the Benedictine order at nearby Sacred Heart Monastery also welcome visitors. Call (701) 974-3315 for an appointment or visit assumptionabbey.com.

Lewis & Clark Trail

Whether you head north of Theodore Roosevelt National Park or follow the Missouri River from the east, you'll find many of North Dakota's most historic and storied places by following the *Lewis and Clark Trail* (lewis andclarktrail.com).

The explorers and their crew bravely headed across uncharted territory to seek a route west across the continent from St. Louis to the Pacific Ocean, meticulously recording their discoveries and adventures along the way. The Lewis and Clark Trail comprises two developed highways along the Missouri River. The highway numbers—1804 and 1806—appropriately match the years that the explorers entered and returned to North Dakota. ND 1804 follows the eastern side of the Missouri River, while ND 1806 follows the western side. Historical sites and recreation can be discovered along both banks of the river.

Fort Union and Fort Buford

On the far western border of the state, astounding history unfolds at the **Fort Union Trading Post National Historic Site** (701-572-9083 or nps .gov/fous), which stands near the confluence of the Yellowstone and Missouri Rivers in the town of **Buford.** Open daily year-round, the site is accessible from ND 1804, a 24-mile drive southwest from Williston. From 1829 to 1867, the Fort Union Trading Post was the "vastest and finest" of a string of trading posts along the northern rivers. In a typical year more than 25,000 buffalo robes would change hands here, along with iron tools, guns, blankets, and other manufactured goods. Twenty-foot-high whitewashed palisades, anchored by two-story stone bastions, surrounded Fort Union. Capitalist John Jacob Astor reasoned that the imposing structure would impress the local Native Americans. Here, Scots, Germans, French, and Spanish bargained with the Assiniboin, Crow, Cree, Blackfoot, and Sitting Bull's Hunkpapa band of Sioux.

Much of what we have learned about the cultures of the Northern Plains Indians comes from Fort Union's adventurous staff and often rich-and-famous guests. John James Audubon, Germany's Prince Maximilian, and renowned artists George Catlin and Karl Bodmer left lasting legacies in their

Glorious Golf Courses

North Dakota has three of the nation's top golf courses, which frame up some of the state's most stunning scenery. It costs $165 to play all of them with the Triple Golf Challenge.

The Links of North Dakota (701-568-2600; thelinksofnorthdakota.com) boasts a pure links style, taking advantage of gently rolling bluff-tops overlooking Lake Sakakawea west of Williston on ND 1804.

Hawktree Golf Club (701-355-0995; hawktree.com) at 3400 Burnt Creek Loop near Bismarck also takes a links-style approach with greens tucked into the Burnt Creek Valley and framed in native grasses.

Bully Pulpit Golf Club (800-633-6721; medora.com), 3 miles south of Medora, looks the most dramatic with vibrant greens tucked into orange, red, and ochre colors of the Badlands.

Famous North Dakotans

Theodore Roosevelt isn't the only famous person to have kicked up his boots in North Dakota. Some famous North Dakotans include:

Warren Christopher, who served as deputy secretary of state in the Carter administration and was awarded the Medal of Freedom on January 16, 1981. In 1993, Christopher was sworn in as the 63rd US secretary of state.

Angie Dickinson, who has appeared in more than 50 major movies and television productions, but is best known for her roles in the movie *Dressed to Kill* and the TV series *Police Woman*.

Phil Jackson, who will go down in National Basketball Association history not only for his dynamic leadership, but also as the only person to both play for and coach teams (New York Knicks, Chicago Bulls, and Los Angeles Lakers) to titles for the NBA and the Continental Basketball Association.

Louis L'Amour, the award-winning western author and screenwriter, who published more than 400 short stories and more than 100 novels. He wrote 65 TV scripts and sold more than 30 stories to the motion-picture industry, including *Hondo,* starring John Wayne.

Roger Maris, baseball's former single-season home-run king, who hit 61 home runs during the 1961 season while he was a member of the New York Yankees.

Lawrence Welk, who became one of the greatest entertainers in the world through his weekly TV show featuring his distinctive "champagne music."

paintings, sketches, and words about this incredible mosaic. You can enjoy the rich tapestry of culture and feel like a part of the past by timing a visit with the annual **Rendezvous** festival. The site is free and includes tours of Bourgeois House and visitor center and the Trade House with living history actors throughout the summer.

Trade flourished here until smallpox ravaged most of the trading tribes. The friendly trade ultimately ended when Fort Union was occupied by the 30th Wisconsin Infantry in 1864. The fort is open from 8 a.m. to 6:30 p.m. from Labor Day through Memorial Day and from 9 a.m. to 5:30 p.m. in the off-season. The Trade House, filled with replicated goods and a costumed interpreter acting as an 1850s trader, is open from 10 a.m. to 5:45 p.m. Memorial Day through Labor Day.

Fort Union dismantled the private enterprise to help construct the military's **Fort Buford,** now a state historic site about a mile upstream. The fort is probably best known as the place where Hunkpapa leader Sitting Bull surrendered in 1881. Chief Joseph also surrendered here after defeat in the Nez Perce War. Buildings here date from the 1870s. The site is open mid-May through mid-Sept. Admission is $5 for adults and $2.50 for children and includes admission to the **Missouri–Yellowstone Confluence Interpretive Center** half a mile away. The center is open year-round and includes exhibits on geology, prehistoric times, geography, and the impact of people, the river, and roads through the area. The best attraction, though, is the chance to see the same magnificent views that Lewis and Clark saw as they reached the confluence (701-572-9034; history.nd.gov).

Twenty-two miles northeast of Fort Buford on ND 1804 is **Williston,** a proud energy town at the epicenter of the oil boom, with a population that has gone from 14,716 in 2010 to 20,850 by 2013. Locals will assure you this isn't the city's first economic boom, and you can glimpse the town's past throughout the summer at the **Frontier Museum,** northwest of Spring Lake Park (6330 2nd Ave. W). The complex comprises a 1910 rural church, complete with furnishings, 2 modern buildings filled with artifacts, a 1903 two-story house filled with antique furniture, an 1887 grocery store, a restored Great Northern depot, and a complete country school. Call (701) 580-2415 for details. The **Williston Tourist Information Center** is housed in the Great Northern depot. Contact the Williston Convention and Visitors Bureau for more information, (800) 615-9041 or visitwilliston.com.

Lake Sakakawea

Williston sits along **Lake Sakakawea,** an artificial widening of the Missouri River named for the young Shoshone woman who guided the intrepid explorers Lewis and Clark from North Dakota to the Yellowstone River in 1805. Garrison Dam, built in 1947–1953, created the lake that's 200 miles long and covers 909 square miles. North Dakota's largest lake draws thousands of visitors each year for superb sailing, camping, hunting, and fishing.

Head 19 miles southeast of Williston on Highway 1804 to reach **Lewis and Clark State Park** on Lake Sakakawea. The explorers were here on April 17, 1805, and you can likewise enjoy the area by land or water. There's a marina and excellent fishing, including walleye, sauger, and northern pike, along with rare pallid sturgeon and ancient-looking paddlefish. There's also a campground, sleeping cabins, and a swimming beach. Winter visitors can snowshoe or cross-country ski, enjoying clear views of the Badlands' rugged buttes in the distance. Go to parkrec.nd.gov/parks/lcsp or call (701) 859-3071 for more details.

If all the Lewis and Clark sites leave you yearning for adventure, the folks at *Lund's Landing Lodge* 23 miles east of Williston on SD 1804 will take guests canoeing or kayaking on the same routes Lewis and Clark followed along Lake Sakakawea. Packages include lodging in their cedar cabins, plus breakfast and evening meals that are likely topped off with their beloved juneberry pie a la mode (701-568-3474; lundslanding.com).

On the south shore of the lake, *Tobacco Garden Bay* was once a stop for steamboats. It's now home to *Tobacco Gardens Resort and Marina* (701-842-4199; tobaccogardens.com), with a restaurant, more than 100 campsites, 2 log cabins, a bait shop, and playgrounds. Nearby, the 2.5-mile *Birnt Hills Trail* offers lovely scenic views of Lake Sakakawea. The name Tobacco Garden Bay is derived from the Sioux and Assiniboin Indian name for the reed that grew in the area.

Fort Berthold Reservation is home of the Three Affiliated tribes (Hidatsa, Arikara, and Mandan Indians) on Lake Sakakawea. The boundaries for the reservation have changed many times since its inception in 1880, and today the reservation encompasses 980,000 acres of tribally and individually owned lands. Historically the Mandan and Hidatsa Indians were a peaceful and agricultural group, stable and not as nomadic as the other Plains Indians. The Arikara, previously part of the Pawnee, separated from their relatives on the Loup River in Nebraska, worked their way north, and eventually joined the Hidatsa and Mandan Indians. At present about 3,696 of the tribes' members live on the reservation.

The *Three Affiliated Tribes Museum* (mhanation.com) is located on the Fort Berthold Reservation about 4 miles west of New Town on ND 23. One of the newest exhibits at the museum honors Fort Berthold World War I veterans. At that time Native Americans were not allowed to vote, yet they valiantly volunteered to serve their country. Memorabilia, photographs, and a 48-star US flag are highlights in the display. The museum is open mid-Apr through November 1. Call (701) 627-4477 for more information.

You can get a feel for the vastness and beauty of the tribes' historic communities with a visit to the *Knife River Indian Villages,* a national park that commemorates Native Americans. The remains of the villages arc along the banks of the Knife and Missouri Rivers, approximately 60 miles north of Bismarck. This is one of the oldest inhabited sites in North America, dating back 9,000 years. The Hidatsa and Mandan Indians, two of the oldest tribes on the continent, lived here in earth lodges, planting and harvesting gardens of corn, squash, beans, and sunflowers, which they exchanged in an ever-growing trading network between tribes. The locally produced Knife River flint has been traced to villages in the far southeastern part of the US. In the winter of 1804–1805, they were gracious hosts to Lewis and Clark and the Corps of Discovery, appointed by President Thomas Jefferson to explore and document America's new Louisiana Purchase territory. The Corps, which departed from near St. Louis, comprised 45 men operating a 55-foot keelboat and five other boats. After arriving in North Dakota for the winter, the explorers met the teenage girl Sakakawea (the Dakotas' alternate spelling of Sacagawea). She helped guide them through her native Shoshone lands as they searched for a water route to the Pacific Ocean. In April 1805 the group left Fort Mandan to continue the westward expedition. Lewis and Clark returned to North Dakota in August 1806 on their way back to St. Louis.

Knife River Indian Villages are part of North Dakota's American Legacy Tour. This world-class archaeological park boasts an earthen lodge at the modern visitor center. Trails lead to three village sites, where remnants of earth lodges and scattered bones and tools are easily seen. Ten miles of hiking and Nordic ski trails offer opportunities to view wildlife. The center is open 7:30 a.m. to 6 p.m. Memorial Day through Labor Day; excluding federal holidays, the center is open 8 a.m. to 4:30 p.m. the remainder of the year. For more information, go to nps.gov/knri or call (701) 745-3300.

Ready for another detour? Take ND 49 North to *Beulah,* which prides itself on being the Energy Capital of the Midwest—and for good reason. The Freedom Mine delivers 6 million tons of coal a year, mostly to the East Coast, but also fuels the nearby Antelope Valley Station, the Leland Olds Station, and the *Great Plains Synfuels Plant.* The synfuels plant consumes about 18,000 tons of lignite each day, turning the coal into 160 million cubic feet of synthetic natural gas. The natural gas is piped to Iowa and distributed to the eastern US. The **Great Plains Visitors Center** offers tours during the week. Call (701) 873-6667 or go to dakotagas.com or basicelectric.com for more details and to make an appointment.

Fort Mandan in Washburn (38 miles north of Bismarck) ranks among the best Lewis and Clark sites, re-creating the Corps of Discovery's winter camp with interpreters explaining their daily life and how they prepared to keep heading west in the spring. Admission is $7.50 for adults and $5 for children and is also good for admission into the nearby North Dakota **Lewis and Clark Interpretive Center.** Among its treasures are a canoe hand-carved from a cottonwood trunk, exhibits on steamboats and frontier trade, and the Berquist Gallery with rare watercolors from Swiss artist Karl Bodmer and written observations from German Prince Maximilian who both traveled through the area in 1833 and lived among the Native Americans. Hours are 9 a.m. to 5 p.m. Mon through Sat, and 9 a.m. to 5 p.m. Sun Memorial Day through Labor Day, and noon to 5 p.m. Sun in the off-season. (701-462-8535; fortmandan.com).

Another jumping-off point for the adventurous is the **Cross Ranch Nature Preserve,** managed by the Nature Conservancy. The ranch is located 30 miles north of Mandan via ND 1806 (a gravel road). This 6,000-acre nature preserve has mixed grass prairies, Missouri River floodplain forest, upland woody draws, and a bison herd. You can hike along self-guided nature trails. The preserve is open year-round to the public. Activities include bird-watching, canoeing, wildlife viewing, and cross-country skiing. The adjacent **Cross Ranch State Park** has a visitor center, 2 log cabins, 70 campsites (both electrical and modern and backcountry), 2 new yurts, plus picnicking and fishing along one of the last free-flowing, undeveloped stretches of the Missouri River. Call (701) 794-8741 or (701) 794-3731 for more information.

Fort Lincoln and the Capital

Most people think of South Dakota and Montana when they hear the name George Armstrong Custer, and for good reason. He led the army expedition into the Black Hills of South Dakota, where he had been sent to quell rumors of gold on parts of Sioux land. Instead he found that the prospectors' tales of extractable quantities of gold throughout the area were bona fide.

Later he and his troops were killed at the famous Battle of the Little Big Horn in Montana. Prior to these illustrious times in history, however, Custer was a young Civil War hero stationed at Fort Lincoln in what was then the Dakota Territory.

You can visit Custer's home at the *Fort Abraham Lincoln State Park* (701-667-6340; parkrec.nd.gov/Parks/FLSP.htm). The only thing dry about these tours might be a sample of hard tack or spicy jerky. The park in Mandan has some of the best living-history actors around, adding a sense of fun with stories on food, manners, day-to-day operations, and old-fashioned gossip from 1875 before the battle. You also can see the central barracks, the commissary store, the blockhouses standing guard over the old fort, and the cemetery where the marked graves of soldiers tell stories never found in history books. Each summer *Frontier Army Days* brings reenactment cavalry and infantry groups—the Frontier Army of Dakota—to Fort Abraham Lincoln for cannon firing, cavalry charges, drills, and the living history of Custer's pivotal presence in the development of the West.

The story of ill-fated Custer isn't the only legend at Fort Abraham Lincoln State Park. Mandan Indians settled *On-a-Slant Village* from 1575 to 1781 with a population once as high as 15,000. They farmed miles of Missouri River bottomland from 10 or 12 fortified cities here on the Slant River. The villages were empty and wiped out by disease by the time Lewis and Clark visited. At the pinnacle of their wealth and power, the Mandans built remarkably cozy, round earth lodges, like those seen at Knife River. On-a-Slant Village shows traces of 75 lodges, including the large ceremonial lodge that is 84 feet in diameter. Visitors also can capture the spirit of the time through trail rides. For more information, call (701) 667-6380 or visit fortlincoln.com.

In downtown Mandan at 401 Main St., the *Five Nations Arts Museum* (701-663-4663; fortlincoln.com) brings the talent of local tribes into the present tense. Inside, the soothing sounds of Native American music can be heard and an amazing selection of native arts and crafts admired. Located in an old train depot, the colonial revival redbrick building affords a unique sense of the architecture in 1929, the year in which it was built. The original interior is still gracefully intact, with stone floors, oak woodwork and trim, and a beautifully meticulous wainscoting of tan tiles. The gallery carries the work of more than 200 artists from the Mandan, Hidatsa, Arikara, Turtle

Mountain Band of Chippewa, and Lakota and Dakota tribes. The gallery is open 10 a.m. to 5 p.m. Mon through Sat.

Just across the Missouri River from Mandan, you'll find **Bismarck,** the state capital and, with 67,034 people, the second-largest city in North Dakota. Located on a natural ford of the Missouri River, Bismarck served as an early-day steamboat port. It was named for German chancellor Otto von Bismarck in hopes of encouraging German investment in the railroad.

For a sense of its history, head downtown to check out its growing number of restaurants and boutiques such as Junk Yard Chic (junkyardchic .com). You'll find plenty of casual, fun eateries, but a fine selection of elegant dining, too.

Among Bismarck's most venerable eateries is **Peacock Alley** (701-255-7917; peacock-alley.com) at 422 E. Main Ave. The former Patterson Hotel was once the off-hours headquarters for state and national politicos and hosted Theodore Roosevelt, Calvin Coolidge, John F. Kennedy, and Lyndon Johnson when they swept through on presidential campaign stops. It's still a posh gathering place, yet with a down-to-earth attitude. Entrees include pecan-crusted walleye, a cowboy rib eye using Dakota beef, sides such as three-cheese hash browns, and prime-beef sandwiches with homemade potato chips. Leave room for desserts such as fresh gelatos, beer bun dough-nut holes, and salted caramel bacon fritters.

For more cuisine worthy of an elegant date night, there's the **Pirogue Grille** at 121 N. 4th St. The chef constantly alters the menu to reflect sea-sonal, fresh ingredients. Choices might include a walleye sampler, house-made venison sausage, a wild rice salad, and bison medallions. For dessert, you can find everything from an artisanal Midwest cheese plate to choke-cherry and chocolate praline ice cream. It's a worthy splurge (701-223-3770; piroguegrille.com).

If warm weather has you craving a meal on an open patio, try the fes-tive Fiesta Villa, 411 E. Main Ave., in a mission-style depot (701-222-8075; fiesta-villa.com) or the Lüft Rooftop Beer Garden at Humpback Sally's, 510 E. Main (701-425-0844).

No trip to Bismarck would be complete without at least a walk or drive past the **State Capitol** (600 E. Boulevard Ave.). If you take 6th Street north 10 blocks, you'll run into Boulevard Avenue and be at the foot of the grand 19-story Capitol, which is topped with an observation tower. It's hard to miss the Skyscraper of the Prairies—it's the tallest building in North Dakota. Built in the 1930s, the Capitol boasts an art deco interior as fashion-forward now as it was then, with exotic wood paneling, stone, and metal. It's open year-round, and free tours are available every two hours from 9 a.m. to 3 p.m. Mon through Fri with expanded hours and weekend tours in the summer. Call (701) 328-2480.

Just in time for the state's 125th anniversary, the **North Dakota Heritage Center** debuted a $52 million expansion in November 2014. The additional 97,000 square feet allows the center to continue its already impressive exhibits on prehistoric times and the Ice Age, Plains Indians, the Old West, pioneers, and bonanza wheat farms while expanding to include more of the past century with World War II, emerging energy industries, and more. Keep an eye out for unique artifacts including a buffalo hide tipi, a mastodon skeleton, and the museum's famous mummified dinosaur that has been seen around the world. Many activities are hands-on (smell a buffalo wallow) and appeal to kids. A new area called the Treehouse is designed for preschool through 3rd-grade visitors and will open in 2015. The museum's open 8 a.m. to 5 p.m. Mon through Fri, 10 a.m. to 5 p.m. Sat and Sun. Admission is free. Call (701) 328-2666 or go to history .nd.gov for more information.

Just a few blocks south at 320 E. Avenue B is the **Former Governor's Mansion State Historic Site** (701-328-2666; history.nd.gov). This restored Victorian mansion was occupied by the state's first families from 1893 to 1960. Interpretive exhibits and governors' portraits now occupy this elegant three-story structure. Tour the mansion for free; it's open 10 a.m. to 5 p.m. Mon through Fri, noon to 4 p.m. Sat and Sun mid-May through mid-Sept.

oldredoldten

If you're itching to ditch the interstate and take the road less traveled on the way west from Mandan to Dickinson, grab the **Old Red Old Ten Scenic Byway.** It slows the pace and the scenery with pretty buttes, wildlife, prairie, and small towns. Go to oldredoldten.com for more information.

To see the great state of North Dakota in a similar fashion to Lewis and Clark over 200 years ago, hop aboard the **Lewis and Clark Riverboat,** a 150-passenger boat. The riverboat offers daily excursion cruises, dinner

BEST BISMARCK-MANDAN FAMILY ATTRACTIONS

North Dakota Heritage Center and the Capitol Grounds
612 E. Boulevard Ave.
Bismarck 58501
(701) 328-2666
history.nd.gov

Dakota Zoo
602 Riverside Park Rd.
Bismarck 58504
(701) 223-7543
dakotazoo.org

Fort Abraham Lincoln State Park
4480 Fort Lincoln Rd.
Mandan 58554
Park Information:
(701) 667-6340
fortlincoln.com

Fort Lincoln Trolley
Departs from 3rd Street
Station in Mandan summer
afternoons, early June
through Labor Day
(701) 663-9018

Raging Rivers Waterpark
2600 48th Ave. SE
Mandan 58554
(701) 663-3393
ragingriverswaterpark.com

Papa's Pumpkin Patch
5001 Fernwood Dr.
Bismarck 58503
(701) 222-1521
papaspumpkins.com
papaspolarpatch.com

cruises with pizza or barbecue, sunset cruises, and special events for the entire family from Apr through Sept. The riverboat is located at the Port of Bismarck on N. River Road, exit 157 off I-94. Prices start at $8.95 for kids (4–12) and $13.95 for adults taking a one-hour cruise. Call (701) 255-4233 or visit lewisandclarkriverboat.com.

North Dakota is again timelessly joined to South Dakota through the **Standing Rock Reservation,** which extends into both states. The people of the Standing Rock Sioux tribe are part of the Yanktonai and Teton Sioux Nation, which formerly controlled a vast domain that extended from the James River in North Dakota and South Dakota west to the Big Horn Mountains of Wyoming. In 1868 the Treaty of Fort Laramie reduced this area to the Great Sioux Reservation, setting the boundaries of a 25 million–acre tract that covered all of South Dakota west of the Missouri. When gold was discovered in the Black Hills, Congress ratified an invalid agreement and took the Black Hills shortly thereafter. The Great Sioux Reservation was broken into six small reservations in 1889, one of which is Standing Rock (formerly called the Grand River Agency), situated on the North Dakota–South Dakota border between the Badlands and the Missouri River. On the western edge of Fort Yates, located on the Missouri River on the North Dakota portion of the Standing Rock Indian Reservation, is the original gravesite of renowned Hunkpapa Sioux spiritual leader Sitting Bull.

You can arrange a tour of the reservation and sites along the Standing Rock Scenic Byway at the new visitor center on the Sitting Bull College Campus in Fort Yates. The center is open from 8 a.m. to 5 p.m. Mon through Fri. It's also a good place to check for campsites or rooms at Prairie Knights Casino and Resort (800-425-8277; prairieknights.com) or to check on pow-wows, rodeos, and other special events in the area (701-854-8125).

Where to Stay in Western North Dakota

BISMARCK

AmericInn Lodge and Suites of Bismarck
3235 State St.
(701) 250-1000
Moderate

Expressway Inn
200 E. Bismarck Expressway
(800) 456-6388
Inexpensive

Kelly Inn
1800 N. 12th St.
(701) 223-8001
Moderate

Radisson Hotel
605 E. Broadway Ave.
(701) 255-6000
radisson/bismarck-hotel-nd
Moderate

Wingate by Wyndham Bismarck
1421 Skyline Blvd.
(701) 751-2373
wingatehotels.com
Moderate

BOWMAN

North Winds Lodge
503 Hwy. 85
(701) 523-5641
Inexpensive

MANDAN

Baymont Inn and Suites
2611 Old Red Trail
(800) 568-8520
baymontmandan.com
Moderate

MEDORA

AmericInn Motel
75 E. River Rd. S
(701) 623-4800
americinn.com
Moderate

Badlands Motel
501 Pacific Ave.
(701) 623-4444
Moderate

SELECTED CHAMBERS OF COMMERCE

Bismarck–Mandan Convention and Visitors Bureau
1600 Burnt Boat Dr.
Bismarck 58503
(701) 222-4308
discoverbismarckmandan.com

Bottineau Convention and Visitors Bureau
519 Main St.
Bottineau 58318
(701) 228-3849
bottineau.com

Dickinson Convention and Visitors Bureau
72 W. Museum Dr.
Dickinson 58601
(701) 483-4988
visitdickinson.com

McKenzie County Tourism
100 2nd Ave. SW
Watford City 58854
(800) 701-2804
4eyes.net

Williston Convention and Visitors Bureau
212 Airport Rd.
Williston 58801
(701) 774-9041
visitwilliston.com

WILLISTON

Missouri Flats Inn
213 35th St. W.
(701) 572-4242
missouriflatsinn.com
Moderate

The Brooks
5515 Hwy. 85
(701) 609-5490
thebrookshotels.com
Moderate to expensive

Where to Eat in Western North Dakota

BISMARCK

Blarney Stone Pub
408 E. Main Ave.
(701) 751-7512
blarneyirishpub.com
Moderate

Bread Poets
106 E. Thayer Ave.
(701) 222-4445
breadpoets.com
Inexpensive

Fireflour Neapolitan Pizza & Coffee Bar
111 N. 5th St.
(701) 323-9000
fireflourpizza.com
Moderate

Laughing Sun Brewhouse and Pub
107 N. 5th St.
(701) 751-3881
laughingsunbrewing.com
Moderate

Sweet Treats Cupcake Bar & Bakery
118 N. 4th St.
(701) 751-3993
sweettreatsbismarck.com
Inexpensive

The Walrus Restaurant
(Italian)
1136 N. 3rd St.
(701) 250-0020
thewalrusrestaurant.com
Moderate

DICKINSON

Brickhouse Grille
2 W. Villard St.
(701) 483-9900
brickhousegrilleonline.com
Moderate

JD's BBQ
789 State Ave.
(701) 483-2277
Moderate

MEDORA

Cowboy Cafe
215 4th St.
(701) 623-4343
Moderate

Little Missouri Dining Room
440 3rd St.
(701) 623-4404
Moderate

Theodore's Dining Room
301 3rd Ave.
(701) 623-4444
Moderate to expensive

WILLISTON

Basil Restaurant Sushi Bar and Asian Bistro
16 E. Broadway
(701) 572-6688
basilwilliston.com
Moderate

Williston Brewing Company
1623 2nd Ave. W.
(701) 609-5439
willistonbrewing.com
Moderate

The Williston
408 1st Ave. E.
(701) 572-0544
thewilliston.com
Expensive

Gramma Sharon's Family Restaurant
1501 16th St. W.
(701) 572-1412
grammasharons.com
Inexpensive to moderate

Central North Dakota

With woods to explore, lush lakes, prairie potholes, and an international garden of incredible magnitude, central North Dakota lures its share of visitors. They come for the world-class birding and outdoor activities, the chance to immerse themselves into the German–Russian or Nordic character of early pioneers, to walk the childhood paths of celebrities, and to experience Native American culture and rare opportunities such as seeing the albino bison the Dakota consider sacred. No matter which direction you point your vehicle, look for the vast patchwork of wheat and brilliant sunflowers that thrive in North Dakota's glacial soils and listen for the songbirds and waterfowl that gather along rivers, potholes, and lakes.

If you enjoy unique graveyards, check out *St. Mary's Church* and *cemetery* in Strasburg. On the National Register of Historic Places, the cemetery is distinguished by ornate iron crosses marking graves—another nod to the area's German–Russian heritage and its craftsmanship.

East of Wishek on ND 13 is the tiny town of *Kulm,* hometown of actress Angie Dickinson and near one of the more haunting sites in the state. *Whitestone Hill*

CENTRAL NORTH DAKOTA

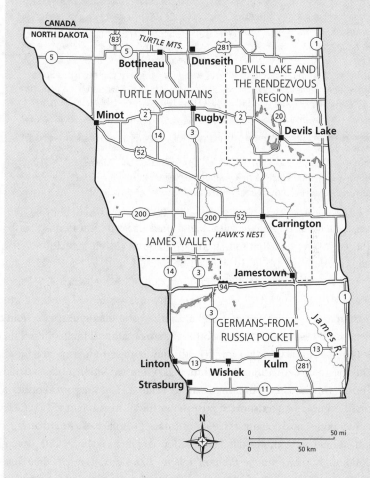

CANADA
NORTH DAKOTA

TURTLE MTS.

Bottineau

Dunseith

DEVILS LAKE AND
THE RENDEZVOUS
REGION

TURTLE MOUNTAINS

Minot

Rugby

Devils Lake

Carrington

JAMES VALLEY

HAWK'S NEST

Jamestown

GERMANS-FROM-
RUSSIA POCKET

James R.

Linton

Wishek

Kulm

Strasburg

N

0   50 mi

0   50 km

South-central North Dakota: Germans-from-Russia

Start in the southern corner of central North Dakota, an easy jaunt from Fort Yates to the home communities of North Dakota's German–Russians: **Strasburg, Wishek, Linton,** and other area towns.

Their European homelands are no longer in Germany. They left Alsace (then a German province, now part of France) around 1804 and resettled in Ukraine to farm and escape the Napoleonic Wars. In 1808–1809 another wave of immigration created Roman Catholic communities along the Kutschurgan River in Russia, with names brought from Germany: Strassburg, Baden, and Selz. Those names arrived in North Dakota with yet another wave of immigration, fueled by overpopulation and Russian desires to turn the Germans into Russians. The name **Strasburg** underwent its second spelling change (Strasbourg, Strassburg, Strasburg), and Selz was bestowed upon two towns, the first of which, near Hague, disappeared. The second, in Pierce County, is still a thriving community. Black Sea Germans, or *Russlanddeutsch,* as they are called, are so far removed from Germany that the customs and language they preserve are ancient history in present-day Germany. Whereas French and Scottish immigrants quickly assimilated into North Dakota society, the Black Sea Germans maintained their cultural identity longer and were generally aloof to community involvement.

Nowadays the residents are eager to share their food and festivities. Oktoberfest, a traditional event in Germany, is replicated in many communities in south-central North Dakota, as well as in the western part of the state. The town of **Wishek,** for instance, has paid homage to fermented cabbage every October for 70 years with

Battlefield Site was the site of North Dakota's most deadly clash of Native Americans and US cavalry. It's truly off the beaten path, a 23-mile detour that heads 15 miles south of Kulm on ND 56, then east on an unimproved road.

The battle lasted about two hours as General Alfred Sully's troops attacked a tipi camp of Yanktonai, some Dakota, Hunkpapa Lakota, and Blackfeet (Sihasapa Lakota) on September 3, 1863. It was part of a military mission to punish participants of the US Dakota Conflict of 1862 that raged through Minnesota's Minnesota River valley and across the prairie toward the Dakotas. By sunset an estimated 150 to 300 Sioux had lost their lives and 156 were taken prisoner. The cavalry's death toll was considerably less: Only 20 cavalrymen died, and 50 to 60 were wounded. There are memorials its *Sauerkraut Days.* Schoolchildren get out of school early for the free wiener-and-kraut lunch. If kraut's not your style, try *knoephla* soup (spelled many ways, but the soup is always buttery with potatoes and dumplings) and *fleischkuekle,* a beef-filled pasty, or pierogi. The festival is replete with food and drink, and you can hear the oompah-pahs of polka throughout the community.

The family histories of the people who live here are strikingly similar to that of "wunnerful, wunnerful" *Lawrence Welk,* the famous Champagne Music Maker. Welk's father had grown increasingly unhappy with life in Russia, and in 1892 he and his wife came to America. Their voyage was financed by an uncle who ran a store in Strasburg. Lawrence Welk was born in 1903, and he spoke only German until he was 21 years old. This was not uncommon for children of German–Russian descent, as parents were reluctant to send their children to school, only allowing them to attend when their work was finished on the farm. Welk was the sixth of nine children, and on his 21st birthday he left for Bismarck. He played his accordion at weddings and dances until his great break came in 1955 with a chance to appear on national TV.

Welk's birthplace, officially known as the *Ludwig & Christina Welk Farmstead,* is nestled among wheat fields north of Strasburg at 845 88th St. SE. Although the home is made of sod, with 3-foot-thick walls, it has white siding on the exterior and wallpaper inside. The site includes a summer kitchen, barn, buggy house, granary, and blacksmith shop. It is open Thurs through Sun from 10 a.m. to 5 p.m. Memorial Day through Labor Day and by appointment. Welk died in sunny southern California in 1992, the year the homestead restoration was completed to its 1920s condition. Admission is $5 for adults; $3 for children age 6–12. For more information call (701) 336-2641.

to both sides of the battle on-site, along with a self-guided tour and a small museum, picnic area, and playground. The North Dakota Historical Society (701-328-3508; history.nd.gov/historicsites/whitestone) operates the free museum mid-May to mid-Sept Thurs through Mon. The local Whitestone Historical Society hosts an annual summer event at the site to commemorate the battle.

Jamestown and James River Valley

Jamestown, nestled in the valley where the James and Pipestem Rivers meet, is appropriately known as Buffalo City, and you can't miss seeing its

Go Birding Along the Central Flyway

North Dakota is a world-class paradise for birds, with 63 National Wildlife Refuges—more than any other state. More than 320 species and an estimated 53 million songbirds, shorebirds, birds of prey, wading birds, upland birds, and nesting waterfowl make their home here in the summer, and even more make it a rest stop on their way north or south, using the Missouri River and the Central Flyway.

What also makes this area unique is its convergence of eastern and western species and the thriving prairie potholes that polka-dot the landscape east of the Missouri River. Check out one of the many birding hot spots throughout the valley.

Arrowhead National Wildlife Refuge, Carrington (25 miles northwest of Jamestown on US 281), has a 5.5-mile auto tour with viewing areas for waterfowl, shorebirds, dancing sharp-tailed grouse, grassland songbirds, and a herd of American bison. The 16,000-acre refuge is also known for sightings such as downy woodpeckers, greater yellowlegs, and belted kingfishers. Look for migrating snow geese in the fall (701-285-3341; fws.gov/arrowwood). A self-guided automobile tour affords breathtaking views of duck broods in summer and migrating snow geese in fall.

Chase Lake National Wildlife Refuge, Woodworth, is one of the country's oldest refuges, established by President Theodore Roosevelt in 1908 to protect American white pelicans, which were threatened at the time. Today it's home to America's largest nesting colony of white pelicans (701-752-4218; fws.gov/arrowwood/chaselake_nwr).

Lake Alice National Wildlife Refuge, Cando, is known for thousands of geese and ducks that use its open waters during spring and fall migration as they pass through the Devils Lake region (701-662-8611; fws.gov/refuge/Lake_Alice).

Long Lake National Wildlife Refuge, Driscoll, is one of the nation's best birding spots, noteworthy for its 2-mile-wide, 16-mile-long lake that draws more than 20,000 shorebirds for a rest stop while migrating or for breeding. You may be able to spot sandhill and rarer whooping cranes in March or April or reserve a spot in a blind to watch the sharp-tailed grouse do its mating dance on the prairie or watch grebes doing their mating dance on water. September and October also are peak bird-watching months. You can watch birds from the public roads or "the butte" a mile east of Highway 83 on the lake's north side (701-387-4397; fws .gov/longlake).

Lostwood National Wildlife Refuge, Kenmare, lies along what's called the Missouri Coteau with rolling and steep hills covered in rich prairie that includes more than 700 plant species and harbors grassland birds such as piping plover, grasshopper sparrow, Sprague's Pipit, and Baird's sparrow. It's considered globally important by the American Bird Conservancy. Close observers might also be able to spot close to 200 ancient tipi rings across the landscape (701-848-2722).

Even if you aren't heading to a wildlife refuge, keep the binoculars handy. Take the roads less traveled and follow the scenic bluffs of the Missouri River. You're sure to spot a wealth of winged creatures.

Birds unique to the pristine prairies include the western grebe (also known for its comical upright two-grebe dance across the water—known as water weaving), ferruginous hawk, Hungarian partridge, sharp-tailed grouse, upland sandpiper, marbled godwit, clay-colored sparrow, and the chestnut-collared longspur.

Several endangered or threatened birds have been documented in North Dakota by the US Fish and Wildlife Service, including the interior least tern, bald eagle, whooping crane, peregrine falcon, and piping plover. For details on the refuges, including maps and trails, go to fws.gov/mountain-prairie/refuges/nd.

You can get complete details on the best birding hot spots in the region of Steele, Carrington, and Jamestown by calling (888) 921-2473 or checking out birding drives.com. The site includes 6 birding routes pulled together by bird experts.

If you like to have company and enjoy the expert eye of a guide, you can find several birding festivals and workshops in late May and early June.

For information on the ***International Adventure Trail,*** a network of 15 notable birding sites in North Dakota and southern Manitoba, go to internationaladventure-trail.org.

TOP HITS IN CENTRAL NORTH DAKOTA

Devils Lake

International Peace Garden
on the US border
(888) 432-6733

National Buffalo Museum
Jamestown
(701) 252-8648

Norsk Hostfest
Sept–Oct, Minot
(701) 852-2368

North Dakota Birding Trail

North Dakota State Fair
July, Minot
(701) 857-7620

Turtle Mountains

"World's Largest Buffalo" sculpture that stands 26 feet tall and weighs 60 tons. It was built in 1959 and was gradually surrounded by historic buildings that the community thought should be saved. That collection grew into the *Frontier Village* and attracts over 100,000 people each year. A post office, trading post, 1881 church, fire department, jail, and barbershop are just some of the structures that re-create small-town life in the 1800s and are open to the public during the summer months. If you have children, be sure to take the stagecoach ride so they appreciate the modern wonders of paved roads and shock absorbers. There are pony rides, too.

You should be able to see the herd of about 30 bison that absolutely deserves a closer look. Native Americans have long revered the rare albino bison as sacred, and Jamestown's *National Buffalo Museum,* at the Frontier Village, 500 17th St. SE, has two. White Cloud has been here since 1997, and she gave birth to an albino calf named Dakota Miracle in 2007. The museum is open 8 a.m. to 8 p.m. Memorial Day through Labor Day. Check the website at buffalomuseum.com or call (701) 252-8648 for details on off-season hours. Admission is $5 for adults, $4 for seniors, $1 for students 7–18, or $10 per family. There is no admission to visit the Prairie Winds Gift Shop.

One of the favorite stops at the Frontier Village is the writing shack of famed western novelist and Jamestown native *Louis L'Amour,* the highest-selling western author of all time. He wrote 117 books and is best known for his frontier books, such as *Mustang Man, The Sackett Brand, Ride the Dark Trail,* and *The Daybreakers*. More than 30 of his books became movies, including *Hondo,* with John Wayne; *Shalako,* starring Sean Connery; and *The Burning Hills,* which featured Tab Hunter and Natalie Wood.

If you want to learn more about the man who lassoed the American West spirit with words, walk the **Louis L'Amour Trail** in Jamestown. The first stop is the Dakota Territory Courthouse, where L'Amour's father worked as the county and the state veterinarian. He also doubled as a deputy sheriff for several years. The courthouse is located at 5th Street and 3rd Avenue Southeast in Jamestown. The Stutsman County Memorial Museum (located in the Lutz Mansion) and the Jamestown City Hall are next along the trail, then the **L'Amour Family Home Site.** This is where L'Amour's boyhood home was originally located, at 113 3rd Ave. SE. The home was later moved to another part of Jamestown and structurally changed.

The First United Methodist Church, the Alfred Dickey Library (one of the young boy's favorite places), Franklin Grade School, and Walz Pharmacy, once owned by L'Amour's friend Reese Hawkins and stocked with all of the writer's books, also are highlighted along the trail.

L'Amour's writing reflects his Dakota roots. "The sort of men and women it took to open the West were the kind of whom stories were told. Strongly individual, willing to risk all they possessed as well as their lives, they were also prepared to fight for what they believed was theirs," he wrote in *The Sackett Companion.*

L'Amour is the only writer to receive the Presidential Medal of Freedom and the Congressional Gold Medal. An elephant handler, a professional

Legend of the White Buffalo

The white buffalo is sacred to the Lakota people. Legend says the White Buffalo Calf Woman brought them their most sacred pipe. This beautiful woman in a white buckskin dress spent four days and four nights showing the Lakota how to smoke the pipe, on which a bison calf was carved on one side. As the White Buffalo Calf Woman left, she walked in the direction of the setting sun, stopped, and rolled over four times. The first time, she got up and became a black buffalo; the second time, a brown buffalo; the third time, a red buffalo; and the fourth time she rolled over, she became a white buffalo. This buffalo walked on farther, stopped, and after bowing to each of the four directions of the universe, disappeared over the hill.

boxer, a seaman, and a journalist, L'Amour, who died in 1988, is warmly remembered in his hometown.

An attractive brochure charting the Louis L'Amour Trail is available at the Jamestown Visitor Center, 404 Louis L'Amour Ln., at Frontier Village, or by calling (800) 222-4766 or (701) 251-9145. They also have information on the area's 30 miles of hiking and biking.

trivia

Louis L'Amour wasn't Jamestown's only world-famous firstborn. Norma Deloris Egstrom, better known as the singer **Peggy Lee,** was also born in Jamestown, on May 26, 1920.

At the north end of town on US 281, the **Fort Seward Historic Site and Interpretive Center** (701-251-1875), which overlooks Pipestem Lake, sheds light on the early military history of the region. The free center is open daily 10 a.m. to 6 p.m. Memorial Day through Labor Day, although the grounds and picnic area are open year-round. Homesteading by covered wagon is commemorated each year in the **Fort Seward Wagon Train** (covered-wagon-train.com). Participants don mandatory pioneer costumes during a one-week wagon train reenactment each June. The wagon train was first organized in 1969 as a one-time experience, but promoters found it so worthwhile they made it a yearly event. The wagon train starts rolling at the crack of dawn, and it averages 3 to 4 miles per hour. At the end of the day, singing and storytelling around the campfire foster camaraderie, pioneer style—a memorable family affair.

The **Stutsman County Memorial Museum,** at 321 3rd Ave. SE, is housed in the George Lutz mansion, a monument to the early-day history of the area. Four floors in the stately brick museum are devoted to the culture and life of the early pioneers. The first floor, with a complete dining room, kitchen, and butler's pantry, highlights items that a pioneer homemaker might have used. Military life and the railroad's strength in the state are featured on the second floor, and pioneer medicine, wildlife, and church relics round out this eclectic collection on the third floor. A room in the basement has been turned into a claim shanty. Many visitors love the home's art nouveau–style stained glass and Tiffany lamps the best. If you want to learn more about history, be there at 2 p.m. Sun June through Aug for Front Porch Chats. The free museum is open Mon through Fri from 10 a.m. to 5 p.m. and Sat and Sun from 1 to 5 p.m. Memorial Day through September 30. For more information, call (701) 252-6741.

Just north on US 281 the 840-acre **Pipestem Dam and Lake** offers year-round recreational opportunities, and the lovely lake fascinates birders, boaters, anglers, and others. Conservation of wildlife and the natural environment is a major objective of the US Army Corps of Engineers, and 4,200 acres of creek valley and rolling upland at Pipestem are home to a wide variety of wildlife and waterfowl. The natural setting has been enhanced by selective planting of more than 250,000 trees around the lake.

For swimming, camping, fishing, and boating, head to the **Lakeside Marina and Recreational Area** at 3225 E. Lakeside Rd. (701-252-1183) by the Jamestown Dam. Camping and tent and trailer sites are available. There is a fee for some activities. Open early May through late Sept.

North on US 281 and 52 is **Carrington,** which, like most of the communities in North Dakota, can trace its development to the arrival of the railroad. By 1882 the Northern Pacific line ran through the yet unnamed prairie settlement. Agriculture formed the base for Carrington's early- and present-day economy. It's home to the state-of-the-art **Dakota Growers Pasta Co.,** which makes pasta from durum wheat harvested by more than 1,100 third- and fourth-generation growers in the region. It has become the third-largest pasta manufacturer in North America.

It's also home to the charming **Dakota Sun Gardens and Winery,** a destination for relaxing among flowers, buying summer fruits, and sipping wines made by owners Bruce and Merleen Gussiaas since 2010. They sell or make wine from familiar fruits, such as rhubarb, raspberries, plums, and

Nicknames for North Dakota

Peace Garden State, the official license-plate nickname inspired by the International Peace Garden since 1957.

Flickertail State, referring to the Richardson ground squirrel that flicks or jerks its tail while running or just before entering its burrow.

Roughrider State, referring to the first US Volunteer Cavalry that Theodore Roosevelt organized to fight in the Spanish–American War. In fact, the Roughriders included several North Dakota cowboys.

cherries, but you'll also find elderberry, aronia berry, chokecherry, and haskap. You can also grab a glass of lemonade and sit on the patio by the 1950s octagonal grain bins. Call (701) 674-3623 for information on visiting.

Pipestem Creek Bed and Birding offers a fresh combination of a birding getaway and taste of a working small grains farm. Owner Ann Reimers Hoffert grew up on the 5,000-acre farm and started a specialty grain business with edible decor for birds when she moved back. Rustic rooms can be found in two historic granaries or guests can rent one of two houses that sleep six to 11 people. Call (701) 652-2623 or go to pipestemcreek.com.

History and art buffs, be sure to check out the **Putnam House** (533 Main St.), an American Foursquare home built in 1907 by Thomas Nichols Putnam, the area's pioneer lumberman, and his wife, Clara Belle Putnam. The 4,300-square-foot home is testament to the precise craftsmanship and architecture of the turn of the 20th century. The grand staircase is a breathtaking focal point, and the dining room features a built-in oak buffet with leaded-glass doors. It's more than majestic, though. It's also a rural cultural and community center, providing an inspiring setting for summer concerts on the wraparound porch, art exhibits, and hands-on classes in stained glass, jewelry, ethnic cooking, and more. For details and upcoming events, call (701) 652-1213 or go to putnamhouse.org.

Just 6 miles southwest of Carrington on US 52 is **Hawk's Nest,** a butte standing 300 feet above the surrounding plains on 100 acres of unfenced

All Creatures Great and Small

As you are traveling along the highways and byways of North Dakota, be on the lookout for small brown-and-white roadside signs featuring binoculars, which indicate one of the state's 80-plus roadside viewing areas.

Watch the birds and beasts from a distance with good-quality binoculars, a spotting scope, or a telephoto lens. If the animals you are watching are watching you—with their heads up and ears facing your direction—or are nervous, you are probably too close or moving too quickly.

Obviously, be kind to these bashful critters. Patience will reward you. Keep quiet and wait for animals to return to or enter an area. The early and late hours of daylight are generally the best times to watch and photograph most wildlife.

land. The area has one of the few remaining stands of buffalo grass and pine oaks. Visitors to Hawk's Nest, which is maintained by the local Kiwanis Club, can hike, camp, and ski there.

Detour straight east of Carrington to Cooperstown for a sobering look at the Cold War era with **Ronald Reagan Minuteman Missile State Historic Sites** (also known as **Oscar Zero**) that opened in 2009. Visitors can descend 50 feet into a concrete capsule to the control center for 10 Minuteman Missiles, each warhead packing more destructive power than what was dropped on Hiroshima and Nagasaki at the end of World War II. The site is one of 15 command centers and 150 missile sites spread out over 6,500 square miles and manned by the Grand Forks Air Force Base. It was set up to defend the country at the peak of the Cold War that began in the mid-1960s. The sites were decommissioned starting in 1991 after the Strategic Arms Reduction Treaty. It's open 10 a.m. to 6 p.m. daily mid-May through mid-Sept and Thurs through Sat and Mon Mar through May and Sept through October 31. Nov through Feb, it's open by appointment only. Call (701) 797-3691 or go to history.nd.gov/historicsites/minutemanmissile. Admission is $10 for adults; $3 for children. The facility is 4 miles north of Cooperstown at 555 113½ Ave. NE along ND 45.

Devils Lake and the Rendezvous Region

Head an hour north of Carrington on US 281 to reach the emerald waters of **Devils Lake** at the crossroads of ND 19 and ND 20. Don't let the name fool you. This spring-fed lake was once dubbed "Enchanted Waters." Some speculate the nickname was mistranslated. Others point to its legend as "Bad Spirit Lake," after a group of Sioux drowned in 4-foot waves while returning from battle. Either way, the name Devils Lake stuck. The state's largest natural lake covers more than 70,000 prairie acres and nurtures forests of hardwood oak, ash, and elm that provide year-round recreation. Walleye and white bass are the top draws, and yellow perch are found in winter. Migrating geese, ducks, and sandhill cranes take over the skies each spring and fall. Devils Lake State Parks comprises three parks and recreation areas. Call (800) 233-8048 or visit devilslakend.com for more information.

On the south shore of Devils Lake, **Sullys Hill National Game Preserve** shelters swans, bison, elk, deer, prairie dogs, and other wildlife with its native habitat. Worth noting: It started out as a national park in 1904 but was redesignated a big game preserve in 1921. Don't miss the beautiful lake overlook, and bring binoculars for the 4-mile auto tour open May through Oct. In the winter, you can ski the trails. Stop in the visitor center for maps, exhibits, and a look at native species in the 180-gallon aquarium. The preserve is 12 miles southwest of the town of Devils Lake on ND 57. Admission is free. Call (701) 766-4272 or visit fws.gov/refuge/Sullys_Hill_National_Game_Preserve for information.

Thirteen miles southwest of Devils Lake on ND 57, one of the best-preserved military outposts west of the Mississippi is found at the **Fort Totten State Historic Site** (701-766-4441; nd.gov/hist). Fort Totten was built in 1867 to protect the overland route to Montana and was the last outpost before 300 miles of wilderness. It later became an Indian boarding school with up to 400 students, a health care facility for tuberculosis, and then a reservation school. Self-guided tours of the 17 original buildings can be enjoyed 8 a.m. to 5 p.m. daily mid-May through mid-Sept or by appointment on weekdays in the off-season. Admission is $5 per adult and $1.50 per child. In the summer months, check out performances at the Fort Totten Little Theatre.

To get a firsthand frontier experience, stay at the **Totten Trail Historic Inn.** The bed-and-breakfast inn right on the historic site is furnished in period style (1870–1910). Rooms are available year-round, with prices ranging from $80 to $110. Some rooms have a private bath, and others share a bath with one other room. A stay includes breakfast and a Victorian-style afternoon tea. Proceeds fund continuing renovations at the fort. For more information, call (701) 766-4874 or go to tottentrailinn.com.

Minot

The town of **Minot,** like other growing North Dakota cities, has welcomed a wave of almost 10,000 newcomers in a handful of years thanks to the oil boom. But even with over 46,300 residents, the population seems small when fall arrives and the town's size almost doubles over the five days of its much-loved annual **Norsk Hostfest.** An estimated 55,000 visitors from around the region and the country gather to celebrate North

America's largest Scandinavian festival, where you can catch a heady whiff of cardamom-spiced sweet breads, tap your feet to fiddles, and enjoy the kaleidoscope whirl of dancers in ethnic costumes. Held each fall for more than 30 years, the Hostfest brings in big-name entertainers on 7 stages and more than 200 artisans and craftsmen with everything from delicate silver jewelry to sturdy tine boxes. Bite into favorite desserts such as *lefse, rommegrot,* rosettes, and *krumkake* or bravely sample the infamous lutefisk. For multicourse fine dining, reserve a seat at En to Tre. Chefs prepare a buffet with traditional dishes such as smoked salmon, shrimp, herring, lingonberry preserves, roasted meats, cold plates, flatbreads, and cheeses to be savored by Norwegians and non-Norwegians alike. Call (701) 852-2368 or check out hostfest.com.

The Scandinavian Heritage Center, at 1020 S. Broadway, is the world's only outdoor living museum that is dedicated to preserving the ethnic heritage of all five Scandinavian countries. Buildings on the premises include a visitor center; a *stabbur* (storage house) from Telemark, Norway; a Finnish sauna; Danish windmill; Dala horse; Stave church museum; an eternal flame brought to North Dakota from Norway; and a 230-year-old house from Sigdal, Norway. Hours vary by season. Call (701) 852-9161 or check scandinavianheritage.org for details.

The must-go summer event is the **North Dakota State Fair** in Minot. How big is it? Think of it by the numbers: 300,000 visitors; 46,000 competitive exhibits; 600 vendors; 24 buildings; 10 free stages; nine days of fun; and three nights each of rodeo contests and rumbling car and truck competitions. The grandstand that opened in 2010 holds 15,000 spectators for a rockin' evening when big names arrive for concerts. Call (701) 857-7620 or visit the website at ndstatefair.com for details on upcoming events. Also on the fairgrounds is the Ward County Historical Society Pioneer Village and Museum, open May through Sept.

10 North Main

Among the eateries generating the best buzz for great food is this restaurant that opened a decade ago across from the historic Soo Line Depot. Among the owners is Josh Duhamel, who was born in Minot, and went on to star in blockbuster movies, including the "Transformers" series. They serve house-smoked chicken and duck, crispy strips of pheasant tossed in an Asian sauce, Icelandic-style dry-cured smoked salmon, elk loin and bison New York strip, and blueberry bread pudding (701-837-1010; 10northmain.com).

The 19-acre **Roosevelt Park Zoo** (701-857-4166; rpzoo.com) is the home of a black-footed penguin collection. No doubt these flightless seabirds enjoy the chilly temperatures during North Dakota winters. Warmer-blooded residents include spider monkeys, kangaroos, a white Bengal tiger, bears, penguins, giraffes, and llamas. Concessions, a children's zoo, a gift shop, and an educational center also are part of the zoo, which is located on the east side at 1219 E. Burdick Expressway. The zoo is open daily (weather permitting) 10 a.m. to 8 p.m. June 1 to the end of Aug and 10 a.m. to 6 p.m. in May and Sept. Admission is $8 for adults, $7.50 for students and seniors, and $4 for children ages 4–12.

The Roosevelt Park and Zoo is the fifth point along the 2.5-mile **Riverwalk,** a walking and biking trail that starts at the Railroad Museum (701-852-7091) at 19 1st St. NE. The museum presents the history and progression of the railroad through photographs and other memorabilia from 1886 to the present. It's free and open 10 a.m. to 2 p.m. Sat. A two-fifths-scale train, **Magic City Express,** located at the north end of Roosevelt Park, travels down a mile-long track.

The second point of interest is the **Lillian and Coleman Taube Museum of Art** (701-838-4445; taubemuseum.org) at 2 N. Main St. The Minot Arts Association renovated the former Union National Bank building as a center for the visual arts, educational programs, and cultural and social events. Hours are 10:30 a.m. to 5:30 p.m. Tues through Fri and 11 a.m. to 4 p.m. on Sat.

As you traverse the Riverwalk, you will also discover **Val's Cyclery** (701-839-4817; valscyclery.com) at 222 E. Central Ave., where Rocky and Rory Schell continue the cycling and fitness tradition started by their father,

Valentine, more than 40 years ago. **Eastwood Park** is the next stop. This is a splendid place to check out the architectural styles of homes from Minot's early days: Princess Anne, English Tudor, and arts and crafts. In 1986 the neighborhood was designated a National Historic District.

Other sites along the Riverwalk are Lowe's Garden Center (701-839-2000), which is housed in a replica of an early North Dakota train depot; North Dakota State Fair and All Seasons Arena; MotorMania, which takes place every Labor Day weekend at the fairgrounds; and the **Ward County Historical Society Pioneer Village and Museum** (701-839-0785; wchsnd .org). Pioneer Village and Museum, located at the west entrance to the fairgrounds, is a collection of preserved and restored historic buildings, housing vintage automobiles and thousands of artifacts that illuminate Minot's past. Put the emphasis on "restored." Volunteers have worked hard to get it back in shape after 2011 flooding. The museum is open from 10 a.m. to 6 p.m. Tues through Sat. For more information about Riverwalk or what's along it, call the Minot Convention and Visitors Bureau at (800) 264-2626 or go to visitminot.org.

The Minot Air Force Base has about 5,000 residents 13 miles north of the city and was built in the 1950s. With aviation a large part of North Dakota's economy—especially here—it makes sense to check out the **Dakota Territory Air Museum** (701-852-8500; dakotaterritoryairmuseum.com), which is adjacent to the northwest corner of the Minot International Airport at 100 34th Ave. NE. It features civilian and military aircraft from 1928 to the present. If you love things that fly, this is the place to be. You'll find civilian aircraft, from a 1928 Waco to a 1946 Piper J-3 Cub, as well as a Lockheed T-33 jet trainer, a Douglas C-47 World War II transport, and a Curtis P-40 Hawk. Also prominently displayed—and still operational—is the Minot Airport beacon, which guided pilots in the area from 1949 to 1993. And the price can't be beat: $2 for adults and $1 for children ages 6–17. The museum is open from 10 a.m. to 5 p.m. Mon through Sat and from 1 to 5 p.m. Sun. The museum is open mid-May through mid-Oct.

trivia

12,002 jobs are attributed to aviation activity in North Dakota

$1.2 billion of economic activity is created each year by North Dakota aviation

Turtle Mountains and Border Region

One of the prettiest places to take a fall drive is along the 28-mile *Des Lacs River Valley,* which kisses the Canadian border and stretches southeast along US 52 to Kenmare, about 50 miles northwest of Minot.

Hop onto the 12-mile scenic drive along Des Lac Lake from near the Baden overpass to a picnic area 5 miles northwest of Kenmare. There are several scenic pullouts and 13 interpretive panels about the area, famous for vast fields of wheat and cheery sunflowers. In the town of Kenmare, look for the 1902 *Old Danish Mill,* a restored flour mill with millstones that weigh 1,800 pounds.

For a truly stunning sight, head to the *Des Lacs National Wildlife Refuge* one mile west of Kenmare. While it's great for picnics, hikes, and birding year-round, it's best known as a staging area for up to 300,000 snow geese as they gather and prepare for migration. Kenmare hosts *Goosefest* in October to celebrate the gathering (701-835-4046; fws.gov/refuge/des_lacs).

About 90 minutes east of Kenmare and only about 20 miles south of the Canadian border, the bustling community of *Bottineau* serves as the gateway to the Turtle Mountain area. Visitors come for every season at *Lake Metigoshe State Park,* a wooded natural area with numerous lakes, making the area one of North Dakota's most popular year-round vacation spots.

It doesn't hurt that it's also a short drive to the *International Peace Garden,* which drew 50,000 people when it was dedicated on July 14, 1932. This lavish garden on the border commemorates peace between Canada and the US. Dr. Henry J. Moore, a horticulturist from Islington, Ontario, Canada, conceived the idea for the garden when he was on his way home from the

Juneberry Ice Cream

For one of North Dakota's best summer treats, head to the Dairy Dipper, an old-fashioned ice cream parlor at **Pride Dairy** at 517 Thompson St. in Bottineau. They make juneberry ice cream—which is rare to find outside of North Dakota—along with flavors like cherry chocolate chip and a coffee ice cream made with locally roasted Mojo beans. If you travel with a cooler, you can load up with butter and cheeses, along with juneberry and chokecherry syrups and more (701-228-2216; pridedairy.com).

1928 annual meeting of the National Association of Gardeners, a US organization. He thought it was a fitting tribute to the peaceful existence between the two countries.

The proposal was approved at the association's 1929 meeting, and the search began for an appropriate site. Moore liked what he saw when visiting the Turtle Mountains. After a plane ride over the area, he remarked: "What a sight greeted the eye. Those undulating hills rising out of the limitless prairies are filled with lakes and streams. On the south of the unrecognizable boundary, wheat fields everywhere; and on the north, the Manitoba Forest Preserve. What a place for a garden!"

The tablet on a cairn of native stone reads: TO GOD IN HIS GLORY . . . WE TWO NATIONS DEDICATE THIS GARDEN AND PLEDGE OURSELVES THAT AS LONG AS MAN SHALL LIVE WE WILL NOT TAKE ARMS AGAINST ONE ANOTHER. The two countries chose a place situated on ND 3, the longest north–south road in the world, and about centrally located on the continent of North America (Turtle Mountains).

asprawling tributetopeace

The International Peace Garden has:

2,339 acres of gardens

150,000 annuals

50,000 perennials and hardy bulbs

5,000 flower shrubs

300 shade and flowering trees

The border walk through the Formal Gardens is a one-of-a-kind chance to see an enormous carpet of flowers in bloom across two nations. The 1.5-mile walk takes you past fountains, pools, cascades, the Perennial Garden, Arbor Garden, arboretum, bell tower, and the renovated Sunken Garden, Conservatory, and Visitor Center.

If you visit between July 15 and August 15, you'll be dazzled by hundreds of orange and yellow Asiatic lilies. Most gardens hit their peak color in August. Self-guided driving tours will allow you to see Lake Udall on the US side and Lake Stormon on the Canadian side.

One of the most touching displays at the garden is the 9/11 Memorial Site, which pays tribute to the more than 2,800 lives lost in the September 11, 2001, terrorist attack. On June 3, 2002, the International Peace Garden received ten 10-foot girders from the World Trade Center wreckage. The girders lie at rest at the 9/11 Memorial Site as an everlasting reminder of the human tragedy that occurred one quiet September morning in New York City, Pennsylvania, and Washington, DC.

The park isn't only for the green thumbs in the family; it's also the perfect spot for the culturally inclined. The **International Music Camp** is held annually during early summer at the park, featuring Saturday concerts with guest conductors and an old-time fiddlers' contest.

The International Peace Garden is one of the prettiest spots in the nation for picnicking, camping, or just sitting back and absorbing the scents and beauty of nature. The grounds are open daily, with camping available May through mid-Oct. For detailed information, call (888) 432-6733 or visit the website at peacegarden.com. To get to the garden from Bottineau, travel 13 miles east on ND 5 until you reach Dunseith; then take US 281 north for 13 miles.

If you drive US 281 south back to Dunseith, check out the quirky Wee'l Turtle statue, made from more than 2,000 tire rims. Then take US 281 east approximately 18 miles, which will take you right through Belcourt, near the lovely town of **Rolla** and the heart of the magnificent Turtle Mountains.

Crossing the Border

If you plan to travel between Canada and North Dakota at any of the 18 border crossings, heightened security measures means you'll need a passport or a US passport card. The card, a slimmed down version of a passport, is good for travel in Canada, Mexico, and the Caribbean. Apply for one and find out more about customs procedures at travel.state.gov.

The best way to avoid delays and hassles when crossing the international border is to be prepared.

In either direction, customs officials will ask you where you live, your citizenship, the purpose of your trip, how long you intend to stay, and if you have any goods to declare. There may be questions about alcohol, tobacco, and firearms. If you made a duty-free purchase, state how much you bought. When returning home, you may be asked what you have purchased, so it's a good idea to save your sales slips and pack your items so they can be easily inspected at the border. Oral declarations are the general rule.

24-hour Ports of Entry

Pembina, North Dakota, and **Emerson, Manitoba**
I-29
(701) 825-6551

Dunseith, North Dakota (International Peace Garden), and **Boissevain, Manitoba**
US 281
(701) 263-4460

Portal, North Dakota, and **North Portal, Saskatchewan**
US 52
(701) 926-4241

All other ports of entry are open daily with varied hours.

Peace among nations is nothing new in this territory. Ancient tribes became nations of Mandan, Hidatsa, Arikara, as well as Yanktonai, Sisseton, Wahpeton, Pembina Chippewa, Cree, and Metis. Each had its own culture, yet many worked together during years of peace and years of turmoil and change. Their traditions, philosophies, and spirituality have made an unparalleled contribution to the sumptuous cultural landscape of North Dakota.

The *Turtle Mountain Band of Pembina Chippewa* live in the wooded, rolling hills of north-central North Dakota. Their ancestors came from the Great Lakes region in the late 1700s, essentially pushed west by the fur-trade business. As trappers, voyagers, entrepreneurs, and caretakers of the land, the Pembina Chippewa formed enduring relations with other indigenous and European peoples, most significantly the Cree and the French. The Chippewa and Metis people built and developed North Dakota's oldest still-existing community: *Pembina,* located east of the Turtle Mountains and tucked into the far northeast corner of the state. The Red River Valley and northern North Dakota were the choice hunting territories of the Pembina Chippewa after the 1800s. As part of the continuing westward migration and following a stir of treaty making, Chief Little Shell III brought his band across the Dakota prairie to the Turtle Mountains, an area much like the woodlands of Minnesota. On December 21, 1882, the Turtle Mountain Indian

Reservation was established. It is now located on 33,100 acres in Rolette County, where the community of Belcourt is situated.

You can explore some of this history at the **Pembina State Museum** with more than 100 million years of regional history. There's also a 7-story viewing tower for an eagle's eye view of the landscape. Call (701) 825-6840 or go to history.nd.gov for hours.

enchantedforests

The oak and aspen forests of the Turtle Mountain State Forest provide refuge to a variety of birds, including rugged grouse, magpies, and vireos. Also commonly seen are deer, moose, and small mammals such as squirrels, woodchucks, raccoons, and snowshoe hares.

The reservation is surrounded by the beautiful **Turtle Mountains,** which offer endless recreational opportunities that include cultural centers, gaming facilities, powwows, fishing, swimming, skiing, golfing, and sundry community-sponsored events. Named the Turtle Mountains 200 years ago by explorers, these hills, flecked with lovely lakes, have long been home to native tribes. One of the safest bets for accommodations and entertainment is the **Sky Dancer Hotel & Casino,** located 5 miles west of Belcourt on US 281. The hotel, which is operated by the Turtle Mountain Band of Chippewa, features 97 guest rooms, the Chippewa Trails Restaurant, and a 37,000-square-foot casino with poker and blackjack tables, bingo, and 525 slot machines. For more information, call (866) 244-9467 or visit skydancercasino.com.

Two miles from Belcourt on ND 5, the **Anishinaubag Intercultural Center** (701-477-5519) offers a hands-on living-history experience in a reconstructed Plains Indian village. In a natural wooded 100-acre setting, visitors can see Native American architecture, villages, a trading post, log cabins, and a log round house used for dances and meetings. Canoe rental also is available at this exquisite lake setting.

Six miles east of Belcourt on US 281 is Rolla, which hosts the annual **International Ragtop Festival** each July. The three-day salute to America's automotive gem—the convertible—rolls out a parade, rock 'n' roll concerts, and other activities. For more information call (701) 477-3610.

Twenty-three miles south of Rolla on Highway 30 is the **Dale and Martha Hawk Foundation Museum,** with North Dakota's largest collection of antique farm machinery and the only known working Hackney Auto Plow. The collection is housed in 5 historic buildings, including a church, a store, and a schoolhouse. It's open 9 a.m. to 6 p.m. 7 days a week May through Sept. Camping also is available. Call (701) 583-2381 or visit hawkmuseum .org.

Where to Stay in Central North Dakota

BOTTINEAU

Norway House
1255 Hwy. 5 E
(701) 228-3737
Inexpensive

Quilt Inn and Suites
10722 Lake Loop Rd.
(701) 263-6500
quiltinn-lakemetigoshe
.com
Moderate

DEVILS LAKE

Fireside Inn and Suites
215 US 2 E.
(701) 662-6760
Inexpensive

JAMESTOWN

Lakeview Meadow
8280 31st St. SE
(701) 252-5100
lakeviewmeadow.com

MINOT

Dakotah Rose Bed & Breakfast
510 4th Ave. NW
(701) 838-3548
dakotahrose.com
Moderate

Holiday Inn Riverside
2200 Burdick
Expressway E.
(701) 852-2504
minotconventioncenter
.com
Moderate

Hyatt House Minot
2301 Landmark Dr. NW
(888) 882-1234
minot.house.hyatt.com
Moderate

Noble Inn
1009 20th Ave. SE
(701) 837-1500
nobleinnhotels.com
Moderate

Souris Valley Suites
800 37th Ave. SW
(701) 858-7300
sourisvalleysuites.com
Moderate

Where to Eat in Central North Dakota

DEVILS LAKE

Cedar Inn Family Restaurant
445 US 2 W.
(701) 662-8893
cedarinndl.com
Inexpensive

Dakotah Buffet
(Spirit Lake Casino)
7889 Hwy. 57
St. Michael
(701) 766-4747
spiritlakecasino.com
Moderate

MINOT

Big Time Bistro
101 Central Ave. W.
(701) 839-2666
bigtimebistro.com
Moderate

SELECTED CHAMBERS OF COMMERCE

Devils Lake Convention and Visitors Bureau
208 Hwy. 2 W
(701) 662-4957
devilslakend.com

Jamestown Tourism Center
404 Louis L'Amour Ln.
Jamestown 58401
(800) 222-4766
tourjamestown.com

Minot Convention and Visitors Bureau
1020 S. Broadway
Minot 58702
(800) 264-2626
visitminot.org

Turtle Mountain Tourism Association
519 Main St.
Bottineau 58318
(701) 228-3849
turtlemountains.org

Souris River Brewing
32 3rd St. NE
(701) 837-1884
sourisriverbrewing.com
Moderate

Sweet and Flour Patisserie
400 Central Ave. E.
(701) 240-3664

Eastern North Dakota

The Red River Valley

As you travel toward the North Dakota–Minnesota border, the alluvial **Red River Valley** defines the history and economy of the far eastern third of North Dakota and has been dubbed the "Breadbasket of the World." It is one of the greatest agricultural regions in the world and is often compared with the Valley of the Nile.

The Red River Valley is the remnant of glacial **Lake Agassiz,** and its waters flow into the Hudson Bay and eventually into the Arctic Ocean. The valley varies from 10 to 40 miles in width from north to south along the border of North Dakota and Minnesota and is relatively flat, with an average elevation of 900 feet. Rich chernozem (black) soils are found in the Red River Valley; promoters in the 1800s hailed the valley as the Garden of Eden, conveniently omitting the fact that early spring flooding or a lack of water coupled with a short growing season could be less than idyllic.

North Dakota's livelihood, nonetheless, has always depended upon its soil, and that soil has made the state the land of plenty, whether in agriculture, crude oil, or lignite

CANADA
NORTH DAKOTA

5

81

29

Grafton

ICELANDIC
COMMUNITIES
AND
GRAND FORKS

2

Grand
Forks

18

29

NORTH DAKOTA

MINNESOTA

200

32

FARGO AND
SHEYENNE
VALLEY

Valley
City

Fargo

94

46

32

Wahpeton

13

29

NORTH DAKOTA
SOUTH DAKOTA

N

0   50 mi

0   50 km

(a brown variety of very soft coal). North Dakotans simply call this long eastern corridor of woodlands in the north and agricultural bounty in the south "The Valley."

In the very northeast corner of the state, the four communities of Walhalla, Pembina, Langdon, and Cavalier successfully meld various traditions and nationalities. The largest Icelandic settlement in America is located within the region—providing a fascinating chapter in the rich history of the frontier West.

Icelandic Communities

The towns of Mountain, Gardar, Hallson, Svold, and Akra were settled in 1873–1879 by Icelanders coming from a sister colony in Gimli, Manitoba. After traversing the fertile Red River Valley, the immigrants reached the Pembina Escarpment, a hilly wooded region that overlooks the valley. They put down roots and thrived here. Quality education for their children was paramount to the settlers, and the vision was not only to assimilate into this new world but also to become its leaders. Icelandic pioneers and other ethnic groups are remembered in the Pioneer Heritage Museum, Akra Hall, Cranley School, and the Gunlogson Homestead at *Icelandic State Park* near *Cavalier.* In Mountain you'll find the oldest Icelandic church in America.

thestateflower

The wild prairie rose (*Rosa blanda* or *Rosa arkansana*) has bright pink petals with a tight cluster of yellow stamens in the center. This rose grows wild along roadsides, in pastures, and in native meadows.

One and one-half miles northeast of Walhalla on ND 32, the *Gingras Trading Post State Historic Site* (701-825-6840, history.nd.gov) preserves the home and trading post established by prominent Metis trader Antoine B. Gingras in the 1840s. (Gingras was one of the signers of the charter of Winnipeg.) His hand-hewn oak-log home and store are among the few tangible remains of the fur trade in the Valley of the Red River of the North. The site is open from May 16 through September 15 from 10 a.m. to 5 p.m. daily. Admission is free.

Today Walhalla is more of a vacation outpost. *Frost Fire Ski and Snowboard Area* is a fully developed ski area, with 2 chairlifts, magic carpet for the tubing hill, Nordic ski trails, a lodge, and spectacular views at 11950 County Hwy. 55. During the summer, musicals draw audiences from near and far. The covered amphitheater, on the slopes of the heavily wooded Pembina Gorge, sees sellout crowds who like to come early, shop in the crafts barn, and grab lunch before the curtain rises. For information call (701) 549-3600 or visit frostfireskiarea.com.

Four miles east of Walhalla on ND 5 is Lake Renwick and *Icelandic State Park,* one of the jewels of the park system. Its newest addition is the historic Akra Hall community center, joining the old homestead, a one-room schoolhouse, and nature trails of the Gunlogson Arboretum, which in winter are groomed for cross-country skiing. The *Gunlogson Homestead and Nature Preserve,* located within the park and the focal point of the Pioneer Heritage Center, illuminates the homesteading days of American history, when immigrants bravely settled land at the edge of the wilderness. The two-story frame homestead was built by Icelandic immigrants between 1882 and 1890. The formidable *Pioneer Heritage Center* is open mid-May through Labor Day (call 701-265-4561 for information). The six time periods that are featured include the early fur-trapping days, as well as the era of pioneers such as the Gunlogsons. For nature lovers, there are trails along the Tongue River, a beach along Lake Renwick, a campground, and 3 sleeping cabins open mid-May through Sept.

If you prefer grander accommodations, head a mile east of nearby Mountain on ND 3 to *221 Melsted Place Bed & Breakfast,* This elegant bed-and-breakfast has hosted Olafur Grimsson, the president of Iceland, who stayed in its Matriarchal Suite, an original bedroom for the maternal

TOP HITS IN EASTERN NORTH DAKOTA

Bagg Bonanza Farm
45 miles south of Fargo
(701) 274-8989

Fargo Theatre
314 Broadway
(701) 289-8385

Fort Abercrombie State Historic Site
Abercrombie
(701) 553-8513

Pembina State Museum
805 State Highway 59
(701) 825-6840

grandparents. It's appointed with an ornate gold-leaf headboard and a king-size bed. There are three other rooms at this historic farmstead built in 1910 by Sigurdur Magnusson Melsted, an engineer, businessman, farmer, and active citizen. He built the impressive estate for his wife, Rosa, her parents, and their 10 children. Savor sweets at the inn's Chocolate Festival in February, enjoy the sight of swans at the Spring Celebration in April, tour the haunted granary in October, or enjoy sleigh rides, Victorian teas, and candlelight dinners during the Christmas season. Room rates range from $80 to $120. Amenities include a spa, evening bonfires, and a host of nature activities, including bird-watching, stargazing, and berry picking (701-993-8257; melstedplace.com).

tip

The Pembina River is North Dakota's only whitewater river, offering excellent paddling through the Pembina Gorge.

The town of **Mountain** holds its own treasures: the 1884 Historic Vikur Church, an Icelandic Festival in August, and the Borg Pioneer Memorial Home.

Two pleasant diversions await travelers heading east on ND 5 at Cavalier and the wooded hills of the Pembina Escarpment. The **Pembina County Historical Museum** (701-265-4941), located at Division and Main Streets, features pioneer replica rooms, rotating theme displays, and a research library. Three buildings contain antique pioneer machinery. The museum is open from 9 a.m. to 6 p.m. daily Memorial Day through Labor Day; closing time is 5 p.m. during the winter. At the **Pembina State Museum** (701-825-6840; history.nd.gov), visitors can see 100 million years of history, dating from the Cretaceous period to modern times, in the permanent exhibit gallery. Or they can view the Red River Valley from the seven-story-high observation deck. It's open 9 a.m. to 6 p.m. Mon through Sat and 1 to 6 p.m. Sun mid-May through mid-Sept. It closes an hour earlier during the rest of the year.

Grand Forks Area

Grab I-29 south from Pembina, and you'll follow the Red River valley to the heart of Grand Forks, the state's oldest community and third-largest city at about 54,932. The junction of the Red River of the North and the Red Lake River has been a meeting place for centuries—first for Native Americans who camped and traded there, then for French, British, and American fur traders who ambitiously peddled their wares across the continent. The regional population of about 100,000 encompasses North Dakota's Grand Forks and Minnesota's East Grand Forks, established on the opposite river bank in 1870 by steamboat captain Alexander Griggs.

The population first grew dramatically after the Great Northern Railroad came to town in 1880. From the 1880s to 1910, pine logs were floated down the Red Lake River or brought in by rail to sawmills in the city. Many homes in Grand Forks were built of regal white pine from the immense forests of northern Minnesota. Through the years, Grand Forks has remained the center of trade and processing for an agricultural area rich with wheat, potatoes, sugar beets, and livestock. The community's also bolstered by a thriving state university, an air force base, and world-class sports facilities.

Locals are mighty proud of the *Alerus Center,* 1200 42nd St. S., which hosts conventions, arena concerts, exhibitions, meetings and sporting events—especially as home to University of North Dakota football. Free walking tours are offered at 2 p.m. Mon through Fri. Call (701) 792-1200 for more information or visit aleruscenter.com.

You don't have to be a sports fan to be bowled over by UND's $100 million *Ralph Engelstad Arena* (701-777-6636; theralph.com). The luxurious 400,000-square-foot, five-story arena, with seating for 11,700, is truly the envy of the NCAA. Chalk it up to an Italian marble lobby, cherrywood leather-padded seats, and 300 televisions sets that can even be found in the bathroom so fans won't miss a bit of the action. The arena hosts family shows, ice events, concerts, and games featuring the Division I National Champion men's hockey team and the up-and-coming women's team. Also on-site are a pro shop and a Fighting Sioux Museum. The Betty Engelstad Sioux Center, a 50,000-square-foot expansion to the arena, houses 4 regulation-size practice volleyball and basketball courts, all of which can be converted into one main game court. Tours are available at 1:30 p.m. Mon through Fri. Call for reservations.

For devoted bakers, the state-owned *North Dakota Mill and Elevator* has been a Grand Forks fixture, supplying high-quality patent flours since 1922. They offer a mind-boggling array of choices such as extra fancy durum, high-gluten flours, pancake mixes, wheat germ, and spring wheat tailored for tortillas and pizza crusts. Most of it goes to food manufacturers, such as those who make pasta or crackers, but you can find some basic flours on grocery shelves. The mill can process more than 80,000 bushels of wheat a day or add value to 23 million bushels of hard red spring and durum wheat each year. A $27 million expansion announced in the fall of 2014 will make the mill the largest wheat-grinding factory in the country (ndmill.com).

trivia

In 1893 miller Frank Amidon invented Cream of Wheat as a creamy white porridge that became a hot cereal staple in kitchens across the Midwest— especially on cold winter mornings.

Although Grand Forks lost several downtown buildings to the flood and fire of 1997, many remaining structures reflect the innate style and grace of the architects who shaped the city at the turn of the 20th century. You'll find architectural styles that include art deco, classical revival, colonial revival, Romanesque, Greek revival, and Dutch colonial.

A better lure than architecture—think creative food and drink—gets most people to the lively downtown that runs along 3rd Street and parallel to the river and flood memorials. At **Dakota Harvest Bakers** (17 N. 3rd St.; 701-772-2100; dakotaharvest.com), smell the fresh-baked bread.

Paul Holje and George Kelley use local honey, eggs, butter, fruits and vegetables, as well as flour from nearby North Dakota Mill for artisan breads, savory soups, and sweet desserts at Dakota Harvest Bakers. They opened in 2004, baking bread in stone-deck ovens, with menu items changing daily and often including vegetarian or vegan options. Try their oatmeal whole wheat or Cream of Wheat bread, buffalo beer chili, red velvet cake with cream cheese frosting, or bittersweet chocolate cookies with sea salt.

In an 1893 building at the other end of the block, **The Toasted Frog,** 124 N. 3rd St., drew fans with its regional, trendy dinners and eventually expanded to Bismarck, as well. They specialize in wood-fired cooking, serving Moroccan-spiced lamb burgers, pheasant lavosh, and pear pie with cinnamon ice cream. Appetizers include fried cheese-wrapped pickles and, of course, frog legs (701-772-3764; toastedfrog.com).

At 22 S. 3rd St., *Sander's 1907* has been a longtime favorite for fine diners seeking Swiss Eiger prime rib, bison barbecue ribs, and wild salmon with a prairie sauce (701-746-8970).

Beyond downtown and at the west end of University Avenue, the *University of North Dakota* (UND), reigns as the state's largest school and its oldest after being started in 1883. It feeds the minds of close to 15,000 students. Many of them are drawn to its highly respected medical and law schools and its internationally known John D. Odegaard School of Aerospace Sciences.

madein northdakota

If you're seeking the perfect souvenir or gift, check prideofnorthdakota.com for a guide to North Dakota–grown and –created products.

The *North Dakota Museum of Art* (701-777-4195; ndmoa.com), located on the UND campus in a renovated gymnasium, is renowned for its cutting-edge contemporary art and human-rights exhibitions. Its collection spans art in all media starting with the early 1970s, including the visual history of the region. Leave time to browse the eclectic gift shop with ethnic gifts, children's books, jewelry, and artwork. The museum is open 9 a.m. to 5 p.m. Mon through Fri, and 1 to 5 p.m. Sat and Sun. Admission is free, but a $5 donation is encouraged.

Also on the UND campus, the *Chester Fritz Auditorium* is a 2,300-seat venue for a wide array of performances, from country acts and classical music to Russian ballet and Broadway shows. There's a permanent photo gallery of past performers at "The Fritz," world-renowned for acoustic brilliance. Call (701) 777-4090 or go to und.edu/chester-fritz-auditorium.

For a tucked-away UND gem, follow the dinosaur tracks to the free Geology Museum in Leonard Hall, open weekdays year-round, with fossil and geological displays and a 70-million-year-old triceratops skull.

Families can continue the prehistoric theme at *Canad Inns Destination Center* at 1000 S. 42nd St. and connected to the Alerus Center. There are 14 kid-themed rooms with bunks and murals with dinos, mermaids, or the galaxy plus a few themed Jacuzzi rooms with Egyptian, Japanese, Mayan, and Dakota decor. The hotel's 40,000-square-foot water park is North Dakota's largest. Non-guests also are welcome to use the water

Crunch into Chippers

Enjoy Red River valley potatoes in an addictive new way at Widman's. Grand Forks' Widman's Candy Shop (106 S. 3rd St.; 701-775-3480) and Carol Widman's Candy Co. in Fargo (4325 13th Ave. S.; 701-281-8664). They drench salty, crispy potato chips in smooth, sweet milk or dark chocolate made from a family recipe. They put a North Dakota twist on other chocolates, too, pouring almond bark across nutty sunflower seeds and coating roasted flax seed in dark chocolate. Enjoy the sweet goodness.

park. Call (701) 772-8404 or go to canadinns.com for current prices and details.

For a history lesson, check out the Campbell House where Thomas Campbell lived and was dubbed the "Wheat King of America" in the early 1900s. He earned his nickname because of the enormous farm acreage he owned. His white, clapboard structure at 2405 Belmont Rd. shares space on the old family ranch with an original 1870s post office, a 1920s one-room schoolhouse, a carriage house, the original log Grand Forks post office, and the *Myra Museum.* The house and property were deeded to the historical society in 1971 and used to house a variety of local artifacts. Buildings are open daily mid-May through mid-Sept, from 1 to 5 p.m. Call (701) 775-2216 for more information.

For an easy weekend getaway and perfect place to introduce children to fishing, check out *Turtle River State Park* (701-594-4445; parkrec.nd .gov), 22 miles west of Grand Forks on US 2 in the breathtaking Turtle River Valley. You can borrow fishing gear at the park office and try catching rainbow trout in the river. Not your thing? Hike, mountain bike, or return in the winter for cross-country skiing and sledding. Camping spots and rustic cabins are available May through Sept.

Fargo

Hit I-29 and head south to *Fargo,* which has soared in population—from 90,700 about five years ago to 113,658 in 2013—and is clearly keeping its claim as North Dakota's largest city and hippest metropolitan area. And despite all the fun Hollywood makes of Fargo (see sidebar), the area continually wins honors for being among America's best small cities with shout-outs from magazines such as *Money, Self,* and *Forbes.*

The town's roots are firmly in agriculture, playing a role as a vital trade and distribution center for sugar beets, wheat, and livestock produced in the rich soils of the surrounding valley. But it's diversified by many other industries, too, including health care and companies such as Microsoft.

trivia

Fargo was established in 1871 where the Northern Pacific Railway crossed the Red River. Its first name was Centralia, but the town later was renamed to honor William George Fargo, who was founder of Wells, Fargo and Co. and one of the railroad's directors. Low railroad freight rates and the land's incredible wheat-producing potential attracted settlers.

Fargo wears its heritage like a badge of honor and brings the past to life with events like *Pioneer Days* during the third weekend in August. Head to *Bonanzaville,* a restored and extensive pioneer village of more than 45 buildings from the early 20th century. It proudly touts itself as "15 acres of valley heritage," including a Plains Indian Museum, train depot, machinery shed, church, general stores galore, log cabins, and even a hangar for historic planes. Plan to spend at least a few hours here or you'll miss the fun details like the telephone company offering local calls in exchange for "two eggs or five cents."

Bonanzaville is named for the large and well-capitalized Bonanza farms (not to be confused with the ranch of 1960s TV fame) that were built by early railroad boosters as a way to attract settlers to this "slice of Eden in the West." Sure enough, settlers followed with their plows and dreams. Between 1879 and 1886 about 100,000 people, many of them Scandinavian and German, came to live in Dakota Territory. This period became known as the Dakota Boom. Several of the Bonanza farms endured to the early part of the 20th century—the last threads in the fabric of a powerful era in agriculture.

Bonanzaville's visitor center does a great job commemorating what was one of North Dakota's most colorful eras. The village (located 4.25 miles west of I-29 on Main Avenue or via I-94, exit 343) is open daily Memorial Day through Labor Day. Admission is $12 for adults, $10 for seniors and

Fargo and Fame

Ah, geez. Thanks to Hollywood, saying you're from Fargo can elicit a snicker and flashbacks to the darkly comic and cultish *Fargo* movie from 1996. It doesn't help that *Fargo* came back as a 2014 TV series. You can find T-shirts that say, "Yes, I'm from Fargo. No, it's not like the movie" or "You betcha." *Fargo* fans can pose with the infamous wood chipper from the movie at the Fargo-Moorhead visitor center. They even provide the furry hats with ear flaps. If you head downtown to the funky Fargo Theatre, you can pose with "Wood-Chip Marge," an 8-foot-tall chainsaw carving of the movie's heroine, Marge Gunderson, a role that helped Frances McDormand score a best actress Oscar.

military; and $6 for kids 4–14. Call (701) 282-2822 or go to bonanzaville.com for details and special events such as Christmas on the Prairie.

Children can have their own lesson on the merits of agriculture through the ***Children's Museum at Yunker Farm,*** 1201 28th Ave. N. Here they can see a display of live bees, then crawl through a honeycomb section designed just for them. The exhibits were constructed to involve kids in demonstrations and hands-on experiments. Housed in a renovated, century-old redbrick farmhouse, the museum is naturally inviting. The 55-acre grounds include a playground, a pumpkin patch, nature trails, and a community garden. Admission is $5 for children and adults. Train rides are $5 and carousel rides are 50 cents. Open 10 a.m. to 5 p.m. Mon through Sat and 1 to 5 p.m. Sun. It's closed on Mon during the school year. Call (701) 232-6102 or check childrensmuseum-yunker.org for details.

For hip, sophisticated fun, head to ***downtown Fargo.*** On balmy Thursday nights, it might be lined with the vibrant colors and throaty rumbles of classic cars. Pick any night, though, and you'll find Broadway hopping with restaurants, upscale stores, and the glowing neon of ultra-trendy Hotel Donaldson on one end and the art deco ***Fargo Theatre*** marquee on the other.

The renovated Fargo Theatre at 314 Broadway hums with the artsy, quirky spirit that has helped independent films thrive in the last decade. They added a second 99-seat theater in 2009, giving patrons the choice of two movies each night when the theater isn't hosting dance groups, comedians, bands, and orchestras. The theater opened in 1926 as a vaudeville and silent-film hall. There are still a handful of rare talents, local men who can improvise the sound effects and background music for silent films with the theater's rare, still-functioning Wurlitzer pipe organ. Your best bet for hearing it is attending the annual **Fargo Film Festival** in early March. Call (701) 239-8385 or visit fargotheatre.org.

For the best view of downtown, head up to Sky Prairie Lounge and watch the sunset from **Hotel Donaldson**'s rooftop gathering place, 101 N. Broadway. It's open to the public 5 to 10:30 p.m. on balmy evenings, Mon through Sat. Guests in the 17-room boutique hotel each enjoy the work of a different artist and can use the hot tub on the rooftop. The centerpiece of its premiere room—No. 17—is a Japanese soak tub with water cascading from the ceiling. The hotel boasts some of the area's most creative dining with an emphasis on local ingredients. Splurge on bison flat iron steak with wild mushrooms and sunchokes, root-beer-braised short ribs, and tapas-style desserts, or go for more a more affordable lunch in the HoDo lounge: gourmet burgers and salads. Head there on Thursday nights for live music (701-478-1000; hoteldonaldson.com).

For a newer option in rooftop dining and tasty food, head to **Rhombus Guys Pizza,** a Grand Forks favorite that has expanded to Fargo at 606 Main Ave. You'll find choices like the meat-laden T-Rex or vegetarian Backpacker and even a s'mores dessert pizza (701-540-4534; rhombuspizza.com).

It would take weeks to check out all the superb dining in Fargo, but even if you've run out of time, at least grab a to-go item from **Nichole's Fine Pastry,** 13 S. 8th St. They create such artful fruit pastries, tarts, and layer cakes, you'll definitely want a photo. Cool down a hot day with a creamy gelato or tart sorbet in flavors such as spicy ginger, tangy rhubarb, or blood orange. The cafe serves sandwiches, soups, and salads, too (701-232-6430; nicholesfinepastry.com).

baseball legend

Fargo athlete Roger Maris vaulted to fame when he joined the New York Yankees and hit 61 home runs during the 1961 season, breaking the long-standing record of the great Babe Ruth. At the Roger Maris Museum exhibit at West Acres Shopping Center, you'll see actual film of Roger's last 12 homers of 1961, along with his uniforms, baseball equipment, and other memorabilia (701-282-2222; rogermarismuseum.com).

If you like edgy, Native American or contemplative art, head to 704 1st Ave. N to the elegantly renovated, turn-of-the-20th-century warehouse that's home to the *Plains Art Museum* (701-232-3821; plainsart.org). It hosts regional, national, and international exhibits, large permanent collections, special events, performances, and art classes. The museum is open daily. Check for current hours. Admission is $5 for adults and $4 for seniors.

You can see the white peaks of the Historical and Cultural Society of Clay County from the North Dakota side of the Red River, but you have to cross the bridge to Moorhead, Minnesota, to see the *Hjemkomst Viking Ship,* a replica built by Robert Asp, a Moorhead school counselor whose dream was to sail it to Norway. Leukemia took him before he could, but his family completed the harrowing, adventurous, and historic Atlantic crossing, landing in Bergen, Norway, in the 1980s. You can get up close to the ship, watch a movie about it, and also go outside to tour the impressive Hopperstad Stave Church. To get the best feel for these Nordic cultures—through sights, music, costumes, and food—time a visit with the Scandinavian

A Spirited Dakota Road Trip: Beer, Wine, and Vodka

Looking for your new favorite drink? Here's just a sampling of the many regional breweries, distillers, and vineyards:

- *Drekker Brewing Company,* hand-crafted beers in Fargo (630 1st Ave. N.; drekkerbrewing.com)

- *Fargo Brewing Company,* artisan beers in Fargo (610 N. University Dr.; fargobrewing.com)

- *Maple River Distillery,* wild plum and native fruit wines, rhubarb, chokecherry and other fruit-infused vodkas, cordials, and fruit brandies in Casselton (628 Front St.; mapleriverwinery.com)

- *Red Trail Vineyard,* wines made from northern varietals along the Old Red Trail along the Maple River valley in Buffalo (redtrailvineyards.com)

For more information and additional sites, check out the North Dakota Beer and Wine Trail Brochure at ndtourism.com or contact the North Dakota Grape Growers Association at ndgwa.org.

Festival the last weekend in June or the Viking Village in late July. Call (218) 299-5511 or go to hjemkomst-center.com.

You can soak up much more art and culture, especially theater and musical performances, with three universities calling the Fargo-Moorhead area home: Concordia College and Minnesota State University at Moorhead and North Dakota State University at Fargo. Check the Fargo-Moorhead Visitor and Convention Bureau for upcoming performances at fargomoorhead .org.

One of the nicest places to enjoy the peaceful Red River is 17 blocks south of Main Avenue. Here, tucked back behind residential streets, you'll find **Lindenwood Park** with spacious, wooded picnic grounds, playgrounds, bike rentals and trails, and places to pitch a tent along this scenic oxbow (1712 5th St. S.; 701-232-3987; fargoparks.com).

Like Grand Forks, Fargo hums with pride when it comes to aviation. Check out the local heritage at **Fargo Air Museum** (1609 19th Ave. N.; 701-293-8043; fargoairmuseum.org). Besides educating the public about aviation and North Dakotans' role in it, the museum celebrates the freedom, thrill, and exhilaration of flight and commemorates those who sacrificed their lives in times of war, from World War II to Afghanistan. Some of the planes on display include the F2G-1D, the world's only flying Super Corsair and one of only three existing in the world; and a Beech Staggerwing, a classic airplane known as Queen of the Sky that was used during World War II on reconnaissance missions and to carry generals. It's open 10 a.m. to 5 p.m. Tues through Fri, 9 a.m. to 5 p.m. Sat, and noon to 4 p.m. Sun. Admission is $8 for adults; $7 for seniors, military, and students; and $5 for kids 5–11. For more information, go to fargoairmuseum.org.

skydive

If seeing planes has your adrenaline going or craving an ultra-rush, you can try a static-line or tandem skydive with Skydive Fargo (701-281-0149; skydivefargo.com).

Wahpeton

If you take I-29 35 miles south through the Red River valley, you'll reach Wahpeton and two more intriguing chapters of North Dakota history. **Fort**

Abercrombie was the first permanent US military fort established in North Dakota and served as a gateway to the frontier from 1857 to 1878. It was the only part of the state besieged by Sioux warriors for six weeks in the late summer of 1862, when the short but deadly US-Dakota War broke out in Minnesota. Only one original building remains, but blockhouses and the palisade wall have been reconstructed, and a museum helps bring that era to life. The museum is open 8 a.m. to 5 p.m. Thurs through Mon mid-May through mid-Sept. Admission is $5, adults; $2.50 for children 6–14. For more information call (701) 553-8513 or go to history.nd.gov.

Twenty miles southwest of the fort, check out the ***Bagg Bonanza Farm,*** at 8025 169th Ave. SE, in Mooreton. This 21-building farm is the sole remnant of the "king wheat" boom that started in the late 1870s when harvesting was mechanized, wheat farms were supersized, and railroads eagerly transported the bounty. Bagg Bonanza Farm was once a 6,000-acre operation—a fairly modest size for that era—but it's the last restorable Bonanza farm in the US and a National Historic Landmark. Guided tours are available from noon to 5 p.m. Fri through Sun or by appointment. The season opens Memorial Day weekend and ends Labor Day weekend. Special events are scheduled throughout the season, including the annual Old-Fashioned

TOP FAMILY ATTRACTIONS

Fargo–Moorhead RedHawks
Professional Northern League baseball games
(701) 235-6161
fmredhawks.com

Red River Zoo
4220 21st Ave. S.
(701) 277-9240
redriverzoo.org

Rheault Farm
(a 1918 farm)
2902 25th St. S.
(701) 499-7788
fargoparks.com

Scheels
(with its in-store Ferris wheel)
(701) 298-2918
scheelssports.com

Thunder Road Family Fun Park
(701) 282-5151
thunderroadfargo.com

Waterparks at the Holiday Inn's Shipwreck Bay
(701) 282-2700 or at the
Best Western Kelly Inn & Suites
(701) 282-2143

AUTHOR'S FAVORITE FARGO SHOPS

Boucle Yarn Studio
616 Main Ave.
(701) 356-9276
Gorgeous, vibrant yarn along with guidance and classes for passionate knitters.

Ecce Art
216 Broadway N.
(701) 298-3223
Fine art and handcrafted gifts from the upper plains and Midwest.

Gallery 4
114 Broadway N.
(701) 237-6867
Cooperative gallery with a variety of local art, from pottery and glass to jewelry and paintings.

O'Day Cache
317 Broadway
(701) 293-2088
These Asian imports add up to beautiful decor, clothing, jewelry, housewares, furniture, and vibrant paper lanterns.

Shannalee
313 Broadway N.
(710) 232-3300
Funky clothing, cosmetics, and accessories.

Vlana Vlee and the Red Shoe
102 Broadway
(701) 297-8533
Home decor and furniture, hip women's clothing and high-end shoes and boots, baby clothes and gifts, and unexpected accessories.

Willi Nilli
412 Broadway N., Suite 3
(701) 235-1164
Three-dimensional accents and sculpted leather purses and accessories.

Zandbroz Variety
420 Broadway
(701) 239-4729
Best bet for beautiful stationery and pens, kitchenwares and cookbooks, jewelry, offbeat and retro kids' toys, and a great read, whether it's a brand-new book or a rare vintage edition.

Fourth of July Celebration. Admission is $5, adults; $2.50 for children 6–12. Concessions and a gift shop are on-site. For more information call (701) 274-8989 or go to baggbonanzafarm.org.

Sheyenne Valley

Head an hour west of Fargo to reach **Valley City,** gateway to the Sheyenne Valley. Two of the valley area's most prominent features are not always found in North Dakota: trees and winding roadways. It's no surprise then that it became the *Sheyenne Valley National Scenic Byway* and one of the Midwest's most beloved fall treks with the valley dappled in vibrant shades of gold, yellow, and red. Of course, it's lovely and relaxing any season of the year as the road curves 68 miles from Lake Ashtabula to Lisbon.

The southern end of the byway, about 30 miles south of Valley City, heads toward *Fort Ransom* and *Fort Ransom State Park.* The community and park inherited the name of a frontier cavalry fort, which was established in 1867 to protect the settlers' path to the Missouri River. Nowadays, the small Norwegian town of Fort Ransom is regarded as a scenic arts community. The *Ransom County Museum* is open 1 to 5 p.m. Memorial Day weekend through Labor Day. Admission is $1 for adults. The *Sheyenne Valley Arts and Crafts Festival* is another popular attraction and takes place the last full weekend in Sept. Call (701) 973-4491 for more information.

Sodbuster Days takes place every summer during the second weekend in July and the first full weekend after Labor Day. Here you can revisit the horse-powered days of threshing, haying, and plowing, and homesteading activities from carding and weaving to silversmithing and blacksmithing. Wagon rides and entertainment round out the two weekends of living history. Admission is $5 per day. For more information call (701) 973-4331 or go to ndparks.com/frsp.

While cross-country skiing and snowmobiling are the major winter activities at the Fort Ransom area, *Bears Den Mountain Ski Area* less than 2 miles away boasts a chairlift, a T-bar lift, and a beginner's tow rope. Call (701) 973-2711 or go to skibearsden.com for more information.

North of Fort Ransom, you'll also find tiny Kathryn with its 1900s main street and Clausen Springs Park, which is popular for camping.

Valley City in the heart of the byway ranks among the state's most beloved small-town destinations. Much of its charm comes from elegant and dramatic bridges—including the impressive *Highline Bridge,* a three-span, 255-foot bridge. At 3,860 feet long and 162 feet above the riverbed, the Highline Bridge is one of the longest and highest single-track railroad bridges in the nation. The first train officially crossed the trestle on May 12, 1908, and regular train service over the bridge began May 20. Because it was of vital importance in moving supplies and men, the bridge was closely guarded during both World War I and World War II to prevent sabotage.

You can learn more about the local history at ***Barnes County History Museum*** at 315 Central Ave. N. (701-845-0966) or pick up a brochure on the bridges at the Rosebud Visitor Center, 250 W. Main St. (701-845-1891; hello valley.com). Give yourself at least a few hours to stroll along the river and back and forth across the pretty bridges, many of which are on the campus of ***Valley City State University.*** Don't miss ***Medicine Wheel Park*** where strategically placed rocks create a Native American solar calendar. Interpretive signs explain how it works, and you can catch celebrations here during the equinox and seasonal solstices.

Twelve miles northwest of Valley City, you can slow down the pace even more with a trip to the beaches by ***Baldhill Dam and Lake Ashtabula*** (701-845-2970; mvp.usace.army.mil). This widening of the Cheyenne River boasts 7 recreational areas where you can swim, fish, boat, picnic, and camp. The ***Valley City Federal Fish Hatchery*** (701-845-3464), one of two such facilities in the state, also is located at the park.

Finally, if you want to grandly cap off a Dakota adventure, head about 70 miles southeast of Wahpeton to 9953 141st Ave. near Havana and almost on the South Dakota border. Here you can nestle into the new ***Coteau des Prairie Lodge.*** Perched gorgeously on the coteau that rises and stretches into South Dakota and Minnesota, its serves up a pure, peaceful Dakota landscape and warm hospitality (701-680-1175; cplodge.com).

Where to Stay in Eastern North Dakota

FARGO

Best Western Plus Kelly Inn and Suites
1767 44th St. S.
(701) 282-2143
bestwestern.com
Moderate

Fargo Inn and Suites
1025 38th St. S.
(701) 282-6300
fargoinn.com
Inexpensive

Hilton Garden Inn
4351 17th Ave. S.
(701) 499-6000
Hiltongardeninn3.hilton
.com
Moderate

Howard Johnson Inn
301 3rd Ave. N.
(701) 232-8850
hojo.com
Moderate

Radisson
201 N. 5th St.
(701) 232-7363
radisson.com
Moderate to expensive

GRAND FORKS

AmericInn
1820 S. Columbia Rd.
(701) 780-9925
Inexpensive to moderate

Canad Inns Destination Center
1000 S. 42nd St.
(701) 772-8404
canadinns.com
Moderate

C'mon Inn
3051 32nd Ave. S
(701) 775-3320
cmoninn.com
Inexpensive

Days Inn
3101 S. 34th St.
(701) 775-0060
daysinn.com
Inexpensive

511 Reeves Bed & Breakfast
511 Reeves Dr.
(701) 775-3585
Moderate

Lakeview Inn & Suites
3350 32nd Ave. S
(701) 775-5000
lakeviewhotels.com
(877) 355-3500
Inexpensive

Where to Eat in Eastern North Dakota

FARGO

Cafe Aladdin
1609 32nd Ave. S.
(701) 232-4200
Inexpensive

HoDo Lounge
101 Broadway
(701) 478-1000
Moderate to expensive

SELECTED CHAMBERS OF COMMERCE

Carrington Area Chamber of Commerce
871 Main St.
Carrington 58421
(701) 652-2524
cgtn-nd.com

Devils Lake Tourism Office
208 Hwy. 2 W
Devils Lake 58301
(701) 662-4903
devilslakend.com

Fargo–Moorhead Convention & Visitor Bureau
2001 44th St. SW
Fargo 58103
(701) 282-3653
fargomoorhead.org

Greater Grand Forks Convention & Visitors Bureau
4251 Gateway Dr.
Grand Forks 58203
(701) 746-0444
visitgrandforks.com

Valley City Area Chamber of Commerce
250 W. Main St.
Valley City, 58072
(701) 845-1891
hellovalley.com

Wahpeton Convention & Visitors Bureau
visitwahpeton.com
(888) 850-9544

Monte's Downtown
220 Broadway
(701) 526-0149
Moderate to expensive

Saffron
3003 32nd Ave. SW
(701) 241-4200
Inexpensive to moderate

GRAND FORKS

Amazing Grains
214 Demers Ave.
(701) 775-4542
amazinggrains.org
Inexpensive

Brick and Barley
9 N. 3rd St.
(701) 757-4012
brickandbarleygf.com
Moderate

Big Sioux Cafe
4401 32nd Ave. S
(701) 738-0441
Inexpensive

The Red Pepper
1011 University Ave.
(701) 775-9671
redpepper.com
Inexpensive

Rhombus Guys
312 Kittson Ave.
(701) 787-7317
rhombusguys.com
Moderate

**Wild Hog Smokehouse
Bar & Grill**
4401 S. Washington St.
(701) 757-4263
wildhogsmokehouse.com
Moderate

Index